Love Songs in Motion

Chicago Studies in Ethnomusicology

A series edited by Philip V. Bohlman and Timothy Rommen

∴

Love Songs in Motion

∵

VOICING INTIMACY
IN SOMALILAND

Christina J. Woolner

THE UNIVERSITY OF CHICAGO PRESS
CHICAGO AND LONDON

The University of Chicago Press, Chicago 60637
The University of Chicago Press, Ltd., London
© 2023 by The University of Chicago
Published 2023
Printed in the United States of America

32 31 30 29 28 27 26 25 24 23   1 2 3 4 5

ISBN-13: 978-0-226-82737-7 (cloth)
ISBN-13: 978-0-226-82739-1 (paper)
ISBN-13: 978-0-226-82738-4 (e-book)
DOI: https://doi.org/10.7208/chicago/9780226827384.001.0001

Publication of this book was supported by the AMS 75 PAYS Fund of
the American Musicological Society, supported in part by the National
Endowment for the Humanities and the Andrew W. Mellon Foundation.

Library of Congress Cataloging-in-Publication Data

Names: Woolner, Christina J., author.
Title: Love songs in motion : voicing intimacy in Somaliland / Christina J.
    Woolner.
Other titles: Chicago studies in ethnomusicology.
Description: Chicago ; London : The University of Chicago Press, 2023. |
    Series: Chicago studies in ethnomusicology | Includes bibliographical
    references and index.
Identifiers: LCCN 2023009369 | ISBN 9780226827377 (cloth) |
    ISBN 9780226827391 (paperback) | ISBN 9780226827384 (ebook)
Subjects: LCSH: Love songs—Social aspects—Somalia. | Songs, Somali—
    History and criticism.
Classification: LCC ML2551.S58 W66 2023 | DDC 782.4209677—dc23/
    eng/20230419
LC record available at https://lccn.loc.gov/2023009369

For K and M, my loves

And in memory of Khadra Daahir Ciige
hooyadii jacaylka oo gacalodaydii

and Cabdinaasir Macallin Caydiid
ustaadkii kabanka oo macallinkaygii

Contents

Figures

Notes on Language and Terminology

Orthography and Pronunciation

The Latin script was officially adopted for Somali in 1972. While in everyday use spellings vary widely, I have used standard Somali spellings throughout the text, including for words borrowed from Arabic (e.g., *xaaraan* rather than *haram*) and when quoting material that was published before 1972 or does not use standard spelling (amending spelling where needed). I have also used the Somali spellings of places and names (e.g., Muqdisho rather than Mogadishu, Maxamed rather than Mohamed). However, Somalis do not always spell their own names using standard spelling. In some cases, I have deferred to common usage or individuals' preferences, notably in the spelling of Xidigaha Geeska. Somali spellings are generally phonetic to the English reader, with the exception of *x* (a throaty "h") and *c*, which is the Somali rendering of the Arabic 'ayn (often transliterated in English as '). Readers unfamiliar with this sound may omit the *c* (e.g., read Cali as Ali). For a full guide to pronunciation, see Orwin (1995).

Language and Translations

The research on which this book is based was conducted in both Somali and English. Many youths in Hargeysa speak English and were keen to practice their language skills with a native speaker (especially those I met at the universities where I lectured, where English is the medium of instruction). My day-to-day interactions and more formal interviews with many of these interlocutors were primarily conducted in English. Most of my interactions with artists, by contrast, took place in Somali. Translations from everyday interactions in Somali are my own; Abdihakim Abdilahi Omar and Kenedid Hassan assisted with transcribing and translating recorded interviews conducted in Somali. Quotations from these interactions and interviews are given in their English translation, though I have periodically included the original when the Somali phrasing is significant or not captured well in translation.

Translating poetry presents challenges even to those far more proficient in the language than me, and the song excerpts that appear throughout this book have thus involved input from multiple sources. Several of the Somali texts and translations in chapter 1 are taken from written sources, but most of the excerpts were transcribed and then translated from audio files. Abdihakim Abdilahi Omar did many of the initial transcriptions and provided preliminary translations. Martin Orwin offered keen-eyed editing advice, while Kenedid Hassan helped finalize translations and chased information on the more elusive metaphoric and technical features of poems. Unless indicated otherwise, the Somali texts in this book were transcribed from audio files, and the translations include input from Abdihakim, Kenedid, and Martin. All errors are my own.

In the song excerpts taken from written sources, I have made some minor updates to the spelling in the Somali texts but have maintained the original translators' punctuation and translations (some of whom take more poetic license in their interpretations than I do). In my own translations, I have aimed to maintain a balance between direct, line-by-line literal translations and more poetically rendered interpretations, though in the final instance I have opted toward more literal translations. I have also decided to include both the original Somali and English translations in the main text. One thing that is inevitably lost in translation is the meter and alliteration that are obligatory in Somali poetry; readers unacquainted with Somali may still read the Somali texts to get a sense of what this sounds like in the original. Most lyrics included in the body of the text are excerpts only; full translations of most songs are available on the book's companion website.

Names and Pseudonyms

Many of the names used in this book are pseudonyms, but I have not changed the names of people who are clearly identifiable by their work. This has inevitably tempered the way that I write about our interactions. I have used pseudonyms for everyone who is not an artist or public figure, and in such cases I only use a first name. I refer to artists using the name(s) by which they are commonly known; this is often a nickname, which I have indicated with quotation marks when introducing someone (alongside their full names), but I otherwise treat these as regular names.

For example, I refer to the poet Maxamed Ibraahin Warsame "Hadraawi" as Hadraawi.

A Note on Terminology

The terms "Somali" and "Somalilander" are both used throughout this work. "Somalilander" is of relatively recent origin and is used to define a citizen of Somaliland; it is a political identifier used to distinguish people from Somaliland and Somalia. The term "Somali," however, may be used as an ethnic, linguistic, or political designation, depending on the context. Most Somalilanders use the term "Somali" to refer to themselves in a cultural sense. As the musical genre at the heart of this book does not belong to Somalilanders alone, I refer to "Somali" music and poetry in a broad linguistic and cultural sense.

Use of the terms "Somaliland," "Somalia," and the "Somali Republic" are also potentially loaded. I use the term "Somaliland" to refer to the self-declared Republic of Somaliland, whose borders coincide with those of colonial British Somaliland. The "Somali Republic" refers to the union created by the independent British and Italian Somalilands in 1960; it was renamed the "Somali Democratic Republic" under Barre and is colloquially called "Somalia." By international convention, the term "Somalia" continues to refer to this political entity; however, when Somalilanders use the term "Somalia," they generally use it to refer to what was Italian Somaliland, to the exclusion of Somaliland. When I use "Somalia" in relation to events from 1960 to 1991, I take it to include Somaliland; for events since 1991, I use "Somalia" like my Somalilander interlocutors, that is, as excluding Somaliland.

Companion Website

While music and language might be considered two sides of the same coin, representing musical sound with language—or what Anthony Seeger called the "linguocentric predicament"—is a very real and enduring challenge. As a partial response to this, readers are encouraged to listen to the musical material discussed throughout this book that is available on the companion website (lovesongs.christinawoolner.com). In addition to audio/video files of all the songs referenced in this book, the website contains supplementary images, field recordings, song texts and translations, and links to further information.

It's about Love, of Course!

This book began in a serendipitous series of events in the spring of 2014. I had come to Hargeysa to carry out fieldwork for a pilot study on ideas of indigeneity in Somaliland's peacebuilding process. As I had done during my first visit to Somaliland a year earlier, I was staying at the University of Hargeysa's guesthouse and teaching at the Institute for Peace and Conflict Studies. My housemates at the time included a handful of other university staff, some foreign, others diaspora returnees. After weeks of grumbling that they could not watch Premier League football, someone had acquired a grainy analogue TV, then spent an afternoon trying to position some rabbit-ear antennae in just the right spot on the roof. For their efforts, we had fuzzy reception of a pirated Arab-language sports station, alongside a few local channels. One afternoon when the football crowd had dissipated, I was left channel-surfing with one of my housemates, Jamaal, a political scientist approaching sixty who had recently returned to his native Somaliland. Soon enough we had settled on Horn Cable TV's twenty-four-hour music video service, and a cheaply produced video filled the screen. A man in military fatigues ambled through the semiarid landscape on the outskirts of Hargeysa. The video cut to shots of a woman, her headscarf blowing in the wind, and then returned to the man, who was singing with memorable gusto. I asked Jamaal what he was singing about. "It's about love, of course!" He responded without skipping a beat, as if the answer was obvious. "We don't sing about war anymore."

This lovesick troubadour left a deep impression on me. Now Somalis are well-known orators—a "nation of poets," as it were—and I had previously done research on the peacebuilding potential of Somali verse. But I had not yet encountered Somali music and had not noticed any on the streets of Hargeysa. This singing soldier was memorable because of the juxtaposition of his attire and the subject matter of his song, alongside Jamaal's matter-of-fact response. But he was also memorable because, on first listen at least, music is conspicuously absent from Somaliland's public soundscapes—a result of the lingering effects of a war that devastated the artistic community and the increasing presence of Salafist groups who decry music as *xaaraan* (prohibited). After my Horn Cable TV introduction, however, I soon started hearing, and then listening out for, songs in sometimes unexpected places. I heard security guards listening to *qaraami* (love songs from the 1940s and 1950s) from radios clipped to their belts as they inspected cars at checkpoints. My ears perked up as pentatonic melodies drifted onto the streets from *majlisyo* (*qaad*-chewing houses), as men wiled away the afternoon chewing, chatting, and reminiscing. I started to recognize the voices of young members of Xidigaha Geeska (the Horn Stars)—Somaliland's preeminent contemporary musical collective—as they escaped from cars with their heavily tinted windows cracked ever so slightly. I found myself unconsciously tapping my foot and nodding my head as bus passengers sang along to familiar hits played by rogue bus drivers, undeterred by Salafist pronouncements against music. And when I began asking around about the music that I was hearing, I found friends eager and enthused to spend an entire afternoon introducing me to their favorite singers, flipping from one song to another on YouTube. Two friends even went so far as to organize private sessions with some local musicians—one during a weekend daytrip to Geeddeeble (a popular picnic area north of the city), another on the floor of the sitting room where I'd fatefully watched a lovesick soldier crooning for his beloved.

By the end of my short research trip, I was hooked. I returned to the UK and completely rewrote my research proposal, this time with love songs (*hees jacayl*) at its center. This was, in retrospect, a conversion moment of sorts for me as an apprentice anthropologist. My previous training had been in peace studies, and it was an interest in locally driven peacebuilding processes that led me to Somaliland in the first place. I did and still do maintain an interest in Somaliland's commendable efforts to establish peace and stability in a region that remains marred by violence and insecurity. But a year of study in social anthropology had vastly broadened my horizons to what researchers might study, how we might approach "the political," and what we might learn from reorienting our gaze—and ears—to the ways that people are constantly working to "make the everyday inhabitable," as Veena Das (2006) puts it. Rather than speaking to a predictable lineup of experts about Somaliland's official peace- and state-building efforts—a topic that has preoccupied international research agendas for decades— love songs seemed to offer something different. Might love songs, I mused in my new proposal, offer us an alternative narrative of politics, of postwar reconstruction, of what it means to live and love in an unrecognized polity?

This was only the beginning, however, and many of my early assumptions about what I might find were quickly put to the test. Love songs, to start, do not wear their politics on their sleeves. Hees jacayl, to be sure, have been "radical and disruptive" (Gioia 2015, xi) from the very start, demanding greater freedom in love and greater freedom of expression since their emergence in the 1940s. In certain political milieus—especially under the strict censorship regime of Siyaad Barre's dictatorship (1969–1991)—love songs have also been commandeered for political purposes. Can't critique the government directly? Complain about your unfaithful and deceitful lover instead! And in postwar Hargeysa's contested cityscape, I found artists who were consciously defiant of certain social, political, and religious expectations in their musicking. But mostly when I spoke to people about their music-making and music-listening practices, I found people who had been broken by love, who found deep comfort and release in singing about their love-pains or listening to the love aspirations and tribulations of others. And far from being an escape from hardship and suffering, more often than not I found a form of musicking that demanded a confrontation with pain. This was not the pain of war, displacement, or insecurity, though love-pain is always also entangled in broader sociopolitical forces. Rather, it was the spine-breaking, liver-shaking, heart-bursting, sleep-depriving pain caused by an all-consuming kind of love. Here I found poets who write words, musicians who make music, and singers who sing to give voice to deeply personal love anxieties and aspirations. These vocal articulations of love(-suffering) in turn invite listeners to feel love, to open their hearts, to dwell for a moment in their own vulnerabilities. And the longer I spent with Somali love songs, the more I learned to appreciate that their real power lies not in the social and political demands that they inherently make but in the intimacy that they distill and invite and the spaces they create for what Somalis refer to as *dareen-wadaag* (feeling-sharing).

My second assumption about love songs that was quickly and thoroughly upended was the notion that love songs might be approached as a kind of stable "object" that I would be able to locate or pin down and therefore study ethnographically. Love songs proved to be very elusive "things." Love songs, in one sense, can be found in predictable places, and early in my research my initial strategy was to go to these places. I thus spent the first few months of my research helping to catalogue dusty cassettes in a sound archive at the Hargeysa Cultural Center. But even as cassettes sit and gather dust, songs do not stay still. Sound, though ephemeral, has a peculiar ability to travel, and voices and ears seemed to make songs anew, to propel them on new journeys, every time a song was streamed on YouTube, played on the radio, shared with a lover via WhatsApp, debated at a majlis, or sung to a live audience. Songs seemed to become increasingly "sticky, or saturated with affect" (Ahmed 2014, 11) as they moved from one place to another, gathering stories, memories, and new intimacies as they traveled. If I wanted to study love songs, I needed to follow them across and through these spaces. I needed to approach songs as "fluid quasi-object[s]," as sites where "subjects and objects collide and intermingle" (Born 2005, 7)—or, as "moments [rather] than wholes" (Agawu 2003, 98). And I needed to pay attention to the voices that animate love songs and breathe life into songs again and again, constantly opening new space for feeling-sharing as they propel songs across space and generations.

This book began in a fateful encounter with a lovestruck troubadour on Horn Cable TV. But the claims that I make about love songs, and the shape of the story that I tell, are rooted in these two more recent refigured assumptions. One claim is about what love songs do: they open space for intimacy. This might seem straightforward—these songs are, after all, about love (of course). The force of this claim is in the nature of the intimacy involved. The intimacy of love songs is a deeply therapeutic, heart-mending, and heart-opening kind of intimacy that helps people make sense of their own love experiences. But it also stretches far beyond relationships between (would-be) lovers to stitch together a public united by their experiences of love(-suffering) and a desire to feel with others. In Somaliland's current religious and political climate, this is a salient political force. Yet it is only this because it is, first and foremost, a deeply transformative force that demands a certain letting go—a willingness to be vulnerable.

Another claim is that love songs' intimacy-opening power resides in the voice. Here again, this may seem straightforward: it is the singing voice that breathes life into songs. Love songs would not be without the voice. But the "voice of love" is not only a musical instrument. Conceived to come from "deep, deep, within the soul," it is the means by which deeply personal sentiments come into the world. Yet the "voice of love" is also a fundamentally *multivocal* voice: it is realized only through a collaborative process of feeling-sharing, and it is fundamentally there to be shared and to be taken up and revoiced by others. It is, in short, a sonic-social phenomenon that communicates and invites intimacy: one that distills and models dareen-wadaag. *Voicing Intimacy* is thus not only part of my title. It speaks directly to my central argument.

One additional claim is both theoretical and methodological: because of the nature of the voices that animate love songs, and because of the way that they constantly open space for intimacy anew, love songs are best approached *in motion*. This claim gives this book its structure. Instead of detailing the musical structure of songs, or dwelling on the genre's history, I document love songs as they come into being and move across different private and public spaces in contemporary Hargeysa. The affective force of love songs, to be sure, is inseparable from the genre's sociopolitical past and the sonic-social expectations that this past has shaped—I detail these in chapter 1. But even though much of the repertoire we will encounter is from Somalia and Somaliland's prewar period, the story I tell is primarily about what love songs do in a much more recent historical moment. Each chapter thus focuses on a particular space and process of bringing love songs to life—or, of voicing intimacy. This includes the collaborative song composition process (chap. 2), the storying of a celebrity's voice in circulation (chap. 3), private listening practices (chap. 4), the process of learning to become a musician able to sound love (chap. 5), and the live staging of love songs (chap. 6).

This book is about the work of love songs in contemporary Somaliland and the power of the intimacy that voices of love enable. But it is also a re-flection on my encounter with love songs and those who bring them to life. This is an encounter, or rather a series of encounters spanning many years, that has profoundly shaped me and my own voice. I hope that this book might be for others what Somali love songs have been for me: an entry into a different kind of narrative about sociopolitical life in a region where love stories are not on most people's agendas; an encounter that destabilizes the way we think of the "voice," as a medium of personal expression, a marker of subjectivity, and a mediator of interpersonal relationships; a provocation to think about what intimacy and vulnerability do in the lives of others but also closer to home; and last but not least, a story "about love, of course!"

FIGURE 0.1. Map of the Horn of Africa, featuring Somaliland. © Stefania Merlo (used with permission).

Love is but the desire of an unguarded moment the heart exposes itself to—
and it is smitten.

al-Mutanabbī

We are social beings by the voice and through the voice: it seems that the
voice stands as the axis of our social bonds, and that voices are the very texture
of the social, as well as the intimate kernel of subjectivity.

Mladen Dolar, *A Voice and Nothing More*

Introduction

"Wait a bit," Hanad said, turning his face toward the window to avoid making eye contact. His voice was audibly agitated by his friends' prying questions. But his tone also suggested he might have something to get off his chest. Gazing out the window at the nighttime sky, he added, "Tonight, maybe I will sing."

Hanad, Khaliil, and Idiriis, all unmarried men in their midtwenties, had been chatting boisterously as I attempted to maneuver an aging white Toyota Crown through Hargeysa's dimly lit streets. Hanad's comments momentarily quieted their conversation, prompting an unexpected moment of contemplation. But the energy among them remained one of tangible excitement and anticipation. It was a springtime Thursday evening in 2016, the beginning of the weekend, and we were on our way to Hiddo Dhawr. Self-styled as a "cultural restaurant and tourism village," when it opened in 2014, it became the first live music venue to operate in Somaliland in over a quarter century. Hiddo Dhawr's opening marked a milestone in the postwar recovery of Somaliland's artistic sphere, and the venue quickly became a beloved destination for both men and women, young and old. The venue was not without its detractors and had drawn the ire of conservative religious leaders for whom music, especially that performed and enjoyed by men and women together (publicly voicing love sentiments, no less), is scandalous, an affront to their understanding of Islamic and Somali values. While aware of the sensitive sociopolitical-religious space the venue occupies, such controversies seemed far from my passengers' minds. When you come to Hiddo Dhawr, Idiriis explained, you come "wearing the shirt of love."

In anticipation of the evening to come, my friends had been teasing each other and speculating about who might sing what during the audience participation time and, by extension, who might have sensitive love woes to get off their chest. Attention had turned to Hanad. I knew from conversations we had had working together on a music archiving project that he had recently stopped dating a woman who had held his heart for years. Flipping with dusty fingers through old cassettes seemed to allow for unusually intimate conversations, and I had learned that he lacked the financial stability her family required in a suitor. But he deflected his friends' inquiries, explaining that these experiences were still too raw and too painful for discussion. Luckily for Hanad, Hiddo Dhawr is beloved not only as Hargeysa's theater. It was also described to me as the city's "frustration hospital," and thus the best place to go to mend a variety of love and life ills. Khaliil and Idiriis seemed to immediately understand Hanad's request for some patience and what it might mean for their love-wounded friend to sing rather than speak about his troubles.

Snaking our way around the heavily fortified UN Development Programme compound, we pulled into the dark side street that leads to the venue, and I flicked on the inside light of the car and popped the trunk. A jovial security guard in military fatigues peaked his head inside before waving us through to the parking lot. We made our way through a second security check, paid for our prebooked tickets, and headed to our assigned table. Inside, the energy of gathering patrons was electric. My friend Huda and some other women arrived, fashionably late, dressed in vibrantly patterned *dirac*—a loose-fitting dress worn on special occasions—and demurely seated themselves on one side of the table. Before long that night's emcee, Mustafe, arrived to introduce the musicians. Conversations quieted down, and attention turned to the stage where a group of artists assembled with an oud and drums. A younger singer opened with a set that included songs by Xasan Aadan Samatar and Cumar Dhuule, two giants of the prewar music scene, before giving way to the venue's founder, Sahra Halgan, who performed a set of songs by Magool and locally born legend Khadra Daahir. Although they were born at least a decade after these songs were originally sung, my tablemates scribbled down lyrics for me and enthusiastically explained the songs. In one song, a man crooned for his faraway beloved, wishing to become a bird so he could fly across the ocean to meet her. In another, a woman chastised those clansmen who objected to her love for a specific man. In another still, a woman sang of a love she could not express, constrained by expectations of modesty and the consequent pain that had overcome her body, splitting her spine in two. These songs, Huda explained, come "from deep, deep inside the soul." And they can make you "feel what [they] feel." The audience sat enraptured, periodically calling out in solidarity or singing along.

When the artists took a break, Mustafe wound his way through the hall with a large orange microphone, soliciting audience members to tell jokes or sing songs. Some avoided the mic, but others enthusiastically volunteered, reveling in the opportunity to make their friends laugh or to lighten themselves of their love burdens. As Sahra Halgan later explained to me, this part of the evening works as a kind of group therapy session, a place for those who need to unburden their hearts to give voice to highly personal sentiments—and, by singing what they feel, finding at least a temporary cure for their love woes. When Mustafe reached our table, Hanad took the microphone without ceremony. In a naked yet quietly self-assured voice he offered his rendition of "Hibooy" (Hey Hibo!), a classic by Maxamed Salee-ban Tubeec, fondly known as "boqorka codka" (the king of the voice). The song questions what has happened between two lovers and speculates about love's mortal consequences: "Hubaal aawadaa cishqiga i hayaa / Ha-dayduu jaran u halis ahayeey" (Surely, the pain of this love that has me / I am in danger of dying). Hanad exhaled deeply and smiled quietly, avoiding sustained eye contact, perhaps unsure of how others would respond to this intimate disclosure, even voiced in the words and melody of another.

After making his way thoroughly around the room, allowing ample op-portunity for anyone who desired or required their voices to be heard, Mus-tafe made his way back to the stage, and the musicians returned. The artists seemed to speak in simple yet knowing glances, responding to the energy in the room, the emotion audible in the singer's voice and visible in their stage presence. They cycled through another set of love songs from more musical giants, like Faduumo Cabdillaahi Kaahin "Maandeeq," Axmed Cali Cigaal, and Maxamed Mooge. As evening turned to night, Sahra marked the close of the performance by singing a short ditty originally written by Rashiid Bullo for Radio Hargeysa: "Tani waa Hargeysoo / Hirarka gabaan / Idin kala hadlaysee / Habeen wanaagsan" (This is Hargeysa, speaking to you from the short waves, good night). Sung out into the cool night, pa-trons lingered outside, reveling in the afterglow of the performance. Hanad stood quietly, lost in thought, but responded without skipping a beat when I asked how he was feeling. "I feel repaired," he said, exhaling deeply, "I just feel, you know, repaired." "Yes," Idiriis added, "when you get the sound of the oud, and you hear those singers' voices, you feel relaxed." Huda con-curred. This music, that sound, those voices, "it heals you."

Reluctantly, we returned to the car. The mood was quiet and contempla-tive as we passed through the unusually quiet downtown, dropping pas-sengers along the way. As we drove in relative silence, the voices of the evening's performers and concertgoers replayed in my head. I recall being especially struck by how these voices echoed in peculiar contrast to the sights and sounds that usually fill the city's loud and colorful streets. And in many moments since, as I have attempted to make sense of the place of love songs in Hargeysa's cityscape, I have been drawn back again and again to the sounds, the feeling, and the voices of an evening spent with friends, sharing in the performance of love songs, "wearing the shirt of love." In a city where music is conspicuously absent from public soundscapes—muted by the lingering effects of war and an encroaching religious conservatism— these voices sing defiantly, staking a claim of sorts to the city. These voices also transgress a host of gendered social norms, which limit the interaction of men and women in public and make open expression of desire incredibly difficult. But, above all else, these voices seem to open space for people to *feel* and to share otherwise unspeakable intimacies with themselves and others. Against both the din and silences of the city, love songs sound in intimate and provocative ways—voicing otherwise unsayable sentiments, providing relief to lonely ears, drawing listeners into the lifeworlds of love-sufferers past and present, connecting people across space and sentiments across generations, drawing people in, and opening people out to a more vulnerable way of being.

This book is about the work of love songs in contemporary Somaliland. It tells a story about the lives and labor of a genre, the singing and speaking voices that give life to these songs, and their entanglement in the mediation and making of intimacy. What, I ask, is a love song? What do love songs do? And how do they do what they do? Based on two years of ethnographic research with poets, musicians, singers, media personnel, and love-suffering audiences, this book tracks love songs *in motion* as they move across and through Hargeysa's soundscapes, from private to public and back again, gathering new voices, stories, and intimacies as they travel. Journeying deep into the musical world of Somali love(-suffering), this book offers a reflection on music's everyday entanglements in the social and political lives of its makers and audiences. And set in a region where stories of love and longing are usually overshadowed by narratives of war— and where some have lamented the "death" of Somalis' artistic soul (Afrax 1994, Samatar 2010)—I tell a different kind of story about what it means to live and love in an unrecognized, postwar polity.

This book is, first and foremost, about the place and power of love songs in Somaliland and the intimacies that love songs distill and invite. Rooted in dareen-wadaag (feeling-sharing), these are intimacies that transcend everyday sociopolitical and economic cleavages and gendered social norms and prohibitions—intimacies that are as personally transformative as they are politically salient. But in telling a story about the voices that sing, speak, and otherwise animate love songs, this book also provides a novel account of the power of music, sound, and voice in an Islamic context. I argue for an approach to music that more fully accounts for the dynamic and fluid nature of song, the affective work of genre, and the way that songs become increasingly "sticky, or saturated with affect" (Ahmed 2014, 11) *in motion*. I pay particular attention to the way songs are continually *envocalized*— voiced and revoiced, storied and restoried, or otherwise animated by an increasing number of voices—as they live and move across time and space. Theoretically, this book is thus a reflection on songs' fluid ontology and the always-in-progress, human activity involved in making songs sticky. Methodologically, foregrounding songs in motion requires a shift in focus from contextual origins, form, or individual performers toward a broader range of actors—poets and musicians, singers and love-suffering listeners, music fans, critics, even ethnographers—who animate love songs and the diverse kinds of spaces, public and private, in which this takes place.

This book also tells a story about the power of the "voice"—as a medium of personal expression, a marker of subjectivity, and a mediator of interpersonal relationships. Attending simultaneously to the sonic and social nature of the voices that animate love songs, I specifically locate the intimacy-opening power of love songs in an "ideolog[y] of voice" (Weidman 2014a, 45) that figures the voice as a deeply personal mode of individual self-expression *and* the multivocal practices by which love songs are composed, circulated, storied, listened to, and performed. I suggest, in short, that it is in the voice that the intimate meets the social and where the social *makes* the intimate. This has implications for how we understand the voice as an index of subjectivity, the nature of multivocality, and the mediated making of not only songs but persons and publics, too.

Finally, this book also tells a story about Hargeysa and my own journey of learning to listen, appreciate, and even feel the place that love songs occupy in the city's sound- and lovescapes. In the remainder of this introduction, I outline the contours of Hargeysa's cityscape, set forward the theoretical orientation of this book, and situate love songs and myself as an ethnographer in this space.

Tani Waa Hargeysa! (This Is Hargeysa!)

Take a walk down the streets of Hargeysa, and your ears will be filled with a cacophony of sound and your eyes met with a tangle of colors and contrasting sights. Car horns blare and buses honk as they jostle with pedestrians and urban livestock for passage down the city's busy streets. The distinctive sirens of qaad-delivery vehicles alert chewers to an imminent delivery, fresh from Ethiopia. At roadside stalls, men talk poetry and politics while sipping sweet cardamom-laced tea. Glass-clad multistorey complexes mushroom through the city center, built by self-made local entrepreneurs and diaspora returnees. Across from the patriotically painted presidential palace, women sell camel milk to government employees in black SUVs on their way home from the Guurti (House of Elders). Moneychangers swap USD for bricks of Somaliland shillings, women hawk bananas from wheelbarrows, and men sell used clothes under ragged umbrellas. Young men in trendy tight trousers and women dressed more modestly in Saudi-inspired *cabaaya* and *jilbaab* (cloaklike outer garments) crowd into new pizza shops, ice cream stalls, and cafes. In the subdued light cast by a sea of orange tarpaulin, shopkeepers in the central market sell mattresses and pots, toothbrush sticks and cloves, camel liver, vegetables, and rolls of fabric. The five daily calls to prayer echo predictably from the loudspeakers affixed to the minarets of hundreds of mosques. Sheep cry, goats bleat, camel bells clink. The city moves and breathes and sings and groans in the steady sunshine and persistent dust of Africa's northeastern horn.

As the capital of the self-declared though yet-unrecognized Republic of Somaliland, Hargeysa is a bustling urban center indelibly shaped by a complex past, a contested present, and an as-yet-undetermined political future. Formerly a British protectorate, Somaliland first gained independence on June 26, 1960. Five days later Somaliland joined what had been Italian Somaliland to form the Somali Republic. The first decade of independence saw the establishment of a parliamentary democracy, including a number of elections that resulted in the peaceful transfer of power. In 1969, however, Siyaad Barre took power in a bloodless coup and for the next two decades implemented a program of Scientific socialism (*cilmiga hantiwadaagga*), while also pursuing a goal of unifying all Somalis—who had been divided by colonial powers into five regions—into "Greater Somalia" (Soomaaliweyn).[1] While Barre's regime made significant investments into education, literacy, and the arts, his regime became increasingly repressive, and in 1977–78 he led the country into a disastrous war with Ethiopia. While rifts between the former British and Italian Somalilands had been present from 1960, Barre's rule exacerbated what those in the north perceived as an unequal distribution of political and economic resources, a feeling that was especially strong among the Isaaq (one of five large Somali clan families, who live primarily in the north; Barre, by contrast, was Darood).[2] By the early 1980s, opposition in the north had coalesced into the Somali National Movement (SNM). In 1988, the SNM led a military campaign to capture Hargeysa and Burco; Barre retaliated with an air raid that razed much of Hargeysa (and a number of other cities) to the ground and forced most of the residents of Hargeysa and the surrounding

FIGURE 0.2. A monument to the 1988 war in downtown Hargeysa, featuring the MiG fighter jet used during Barre's air raid of the city. Photograph by the author.

area to flee to refugee camps. The MiG fighter jet now on display in the city center stands as a reminder of this destruction. For the next three years, the SNM waged a military campaign against Barre's regime, triumphing when Barre's Muqdisho-based regime capitulated in 1991.

While the SNM was not originally a secessionist movement, on May 18, 1991, Somaliland (re)declared independence from Somalia. Somaliland's early years of independence were tenuous. Violence between Isaaq sub-clans, no longer united by a common enemy, as well as between Isaaq and non-Isaaq clans, threatened the new polity's stability. But since a series of grassroots-led peace conferences throughout the early to mid-1990s, during which the former SNM leadership transformed into a government, Somaliland has functioned as a de facto state—complete with a flag and currency, a constitution, an independent judiciary, legislative branch, and bicameral parliament comprising a house of elected officials and the Guurti, a house of appointed elders. While the country's first two presidents were chosen by indirect elections, the last three have been elected in popularly contested general elections. During my longest stretch of research, the president was Axmed Maxamed Maxamuud "Siilaanyo," who was elected in 2010; he was replaced by Muuse Biixi Cabdi, also of the Kulmiye Party, in 2017. The local-led state-building process and the plural political-legal system that resulted from this—which incorporates traditional elders and elected officials, customary law (*xeer*), Sharia, and elements of the colonial legal system—is often praised as a model of indigenous peacebuilding. For good reason, Somaliland has gained a reputation as a bastion of peace and stability in a region marred by violence and insecurity.

Three decades after declaring independence, Hargeysa is a city that pulses with possibility. Home to just over a million people—roughly a quarter of Somaliland's 4.2 million—the colorful and noisy streets beat with pride at Somaliland's postwar political-economic achievements, largely attained without international assistance. The presidential palace and parliament stand as a constant reminder of the democratic advancements Somaliland has made. Shops painted patriotically in red, green, and white—the colors of Somaliland's flag—showcase the pride that ordinary residents have in their country. The shiny new facades of Dahabshiil, Telesom, Omaar, and Somcable buildings are a tangible reminder of the entrepreneurial spirit that has helped to rebuild Hargeysa from the rubble left by Barre's 1988 bombing campaign. And the bustling marketplaces, colorful streets, and youth sporting trendy new fashions as they sip cappuccinos between university classes pay tribute to the resilience and spirit of independence that has seen this region through immense political turmoil and adversity.

But a palpable precarity also hangs in the air. There is a sense here of being not out of time but afflicted by a kind of "stunted temporality" (Navaro-Yashin 2012, 7), caught between a war and its aftermath and subject to a perpetually uncertain political future. As one friend put it, Somaliland remains "hostage to [political] recognition." The conspicuous absence of buildings that predate the 1990s, and the shattered remains of places like the old National Theater, haunt more recent developments. The ubiquitous presence of urban livestock and makeshift *aqallo*—nomadic dwellings historically fashioned from wood and textiles, now piecemeal constructions of plastic jerry cans and hammered oil tins emblazoned with the logos of international relief agencies—are a constant reminder of the waves of forced migration that have swept over the region, precipitated by periods of violence and, more recently, the unmitigated effects of climate change. These dwellings often sit uneasily beside new malls and pizza shops, a visual reminder of the often vastly different fates of those who never left the region and those who resettled in Europe or North America and returned more recently. Such contrasts also reveal a complex economic picture. While

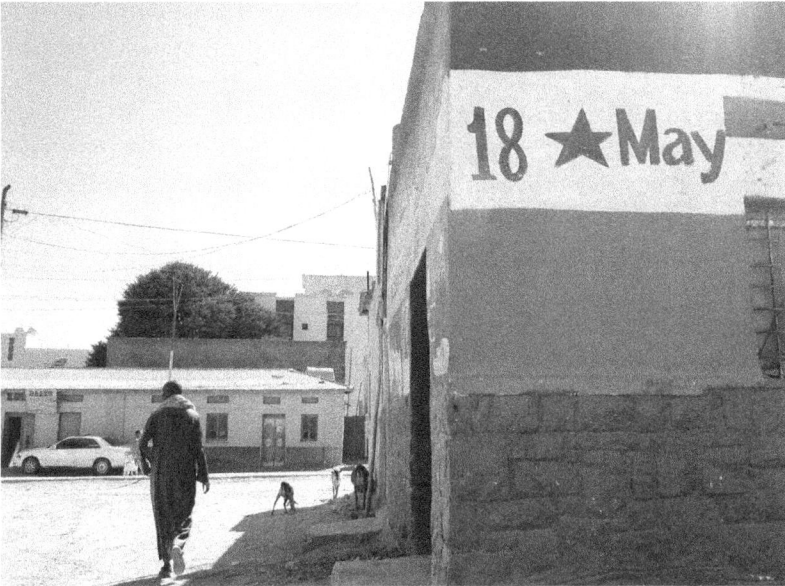

FIGURE 0.3. A shop in Hargeysa with a mural celebrating Somaliland's (re)independence day, May 18, 1991, in the colors of the Somaliland flag. Photograph by the author.

Somaliland's deep tradition of pastoralism is still a mainstay of the country's economy—an estimated 30 percent of the GDP comes from the livestock trade—an even greater proportion of the GDP (anywhere between 35 and 70 percent) comprises remittances from the diaspora (Pegg and Walls 2018, 336). As a result, pastoral-urban dynamics and local-diaspora relations are often fraught.

Other features of the cityscape speak to more recent anxieties and contestations. Large billboards on the main road to Wajaale warning of the dangers of irregular migration to Europe (*tahriib*) are a stark illustration of the challenges facing the country's young population. With unemployment rates estimated at upward of 75 percent, disillusionment with domestic future prospects among the postcollapse generation have led scores of youth to undertake this incredibly dangerous form of migration.[3] The predictable queues of men at qaad stalls also reveal a kind of collective angst—or at the very least the need for distraction. While once an occasional social and religious activity—notably featuring in Sufi gatherings and music-making events—chewing qaad (a leafy plant with stimulant properties, also known as qat/khat) is now more or less a national pastime (for men) that drains both resources and time (though an important source of income for some women). A contest for audiences between well-funded Salafist religious leaders (whose presence has grown since the early 2000s) and members of Sufi brotherhoods with much deeper roots in the region play out audibly in the city's streets: *qasaa'id* (Sufi praise songs) broadcast from defiant Qaadiriya mosques echo uncomfortably alongside the sermons of Salafist preachers who, among other things, preach the evils of music. And while many accounts of Somali politics overdetermine the importance of clan, in the context of war and weak state institutions, the security of kin networks has been a lifeline for many, even as relationships of trust or distrust have formed along these same lines. These lines of (dis)trust influence myriad aspects of sociopolitical life: from business partnerships, marriages, and the neighborhood in Hargeysa where one might live, to the delicate balancing of alliances between the major Isaaq subclans and non-Isaaq clans that defines Somaliland's multi-party democracy.[4]

Much like hees jacayl, Hargeysa is a city simultaneously animated by joy and suffering, memories of pain, and an almost defiant sense of hope for a different future. I have only scratched the surface here of the complex possibilities that characterize contemporary Hargeysa and the sometimes competing sociopolitical and religious influences that define the city's urban landscape. I will return in more detail to some of these specific dynamics below. But first let me outline what I have in mind by an ethnography of love songs in motion—and an account that centers voices that sing and speak about love.

Toward an Ethnography of Songs in Motion

At the heart of this book are a number of interrelated claims about what love songs are, what love songs do, and how love songs do what they do. This argument begins in a specific theoretical and methodological orientation toward "song." In short, I argue for approaching love songs as "quasi-objects" (Born 2005, 7) that are defined by certain socioaesthetic conventions but that are also always in the making, realized and experienced in "moments [rather] than wholes" (Agawu 2003, 98). Ultimately, this necessitates what I call an ethnography of songs *in motion*. This approach finds affinity in recent work that has challenged traditional ontologies of music, often by highlighting the "multiple and elaborative" processes by which music is encoded and that inevitably "set into motion connections that cross many different sensory modalities and enter other aspects of experience" (Shelemay 2006, 27).[5] But this is an approach that ultimately emerged out of my encounter with love songs themselves. The longer I spent with songs and with the people who create songs, listen to them, share them, and story them, the more songs revealed themselves to be more than simply the sum of some formulaic parts or "objects" that I could pin down. Let me explain.

When I began my research, I was determined to place love songs at the center of my project. My reasoning was multifold. I was motivated, firstly, by accounts of popular culture that highlight how popular art forms are uniquely germane ethnographic objects—objects that represent the "episteme of the everyday" (Newell and Okome 2014), and "give us 'history from below' and ethnography from within" (Coplan 1997, 29). I had seen this to be the case in the rich body of literature on African popular music and art,[6] as well as in previous studies of Somali orature that have used poetry as a source of commentary on issues ranging from pastoral life and migration to nationalism and gender relations.[7] But I was also wary of studies that seemed interested in these art forms merely as "windows" into some other aspect of sociopolitical life rather than worthy of investigation in their own right. So, I began my research committed to centering love songs as "the terrain to be studied" (Barber 2007b, 9), rather than an undercover way into understanding, say, gendered relations or politics (though of course I expected to learn about these things too). Hees jacayl, furthermore, have historically received short shrift. Most scholars have gravitated toward more "serious" genres of Somali verse, viewing love songs as "frivolous" and not worthy of extended attention (as some Somalis view them).[8] The same might be said, I should add, of love songs *everywhere*, which have never received as much attention as other forms of popular music (Gioia 2015). And given the prevalence of "Afropessimist discourses of 'disease, despotism and destruction'" (Barber 2018, 2, quoting Zeleza 2003, vii)—which are especially pronounced in the Somali Horn—I was committed, perhaps somewhat defiantly, to researching love songs *as love songs*. When asked what I was studying, I frequently simply said "love songs," resisting persistent requests to reveal that what I was really doing was studying "love songs and [fill in the blank with some more 'serious' research agenda here]."

I remain firmly committed to foregrounding songs as ethnographic objects worthy of attention in their own right. What has shifted is my understanding of the nature of songs' "objectness." In one sense, love songs exist as discreet "things" with some immutable components: words that reflect on the pain and promise of love, pentatonic melodies, and a voice with instrumental accompaniment. Songs can also be found in predictable places—on old cassettes, as digital files online, and sometimes as live performances. Mention the word "Beledweyn," for instance, and any lay listener could hum a specific melody, recite a specific set of words, and quickly find a recording on YouTube. "Beledweyn" is, in this sense, a clearly identifiable "object." But at the same time, the shape and feel of this song, and sometimes even its sound or voice, varied from place to place. In the archives at the Hargeysa Cultural Center, it announced itself as a classic hit penned by someone widely considered to be one of the greatest Somali poets ("Hadraawi is our Shakespeare!"). For many the song was a story, re-counted to me frequently, about a now-infamous encounter Hadraawi had while on tour in the town of Beledweyn, in southern Somalia. For others, this song was a slight against the north (now Somaliland) by an Isaaq poet some thought was too slow to disavow the idea of Soomaaliweyn (Greater Somalia) and Barre's regime (though Hadraawi quickly became a staunch critic of Barre and was imprisoned for his poetry).[9] This interpretation set off a poetic feud between Hadraawi and Cabdi Aadan "Qays," another northern poet who had opposed Barre from the start. (Qays's response? A song that went to great lengths to describe the beauty of a woman from the *north*.) For others still, "Beledweyn" indexed deeply personal moments in their own love lives. On occasion, it was performed live at Hiddo Dhawr, or sung by patrons who needed to get certain love sentiments off their chest. "Beledweyn" was not just one of these things: it was all of them. As a song, it was "fixed" at a certain historical moment. But it lives and moves in all of these moments in the decades since, somehow made and remade each time it is streamed on YouTube, debated, or performed. Centering songs as my primary ethnographic "object" would require an approach that accounted for the way that songs seemed to be continually in the making and to come most fully alive once set in motion.

In attempting to make sense of the fixed yet fluid nature of the songs that I encountered, two ideas have been especially useful. The first is a particu-lar understanding of song *as text*.[10] By text I do not simply mean words on a page or notes on a score. From the Latin *texere*, meaning "to weave," texts are forms of intentional human activity meant to make a mark, "utterance[s] (oral or written) that [are] woven together to attract attention and outlast the moment" (Barber 2007b, 2). In the first instance, texts come into being through a process of *entextualization*, during which "social actors turn on-going discourse and social interaction into text-artifacts" (Stokes 2010, 6). This is, in short, a process in which utterances are made to "stick," attract attention, and outlast the here and now (Barber 2007a). This initial fixing, however, is only the beginning, as ultimately what this does is set texts in motion to be detached and reembedded or recontextualized in future so-cial interactions. Songs-as-text, then, are always in the making, stitched to-gether by a range of actors across time and space. Or, as Agawu (2003, 97) puts it, songs-as-text are "woven by performer-composers who conceive and produce the music-dance, by listener-viewers who consume it, and by critics who constitute it as a text for the purpose of analysis and interpretation."[11] This ongoing process of text (re)creation is a constant, fluid, deeply dialogic and often improvisatory one in which text producers and their audiences are always highly entangled. It is also a process that both distills and produces social relations and that draws attention to the intentional social activity involved not only in fixing a text but also in ensuring that texts survive across time and space. Not all text-artifacts, after all, endure (Barber 2007b, 28). Rather than foregrounding contextual origins or individual performances, when I speak of love songs *in motion*, I do so to draw attention to this always-in-progress process in which poets, musicians, singers, listeners, and myriad others (including ethnographers!) are engaged.

This notion of song-as-text provides a kind of scaffolding for an ethnography of songs in motion. But the ways in which texts are fixed and draw attention to themselves and the channels through which they circulate and are reembedded critically depend on their form. To make sense of how this works, we also need to consider *genre*. Following recent work by anthropologists and others,[12] I approach genre not simply as a way of categorizing literary forms but as a sociohistorically contingent, dynamic, and emergent orienting framework that helps us understand the relationship between different types of texts, the expectations brought to bear on any given text, and a text's possible "trajectories" (Maybin 2017). As Barber puts it, genre works as "the pivot between producer and receiver of a text, the hinge between past creations and future ones, and the interface between coeval texts" (2007b, 44). Genre has something to tell us about the sociohistorical conditions in which a text artifact emerged. "Each word," Bakhtin says, "tastes of the context and contexts in which it has lived its socially charged life" (1981, 293). Yet genre is also dynamic and emergent, "created retrospectively and . . . always under revision" (Barber 2007b, 440); the "porosity" and intertextuality of genre is frequently key to understanding its social power (Gray 2013, 5). And genre plays an indispensable role in shaping the production and reception of texts. Textual producers carry out their work expecting audiences to receive their texts in certain ways (Barber 2007b, 33; Frow 2005). Genre, we might say, provides a framework for the processes of entextualization and recontextualization, guiding not only the form a text artifact takes but also how it is reembedded in new situations.

Because genre links past texts to future ones and provides cues for recognizing and responding to a text, recent scholarship has also highlighted the ways in which genre shapes not only verbal discourse but also *feeling*. In exploring a genre that, my interlocutors tell me, has the power to "make you feel what [others] feel," I also take up work by scholars who have highlighted the ways in which genre provides a framework or structure for feeling—"a form for feeling and a form for its contagion" (Gray 2013, 8)—for producers and audiences alike.[13] Part of the work of genre is *affective* (Gray 2013, 8; Hardt 1999). As such, Gray (2013, 5) suggests that genre is a form/force that is agentive in its own right, "an affective aesthetic force field" around which memories, stories, biographies, fantasies, and affect congeal. In focusing on the lives of love songs in motion, I grant songs themselves a certain agentive force, not least because love itself is locally conceived as agentive, frequently compelling itself into song, which then serve as "structures of feeling" for others (Williams 2015 [1977]). Love songs sometimes seem to live lives of their own, to move about of their own volition, and to move people unexpectedly. They are also especially prone to what Turino (1999, 235) refers to as "semantic snowballing": the continued layering of indexical affective meaning. Yet I am equally concerned with the intimate human activity always involved in infusing songs with their affective stickiness. Approaching love songs in motion allows us to hold together the human activity by which songs are continuously entextualized and recontextualized—or made to stick—and the affective power that sticky genres themselves seem to hold.

Documenting love songs in motion has one additional implication that, in a sense, brings me full circle to my early determination to approach love songs as the terrain itself. While resistant to approaching love songs as merely a window into something else, I did have a sense that I would encounter a range of themes central to contemporary Africanist anthropology and that these would provide important background information, or what is often thought of as "context." These themes include gender relations and evolving expectations and practices of love and marriage;[14] the world-building strategies of youth facing uncertain future prospects;[15] the force of nostalgia in the midst of profound sociopolitical-religious transformations;[16] and the politics of postcolonial belonging. But if songs are quasi-objects at best, constantly being produced as the result of intentional human activity, then the idea that they might ever constitute a two-dimensional window dissipates. So too does the idea of context as some objective field that exists prior or separate to texts.[17] Songs in motion are *process*, not object in location. They are themselves a "weaving together" (as the original Latin roots of "context" imply: *con* = together, *texere* = to weave). Figured thus, songs are not a window into understanding, for example, gender relations, just as gender relations are not simply context for understanding love songs. Love songs in motion, rather, *are themselves a story about* gender relations. Songs in motion are also a weaving together of expectations of romance and marriage, the anxieties and aspirations of youth, the intimate and political memories and longings of an older generation, and the complex politics of belonging and becoming in Somaliland.

This book tells a story about love songs *as songs*. But in so doing, this is also fundamentally a story about the way that songs and a range of sociopolitical processes and relationships congeal and reshape each other as they "collide and intermingle" (Born 2005, 7).

Now at the outset of this introduction I used the term "en*vocal*ization," rather than "entextualization." This is not to suggest that the textual nature of songs is unimportant but rather to draw specific attention to the centrality of the "voice" to the genre's textuality. In the case of hees jacayl, every act of entextualization is also an act of voicing, and an *articulation of voice*—or what I will be referring to as acts of *envocalization*. But for this concept to make sense, we first need a theory of "the voice," and, in particular, the kinds of voice or voices that animate hees jacayl.

Voicing Intimacy

In an effort to understand both what makes love songs sticky and what makes them stick, this book extends research on African popular culture and entextualization by attending to "voice" as both an ethnographic object and analytic frame. As a sung musical genre, it is through the voice that love songs come into the world and through an ever-expanding number of voices that love songs are animated and kept in motion. It is also in the voice that musical and linguistic forms of signification converge, and where referential, discursive, affective, and social meaning collide.[18] The voice, in short, has a high "semiotic density" (Turino 2014, 189). And as my title suggests, it is in the voice that the intimate meets the social, and the social makes the intimate.

In centering the voice ethnographically and analytically, this book contributes to efforts within the "sonic turn" in anthropology to more holistically attend to the sonic-affective social elements of (musical) texts (Faudree 2012), and to efforts in ethnomusicology to more fully elaborate the diverse socialities of song and singing. Summarizing this emerging anthropology of voice is beyond my current scope, but I will highlight a few critical insights. The first is that the voice exists as both a sonic, material, embodied thing—sound, produced by bodies, that is heard by others—and as a social phenomenon that is often elaborated to speak about issues of subjectivity and power. And scholars have shown ethnographically that these two sonic and social registers are fundamentally linked. Harkness (2014), for instance, highlights that the clean European-styled voice cultivated by Christian singers in Seoul cannot be separated from an emerging ethnonationalist Protestant Christian identity that sets itself apart from a rougher pre-Christian past. Similarly, Fox (2004) shows that the vocal stylings of country music singers in Texas both shape and are shaped by a certain kind of working-class culture. Importantly, what gives the sonic voice its social power in each of these circumstances, Weidman suggests, are distinct "ideologies of voice"—that is, the historically and culturally specific ideas that people hold about the voice that determine the links we make between vocal quality and character, the relationship between voice-as-sound and voice-as-subjectivity, and "the conditions that give sung or spoken utterances their power or constrain their potential effects" (2014a, 45). Attending to the linkages between the sonic and the social, ethnographic accounts of "the voice" have worked to correct "overly-discursive" (Feld et al. 2004) approaches in the social sciences that neglect the voice's material-sonic qualities. They have also successfully "provincialized" Euro-American assumptions often made about the "naturalness" of the voice as a medium of individual self-expression and its link to subjectivity (Kunreuther 2014, 33; Fisher 2016, xix).

This book takes up the project of "provincializing" the voice by trying to make sense of the sonic and social "voice" of love (songs). Indeed, I argue that understanding what love songs do and how they do it requires attending to the ideologies of voice that lend the genre its affective-aesthetic power. However, this is only half the story. I also suggest that we must simultaneously account for the *practices of voicing* by which the genre is kept in motion. Here is where I propose the concept of *envocalization* might be useful. In the first instance, en*vocal*ization draws attention to the *vocal* nature of songs as texts. Love songs' initial fixing as texts requires the voice as musical instrument, and their continued animation relies on the voice as medium of communication and personal expression. Their vocal nature, in short, is critical to how they are entextualized and recontextualized. While studies of entextualization have highlighted that "talk and text" are inseparable (Maybin 2017), this scholarship often tends to slip into the metaphorical. En*vocal*ization resists this trend, and calls attention to the role of actual voices in propelling songs as text across time and space. This is a *sounded* process that resonates and reverberates metaphorically and literally in unexpectedly profound ways. But in approaching the voice as a sonic *and social* phenomenon, I also use envocalization to highlight how a range of voicing practices *articulate* with an ideology of voice. We will see throughout this book that specific ideas about the voice shape the practices by which love songs are animated and imbue songs with their intimacy-opening power. Envocalization, in short, draws attention to the way ideology and practice, sound and the social, are linked at each turn.

Love songs' very in-motion nature demands an approach that accounts for this articulation of vocal ideology and practice. Yet attending to processes of envocalization quickly surfaces what first appeared to me as a paradox. We will see in the stories to come that love songs quite clearly find their affective-aesthetic purchase through a vocal ideology that figures the voice as a deeply personal mode of individual self-expression. Middleton (2000) glosses this as an "aesthetics of sincerity," which is common to a range of musical genres that privilege authenticity of expression. Elsewhere, this aesthetic is closely linked to an Enlightenment ideology that figures the voice as the personal property of an individual—as constitutive of the subject itself—and that is thus able to provide unmediated access to the interior sentiments, thoughts, and feelings of a unique individual (cf. Keane 2002, Englund 2018). This is a vocal-aesthetic ideology in which "the voice as musical instrument" and "the voice as instrument of self-expression" seamlessly align (Bicknell 2015, 49–50). My interlocutors used similar ideas when speaking about hees jacayl. The voice of hees jacayl, they said, is a God-given and natural voice, something that is "in one's genes," and that emerges from "deep, deep, within the soul." It is a voice that sounds from the heart. And it is through this voice that listeners said they could taste the emotion of another's love(-suffering) experience and feel what another feels. In Peircean terms, the affective power of songs rests in the voice's status as an "iconic index" (Harkness 2015, 575). Iconically, the voice conveys emotion in its sonic materiality or "grain" (Barthes 1977)—in its embodied color, timbre, tone—and in its musical expressiveness, especially in the shape of the melody. And indexically, the voice points toward a body, a flesh-and-blood person who has experienced love(-suffering).[19] This "voice," at first, looks and sounds very much like the kind of modern Euro-American voice-as-subjectivity "voice" that ethnographers have worked to provincialize, and that has been especially critiqued by Africanist scholars, wary of viewing the voice as the property of an individual (Englund 2015, 2018).

While love songs' intimacy-opening power rests firmly in an ideology that figures the voice as a deeply personal medium of expression, attending to love songs in motion very quickly reveals their fundamentally *multivocal* character. In the chapters to come, we will see that the voice of love songs is, in practice, never singular, and that hees jacayl are multivocal at every turn: from the way they are collaboratively produced and performed, to the ways people talk about songs and singers, to the ways that listeners take up songs into their own love and life agendas. This is unsurprising. Such is the nature of speech, and the varied participant roles we may hold in relation to any given voice (Goffman 1981, Fisher 2019, Weidman 2021). As Kunreuther (2014, 22) points out, paraphrasing Bakhtin (1981), "No word or utterance is every completely 'one's own,' and all discourse is saturated with prior utterances and voices." Indeed, by drawing attention to the ways that different (inherently multivocal) voicing arrangements enable forms of communication and social relations that may not be possible otherwise, a number of ethnographic accounts of the voice have persuasively shown that is it precisely the "heteroglossic," "polyphonic," or "delegated" nature of the voice that lends it its sociopolitical, moral, and affective power.[20] Such accounts have persuasively established that the voice is never the property of a single individual and that multivocality "is a condition endemic to social existence" (Englund 2015, 258; referencing Keane 2010, 77).

At first, the very multivocality of love songs struck me as a paradox—or at least as a crack in the logic of an aesthetics that privileges singing from the heart. If a voice is made by others, inflected by others' experiences and desires, how can it also be uniquely one's own? How can a multivocally produced voice provide access to the most personal of feelings—sentiments that seem to spring from "deep, deep within the soul?" But the longer I have spent trying to make sense of love songs in motion, the more I have come to understand that the very multivocality of love songs both produces and is produced by a voice that sounds "from the heart." In each act of envocalization, this vocal-aesthetic ideology articulates with a different (multivocal) voicing arrangement to distill, model, create, perform, or otherwise open space for intimacy. While each act is multivocal in one form or another, in no case does this make the voice any less personal or intimate. Rather, each instance of envocalization inflects love songs with deeply personal sentiments and, in turn, makes songs increasingly sticky. In the same way that scholars have highlighted how immediacy is an effect of mediation, not something prior to it (Mazzarella 2004, Meyer 2011, Kunreuther 2014), I argue that the deeply personal voice of hees jacayl is made intimate by its very multivocal sociality. Love songs are, after all, always simultaneously emerging from and shaping specific (intimate) experiences and relations.

After detailing the sociopolitical and affective history of the voice of hees jacayl as a genre (chap. 1), each chapter in this book centers a specific process or act of envocalization. In each case, we will see how love songs' multivocality makes and is made by a voice that sounds from the heart. The initial fixing of songs as texts, for instance, involves a collaborative process in which multiple contributors work together to distill love experiences into a voice that sounds from "deep, deep within the soul" (chap. 2). This deeply personal and seemingly singular voice then opens out into stories and talk that work to make and remake the voices of singers in incredibly intimate terms (chap. 3). In other moments, this collaboratively produced voice stands in for the tongue-tied voices of love-suffering listeners, helping them to make sense of their experiences and realize intimacy in their own lives (chap. 4). The process by which musicians learn to sound love, to sing and play from the heart—yet with and through the voices of others— infuses yet another layer of intimate possibilities into hees jacayl (chap. 5). And when performed on stage to a live audience, the voices, memories, and love experiences of artists and audience members collide to open space for a form of intimacy that is as politically salient as it is personally transformative (chap. 6).

I should note, finally, that my argument about the affective power of love songs' voice(s) rests on a particular understanding of intimacy. Intimacy is, after all, a notoriously "slippery" term (Geschière 2013, xix), and its "generative imprecision" (Weston 2017, 7) has led scholars to apply it to a variety of social and musical phenomena.[21] This book is, in one way, about intimate relations of the romantic and potentially sexual variety and thus contributes to efforts to remediate the sparse attention generally paid to love in Africa (Thomas and Cole 2009). The love that hees jacayl voice is often the love of romantic longing, and these songs undoubtedly help listeners and artists to make sense of these feelings in their own lives. Yet when I say this book is about *intimacy*, I also have something more than romance in mind. Following Wilson (2012, 48), I approach intimacy as a concept that is "unfixed but legible," and that "works to cover an open-ended array of relations" that exceed categories of kinship and the assigning of fixed identities. But I also take intimacy to be fundamentally about "deeply felt orientations and practices that make up what people consider to be their 'personal' and 'private' lives and interior selves" (Wilson 2012, 32). Like a voice that sounds "from the heart," this notion of intimacy rests on a specific notion of an individuated self with an interior life (Kunreuther 2014, 128). Yet the intimacy of love songs is ultimately about *sharing* parts of this interior self with others. As Berlant puts it, intimacy is about "an aspiration for a narrative about something shared" (1998, 281). Indeed, when speaking with my poet-friend Weedhsame about the closest concept in Somali to capture this, his suggestion was the term *dareen-wadaag*, which literally means "feeling-sharing." This "feeling-sharing" intimacy, we will see, is predicated on a kind of inter- and intra-personal vulnerability that is animated by a desire to know that one's love-suffering experiences are shared. We might say that this intimacy is less about a blurring of boundaries between self and other and more about the possibility that these boundaries might be permeated by *feeling*. This permeation is, critically, made possible by and through the voice.

Voices of Love in Hargeysa's Contested Cityscape

Much of what I have suggested in the preceding two sections could be said to be true in a range of ethnographic settings. And, indeed, I propose *envocalization* to be a framework that may account for the way that musical genres and other forms of speech find their affective power in a range of contexts and as a way for thinking through voice and practices of voicing in diverse settings. But processes of envocalization are themselves shaped by sociopolitical structures and cultural norms and expectations, which enable and constrain acts of voicing—or what we might call a "politics of voice."[22] The personally and politically transformative nature of the intimacies that hees jacayl distill and enable are fundamentally shaped by (and shape) the contested cityscape in which songs move and do their work. This is a cityscape where a certain politics of voice shapes who can speak, about what, for whom, and how, and where voices that sing and speak about *love* are circumscribed by a range of political, religious, moral and economic factors.

Among a population frequently and fondly referred to as a "nation of poets," the voice (*cod* in Somali) has long occupied a privileged position as a medium of communication. Historically, the poet (or *abwaan*) served as the principal spokesperson in interclan affairs, and oral poets continue to be revered for their ability to put into words the thoughts, feelings, and sentiments of their communities. It is in many ways the poet's "duty" to use their gifts of oration to do so—to be, as multiple poets put it to me, "a voice for the voiceless." Significantly, for Somalis, poetry is not simply a form of art or self-expression. Rather, poetry is a form of action in the speech-act sense. Poetry has been known to both start and stop wars, and an insult thrown in verse may sting more than the cut of a blade (see Laitin 1977, Samatar 1982). Somalis' reverence for the spoken word, and the political and affective potential of the human voice are, furthermore, deepened by the long influence of Islam in the region. While forms of religiosity have shifted in recent decades, common to all Islamic interpretive traditions is a deep reverence for the power of the human voice, both as a medium of language and *as sound*, to move listeners and to orient them toward God, whether this be through Qur'anic recitation, sermons, or in certain interpretive traditions (especially Sufism), through music. It is this reverence for the affective power of the voice that, in fact, lies at the heart of Islamic debates about the permissibility of music. Additionally, in both Somali poetic traditions and Islam, a reverence for the voice is accompanied by a recognition of the interpretive responsibility of listeners, whose "listening acts" (Kapchan 2017) shape the power of the voice in significant ways.

Perhaps precisely because of a deep-seated recognition of the powers of the human voice, Somaliland's speech and sound environment is circumscribed by a combination of political and religious forces, sometimes to contradictory effect. Somaliland today boasts a relatively free speech environment, especially compared to the mediascapes of neighboring Djibouti and Ethiopia and the strict censorship regime previously imposed under Barre. Somaliland has a vibrant print, TV, and online media environment, where new and old love songs circulate alongside Bollywood films and Turkish soap operas, Islamic sermons, Premier League football games, and a host of news programs that often openly critique the government. As one poet put it to me when I asked if he ever veiled political critique in love songs: "Today you can criticize Siilaanyo [the then-president] to his face!" This open speech environment recently manifested in a poetry debate chain (*silsilad*) known as Miimley, which took the government to task in scathing terms for mismanaging public resources.[23]

But at the same time there are clear boundaries to freedom of expression. While criticizing politicians is generally permitted, or at least tolerated, speech (or other acts) deemed to undermine Somaliland's independence are treated as treasonous. In October 2015, some members of the musical collective Xidigaha Geeska were arrested at the airport on their return from a concert in Muqdisho. Their crime? Waving the Somali flag, or simply going to Muqdisho in the first place. In 2019, the young poet Naciima "Abwaan" Qorane was sentenced to prison after her poetry, which lamented the loss of Somali unity, was labeled "anti-national activity."[24] And in what is perhaps the clearest evidence of the continued power of "the voice," private radio, by far the most influential news medium, is illegal: only state-run Radio Hargeysa, Voice of America (VoA), and the BBC Somali Service are permitted to broadcast. Finally, the public speech environment remains mainly the purview of men. There have been notable shifts in recent decades in women's participation in public debate—including in Miimley—but in the public sphere women's voices still feature far less frequently than men's.

Beyond the realm of overtly political speech, other forms of speech and behavior are curtailed by long-established (gendered) cultural norms and the current religious environment. These forces shape everyday public (and private) relations and have a marked effect on music and attitudes toward love and marriage. As I detail in chapter 1, music and the expression of love have *always* been complicated; hees jacayl have long been a site of celebration and contestation. This past remains present in contemporary attitudes toward music and the ambiguous space that artists occupy. But the current place of music and musicians is also shaped by more immediate political and religious forces. Artists have yet to fully recover from the near-complete destruction of the artistic sphere in the late 1980s and 1990s. This included not only the physical destruction of the National Theater and many instruments but also the collapse of the state that had supported the sector and, in the years that followed, a deep decline in artists' morale (Ducaale 2002). In a socialist holdover of sorts, the Ministry of Information and Culture employs about 100 artists, who are expected to perform at national events and to support national causes (like voter registration); the remuneration they receive, however, is far from a livelihood, and the government's relationship to these artists remains ambiguous at best. After two decades of almost no domestic musical production, the establishment of Xidigaha Geeska in 2012, and the opening of Hiddo Dhawr in 2014, marked critical moments in artists' postwar recovery. But artists continue to carry out their work against significant financial hardship and cultural currents that devalue their work. Artists often summarize their position thus: "Fanaanku waa ubax guddaafad ka dhex baxay" (Artists are like flowers growing from the rubbish).

The place of music and a variety of other activities has also been reshaped by Salafist groups that have gained in political and moral influence since the early 2000s. These Wahabi-influenced groups, who categorically reject music as xaaraan, are reshaping Hargeysa's soundscapes in fundamental ways. Most overtly, they have effectively silenced the city's public speakers of music. Whereas music lovers reminisced about the prewar roadside vendors who copied cassettes for passersby, or buses that competed for passengers with the soundtracks they played, opportunities for "ubiquitous" music listening (Kassabian 2013) are now basically nonexistent. During the course of my research a number of restaurants and cafes that piped music into their dining rooms met such resistance from local imams and their followers that they stopped playing music. In the case of Cup of Art, which also hosted open mic nights, harassment escalated into accusations of facilitating prostitution, and within eighteen months of opening, the venue had completely shut its doors. The conservatism of these groups also holds sway in certain parts of the government. Guddida Wanaag Farista iyo Xumaan Reebista (Committee for Morality and the Eradication of Bad Behavior) keeps a watchful eye over the city's youth, especially diaspora returnees, who are reprimanded for breaching unspecified moral codes, including things like men wearing their hair long. And in 2016, the minister of religion canceled a concert by Puntland singer Nasteexo Indho, ceding to complaints by religious leaders that her online videos showed she had a "bad culture" and that she "didn't behave like a Muslim" (she was filmed unveiled). In February 2018, this same minister banned the celebration of Valentine's Day, formally prohibiting would-be romantics from giving flowers or going to the beach in Berbera. In a tongue-in-cheek reference to the most famous Somali example of thwarted love—the story of Cilmi Boodhari, a 1930s baker-turned-poet who died from love—on February 14 my Facebook feed was filled with good wishes for a "Happy Cilmi Boodhari Day." Less overtly but equally significant, many of the postcollapse generation who were schooled in Salafist-funded institutions are more likely than older listeners to simply label music as xaaraan. This does not make music less popular but does manifest in a kind of listening guilt.

The place of hees jacayl, of course, must also be understood against prevailing attitudes and practices related to romance and the appropriate expression of love. As I will detail in chapter 1, there have been significant shifts in marriage practices and ideas about love over the last century: more and more couples aspire toward companionate marriage, dating is now fairly commonplace (though usually done in secret), and both men and women increasingly desire romance. These aspirations, however, continue to be thwarted on multiple fronts. Expectations that women marry by a certain age, to suitors of specific family and financial backgrounds, mean that women frequently accede to their parents' wishes in a choice of spouse. While exogenous marriage was historically preferred by pastoralists, a decades-long trend toward endogamy among urban populations has become especially pronounced in the wake of political violence.[25] Marriage between members of different subclans, and especially to southerners or minority Gabooye groups, can be fraught. And despite recent narratives of "Africa rising" (Taylor 2014, Frankema and Waijenburg 2018), rates of unemployment in Hargeysa are high; this economic precarity frequently leaves young men in a perpetual state of "waithood" (Honwana 2012), unable to afford the Islamic and Somali bridewealth payments, the costs of a wedding, and furnishing a house (cf. Masqualier 2005). As one friend put it, "Clan and money draw a line around love." Once married, the place of love in sustaining unions is also not straightforward. I met youth who spoke eloquently about the need to overcome long-standing cultural prejudices that treat love as irrelevant to marriage (as one Somali saying puts it,

"Maxaanu iska jeclaan waanu is qabnaaye" [Why should we love? We're already married!]), often drawing inspiration from Qur'anic teachings about the importance of respect and love between husband and wife. But in practice, old attitudes die hard, and marriages are often incredibly fragile. While divorce and serial monogamy is more common, the possibility of polygamy colors even companionate marriages.[26] Many friends thus frequently lamented the "love gap" that exists between the love they aspire to and "the love we practice in real life."

Finally, while expectations of love and romance are in constant flux, one more constant feature of Somali lovescapes is the relative difficulty that people have expressing love in both public and private settings. This is the case not only because of religious attitudes that lead government ministers to ban Valentine's Day but because of deep-seated cultural ideas about the appropriate expression of emotion and desire. For men, expectations of emotional stoicism mean there is still a great deal of shame attached to showing affection, even for one's wife—taking your wife out for dinner, or spending time at home rather than with other men, might lead to ridicule or a reputation of soft-heartedness. And while women increasingly demand romance from their partners, public displays of affection remain decidedly taboo, and the potential shame of showing affection even in private often puts men in awkward situations. The dapperly dressed Somali-British owner of Somaliland's first flower shop recounted to me some amusing purchasing arrangements he had developed with customers. While business was booming, he was frequently asked by male customers to discreetly wrap flowers so no one would know they were flowers. On one occasion, he even agreed to throw a disguised flower bundle out of the window to a customer waiting below who was too ashamed to be seen entering the shop. For women, expectations of extreme modesty and shyness (*xishood*), including toward one's husband, mean that it is nearly impossible to voice desire even within committed relationships; even saying "I love you" to one's husband is unthinkable for many. Suffice it to say that the expressions of desire found in love songs stand in stark contrast to everyday ideas about the appropriate expression of love. Love songs, quite literally, "sing what cannot be spoken" (Agawu 2001, 4).

The sociopolitical, moral, and sonic landscapes of Hargeysa are complicated to say the least. These are defined by the lingering effects of war, the near-complete collapse of the artistic sphere, ongoing contests for political-religious control of an unrecognized polity, romantic aspirations often thwarted by material and social realities, and a politics of voice that shapes both music-making and the voicing of love. And it was in this sometimes-bewildering urban space that my field research took place.

Intimate Entanglements

When I arrived in Hargeysa in 2015 to begin my longest (eighteen-month) stretch of research, I had little idea of what awaited me as a *caddan* (white) woman living in Hargeysa, or as an ethnographer of love songs. These experiences included some of the most difficult but also the most joyous periods of my adult life. They have also indelibly shaped the kinds of conclusions that I make in this book—both the arguments I put forward about "song" and "the voice," as well as the conclusions about the nature of the intimacy that love songs distill and invite.

Eager to settle into a routine and get to know hees jacayl, I spent the earliest days of my research at the Hargeysa Cultural Center (HCC) helping to catalogue cassettes for the center's newly established sound archive. But in an effort to "follow the thing" (Appadurai 1986, Marcus 1985), I quickly found myself catapulted from the archives into a range of encounters that were often perplexingly varied. My research took me from archives to informal home studios, from live performances to intimate domestic spaces, from Facebook and YouTube to cafes, hotels, and majlisyo, and, at times, beyond the bounds of Hargeysa, from Boorame to Berbera to Burco. While this often felt disjointed, and I sometimes longed for a more bounded field site and predictable schedule, attending to the ways that love songs move in and through these innumerable spaces gave me an acute appreciation of how songs serve to link otherwise disparate persons and places, moods and associations, gaining value in motion. As a friend from Boorame put it, when I explained to him, somewhat exasperated, the various directions my research often seemed to be pulling me: "What unites these things, Christina, seems to be love songs!"

As I followed love songs across these divergent spaces, I did so through an expanding network of friends, music lovers, artists, and cultural commentators, whose voices animate not only love songs but the stories I tell in the chapters to come. Colleagues at HCC, students at a number of local universities where I lectured, and the networks I developed through these venues proved a receptive audience for my incessant questioning. Frequent trips to Hiddo Dhawr allowed me to witness the real-time effects of love songs on both persons and place. Afternoons spent discussing friends' favorite songs—streaming videos on YouTube and often being taken on a journey through friends' love lives as a result—provided an intimate window into people's listening practices and the deep entanglement of love songs in people's own love journeys. And prompted in part by a friend's observation that if he was researching love songs he would start by interviewing the (aging) "big guys" before it was too late, I also spoke to as many artists as possible, who were active from the 1950s through to the 2020s—from members of Walaalaha Hargeysa and Waaberi to Xidigaha Geeska, among others. Alongside speaking with media personnel and other key actors in the arts sector, these interviews gave me an understanding of the development of Somali music, continuities and discontinuities between the pre- and postwar artistic scene, and artists' varied biographies and musical practices.[27]

These interviews also turned out to be a good initial entry into a network of artists and several informal spaces of music-making. These eventually became some of the most important spaces for my research. The unlikely friendship I struck up with Khadra Daahir early in my research was a crucial initial entry, and the time I spent with Khadra, and with other artists in her home, was pivotal to my research. It was a privilege to have been able to learn about the golden era of Somali music from one of Waaberi's leading female voices and to witness in real time the continued relief that the presence of singers like Khadra brings to their fans. Contacts that I made via Khadra also eventually led me to Cabdinaasir Macallin Caydiid, who took me on as an oud apprentice. In Cabdinaasir's home, I also got to know the young artists of FanSan, who regularly gathered there to spend time together and make music. The many afternoons I spent hanging out and fumbling through songs on the oud in Khadra's and Cabdinaasir's homes proved critical to my understanding of what it means to make music in Somaliland and how musicians are made—both how they are socialized and trained into music-making and how their legends are coconstructed in their interactions with fans. As will become evident in the chapters that document these experiences more closely (chapters 3 and 5), my time in the presence of these artists was both intellectually and personally transformative.

All of my research encounters were shaped by my more general experiences living in Somaliland. Unlike most white foreigners, who live in highly securitized compounds, hotels, or guesthouses and travel around with military escorts, I drove myself around in an old Toyota (prone to losing parts mid-journey) or took public transit, and lived in a regular house in a regular neighborhood—most of the time with my husband, whose family is originally from Arabsiyo (a town west of Hargeysa), and, for a shorter period, with members of his extended family (a female-headed household with five children). In public and in private domestic spaces where men were present, I adhered to the strict dress codes expected of local women and did my best to navigate the city as other Somalilander women do. From learning to negotiate a fair price for vegetables and navigating the busy potholed roads to learning to make *laxoox* (sorghum pancakes) and stay on top of domestic chores in a city of all-pervasive dust, my living situation afforded me a more intimate perspective on daily life than that open to most foreigners in the city.

I am not, however, like any other Somalilander, and my position as a white woman and a *dumaashi* (sister-in-law) indelibly shaped my experiences. Sometimes this positionality worked in my favor. While I adhered to local dress codes and my presence was certainly not genderless, my white womanhood was not neatly assimilated into local gender categories. This meant that I had access to domestic spaces that would have been off limits to a man (Somali or non-Somali), yet as a *white* woman I was, to a degree, freer to interact with men than local women would be. I was also able to speak about intimate matters with both women and men—or at least men of a similar age—in ways that would not have been possible were I a white man or a Somali woman. My white-woman foreignness also made me a kind of novelty, and people's curiosity about the "lady musician from Canada" (as someone who recognized me on the street once called me) was frequently helpful in facilitating contacts. And in circumstances where being an outsider would have raised difficulty and suspicion, my dumaashi (sister-in-law) status afforded me valuable protection. Being treated as a de facto member of my husband's subclan came with tangible benefits, like informal car insurance and easier passage through checkpoints when traveling outside of Hargeysa (especially to the west, where his family is from). My dumaashi status also made it easier for people to locate me within a familiar network of relations, and this often facilitated developing connections and building relationships.

This same positionality, however, was also frequently a source of frustration. Many of the relationships I attempted to build brought with them expectations that caused unease and served as a constant reminder of the asymmetrical power dynamics inherent in research in postcolonial (and many other) contexts. Awareness of my own privilege and what my presence meant did at times lead me to do things that caused discomfort, like being interviewed for TV, or appearing on stage in ways that highlighted my novelty status. My foreignness also marked me as an eternal outsider, frequently the site of unwanted attention and unsure of the footing on which I could build relationships. My dumaashi status was not obvious when I moved around the city alone and gaining this foothold of acceptance required disclosing aspects of my personal life that I did not always want to disclose; it also came with a whole host of other social, religious, and familial expectations. Alongside the everyday stresses of life in a precarious unrecognized state, my position as a caddan-dumaashi-outsider researcher was frequently the cause of sometimes profound personal and professional anxiety.

I do not intend here to resolve the challenges that have long dogged (and should continue to trouble) researchers working in postcolonial (or other) settings. What my anxiety regarding my own positionality did afford me, however, was an even greater appreciation of the kinds of spaces that music-making and love songs open. I felt most at ease in the homes of artists, themselves hyperconscious of what it means to live a life perennially on the edges and, consequently, more welcoming of a stranger in their midst—and more willing to overlook certain unintentional transgressions. And once I let down my own guard and learned to reciprocate the types of feeling-sharing that listening to and talking about love songs affords (or demands), I started to appreciate more deeply love songs' work as a radical social leveler and my interlocutors' refusal to sing, hear, or experience love songs as primarily political. If suffering from love is an inevitable, universal human experience—and in this setting, it is most certainly understood as such—then love songs open the possibility of sharing in something that transcends those aspects of everyday life that usually divide, of belonging to each other on the basis of shared vulnerability.

Writing about his fieldwork in Zimbabwe, Matthew Engelke observed that "it was almost always in singing that I forgot my place as an anthropologist" (in Chrysagis and Karampampas 2017, 10). For me, it was in the moments of vulnerability that love songs opened that I think I both lost *and found* myself as an anthropologist. When friends and family asked me from afar about my research, I would usually answer with some variation of "Somaliland is not an easy place to live"—then, later, "writing a book is hard"—yet invariably followed this up with "but I still love my topic." I have retrospectively come to understand this answer as the work of love songs on me—the work that love songs performed and continue to perform for/on me to open spaces for intimacy, vulnerability, and escape in the midst of the challenges of carrying out long-term ethnographic research and attempting to represent these experiences on the page. And the more time I have spent with these songs, the more encounters, relationships, memories, and spaces the affectively charged words, melodies, and voices of songs have come to index, the more potent their effect has become. I have lost (or found?) countless afternoons of scheduled writing to the wonders of YouTube, where one song leads to another and then another, Maandeeq's voice gives way to Cumar Dhuule, then to BK and Khadra Daahir, perhaps subconsciously needing the kind of "relief" that Hanad described above.

Love songs' reparative powers have recently taken on new resonance for me, as my friend's advice that I should interview the "big guys" before it was too late has truly hit home. In the years since my main research period in Hargeysa, several artists I interviewed have passed away: Maxamed Saxardiid "Jebiyey" of Walaalaha Hargeysa; Rashiid Bullo of Radio Hargeysa; Cabdiraxmaan Dheere of General Daa'uud; Aamina Cabdullaahi of Waaberi; Maxamed Miyir, the talented lead musician of Xidigaha Geeska, who died long before his time; and the prolific and highly revered poet Maxamed Ibraahin Warsame "Hadraawi." The deaths of each of these artists represent an immeasurable loss to the Somali artistic community—and beyond. But it was the recent deaths of Khadra Daahir Ciige and Cabdinaasir Macallin Caydiid, in July and December 2022 respectively, that have affected me the most deeply. Khadra and Cabdinaasir were unequivocally the two people who most profoundly shaped my research experiences in Hargeysa. They each, in their own way, made Hargeysa feel like home. This book, quite simply, would not be what it is without them. In the immediate wake of each of their deaths—when I was also finalizing this manuscript—I found listening to their music to be incredibly painful. But eventually I also found comfort in the opportunity to spend time with them in this way, and a quiet joy in the knowledge that their voices, memories, and legacies will unquestionably live on. I am honored to have been able to call them both friends. I hope that I have done justice to their stories, their wisdom, and their voices in the pages to come.

Given these intimate entanglements, what follows in this book is a deeply personal yet simultaneously multivocal account of a genre, written in a voice constrained by the expectations of a different genre—yet nevertheless a voice that now joins many others in the intimately social work of animating love songs.

[CHAPTER ONE]

Anatomy of a Love Song

Ciil iyo caashaq ayaa loo gabyaa.
Poetry is made from oppression and love.

Somali saying

"Well, if you want to study love songs, then you've come to the right place!" Sada remarked, in response to my brief explanation of what had brought me back to Hargeysa. "But I'm not sure if we should really call them *love* songs," she continued. "They are more like sadistic torture lessons in anatomy. About your internal organs being squeezed, your ribs broken, your heart exploding. For some reason, Somalis always associate love with pain. It's no coincidence that our greatest love story is a story of unrequited love."

Sada and I were sitting in a makeshift office at the Hargeysa Cultural Center, sheltering from the afternoon sun on a dusty summer's day in August 2015. We had run into each other by chance, though in those early weeks of my research I was spending most days at the center, alternating between language lessons and helping to catalogue cassettes for the center's new sound archive. Established just months before I had returned, this archive was meant to preserve and celebrate the music and poetry of prewar Somaliland.[1] Hanad and I had been tasked with labeling cassettes, most of which were purchased from studios abroad or donated by individuals who had safeguarded cassettes during the insecurity of the late 1980s and 1990s. A local student in his midtwenties, Hanad seemed to have an encyclopedic memory when it came to Somali music, and our work was regularly distracted by the stories that different songs elicited about the songs' origins and Hanad's first encounters with this music, most of which was composed decades before he was born. And when we finally acquired a secondhand cassette player after days of scouring the central market, these stories were accompanied by the songs themselves. This caused our cataloguing work to progress exceedingly slowly. But as we worked with dusty fingers, old cassettes piled high around us, I was beginning to get a sense of the artists behind these works, the complicated political context in which many of these songs were produced, the continued appeal of prewar love songs to Hanad and his peers in the postcollapse generation, and the political statement that, like Hiddo Dhawr, an archive such as this was making in Hargeysa's contested soundscapes. I was also starting to get a sense of Somali conceptions of love, its unruly and transformative power—not least because nearly every song we encountered seemed to be about love-*suffering* of one sort or another. But Sada's suggestion that love songs might be better conceived as "sadistic torture lessons in anatomy" cast the theme of love-pain in especially poignant terms.

This was not the first or the last time that I would hear comments to this effect. On the contrary, wherever I encountered love songs I also seemed to encounter the expectation of hearing about another's love-pain, of sharing in the deeply felt sentiments of some man or woman who had been squeezed and broken by love. The songs that I catalogued with Hanad spanned many decades of profound sociopolitical change: the end of colonialism and the birth of the Somali Republic, the rise and fall of Barre's military regime, increasing urbanization, a series of wars and their aftermath, and ever-evolving expectations regarding romance and marriage. These songs were inevitably inflected by the historical contexts out of which they emerged. Their sound and instrumentation indexed changing musical influences and historical circumstances. But there also seemed to be a clearly identifiable thread that linked these songs. The "anatomy" of these songs, we might say, remained familiar, even as their external styling evolved. Among their most easily identifiable parts was a "voice" that sang of deeply felt internal sentiments, a first-person voice that often seemed to be simultaneously transgressive and much beloved for the intimate anxieties and aspirations that it sounded in the world. And, as Sada memorably pointed out, many of these songs contained quite literal lessons in anatomy.

This chapter is about the anatomy of hees jacayl. I explore why it is that love songs might be conceived of as anatomy lessons in the first place by providing a kind of dissection of the crucial component parts of love songs as they took shape in a particular historical moment, in a specific voiced form. I am especially interested here in two features that link otherwise quite diverse-sounding songs and that are central to the affective force that songs continue to wield: the nature of love(-suffering) in these songs and the voice that gives songs breath. Teasing out the love imaginaries that give flesh to Somali love songs is a task that gets us some way to understanding why anatomy lessons seem to be a key feature of the genre's own anatomy, while also providing critical insight into the kinds of intimacies that love songs continue to distill and invite. At the same time, the voice of these songs is equally critical to the work that they do. This is a voice, we will see, with a particular history, shot through with certain religious and sociopolitical sensibilities. And distinct from other genres of orature, this voice indexes, both sonically and metaphorically, a particular kind of voicing subject. Taking genre to be sociohistorically contingent, yet also a dynamic and emergent "affective aesthetic force field" (Gray 2013, 5), I tell a story about the sociopolitical-historic conditions that gave rise to vocal expressions of intimate love sentiments, as well as the affective expectations and ideologies of voice that have attached themselves to love songs as a genre—and that inevitably inflect how love songs are heard, circulated, and voiced today.

I will note two things at the outset. The first is that I approach hees jacayl, like Somalis themselves do, as a broad genre of orature that encompasses songs composed and performed from the 1940s onward, on the theme of love, by and for both men and women, and set to instrumental accompaniment. The term itself—which simply means "love song" (*hees* = "song," *jacayl* = "love")—only came into popular usage from the 1960s or 1970s but is retrospectively used to describe earlier songs, like qaraami, that share these characteristics. The genre encompasses a range of subgenres that describe specific types of love experiences: *calaacal* depict painful experiences of longing or mistreatment; *riyaaq* detail instances of requited love; *foorjo* contain rebukes of scorned lovers. In Somali orature more generally, genre (*bad*, which also means "sea") is sometimes used to describe quite technical features of verse (especially meter) but is also used as an affective-aesthetic classifier linked to the social circumstances and "work" that particular types of poems perform.[2] At the broadest level, poetry can be divided into *maanso* and hees.[3] Maanso poems were considered the more serious and prestigious and include genres like *gabay*, historically the preferred (male) genre for politics and philosophy; *geeraar*, a genre originally used in warfare; and *buraanbur*, a women's genre. Hees, by contrast, were considered less serious and include shorter poems sung to accompany various work activities (*hees hawleeddo*, "work songs") or dances (*hees ciyaareed*, "dance songs"). Both maanso and hees deployed a meter associated with that genre alone, often related to the activity the genre accompanied (e.g., *geeraar* uses a meter that mimics a horse's cantor) and were performed to a genre-specific melody or melodic mode (*luuq*).

Beginning in the late colonial period, Somali orature underwent significant transformations. The general categories of maanso and hees still stand and exist in a hierarchical relationship of sorts, but the content of what they describe has evolved, as has their sound. The category "hees" came to be used to designate poems sung to a unique *laxan* (melody) with instrumental accompaniment, or what might simply be described as "popular song" (sometimes referred to as "modern song"). The overwhelming majority of newer hees are love songs, though there are also songs that comment on politics (*hees siyaasadeed*). There is also now crossover in the types of meters deployed, with both maanso and hees making widespread use of the short-lined *jiifto* meter.[4] Maanso continues to describe poetry considered more "serious," but the gabay meter has decreased in popularity, and luuq are rarely used—though listeners know how the gabay meter sounds, and the use of specific meters in certain contexts can carry affective or political force. A gabay composed by a woman, for instance, makes an implicit claim to public spaces historically reserved for men. What is pertinent to bear in mind is that hees jacayl is both a fixed and fluid category—much like seas are distinct bodies of water but still quite literally fluid. And as all genres, love songs find their affective-aesthetic force in a particular history and in the ways that they are related to and distinct from other genres of orature.

The second observation relates to the fluid and always emergent nature of love songs. This chapter is, on the one hand, a kind of history of voices that speak and sing love in Somaliland. I trace nearly a century's worth of love poetry and song, much of which can be found in the archives at the Hargeysa Cultural Center. Yet it is equally important to highlight at the outset that these songs remain very much alive, and the stories that continue to animate these songs are not stories only of the past. In part because of the impact of the war on musical production, much of the prewar music I discuss below remains in wide circulation today. And while conversations with Hanad provided me with an early clue to the historical significance and enduring appeal of these songs, it was the more everyday encounters, like the one with Sada, that gave real flesh to the songs and unequivocally demonstrated how the genre's past continues to be storied and animated. I have organized this chapter around key historical figures and developments, highlighting the nature of love and the voice at each turn, as well as how each earlier iteration of the genre has shaped what comes next. But these voices always resound in multiple directions, simultaneously echoing forward and backward. I hope to give a sense of this continued and multivalent sounding in the narrative below, weaving together the texts and contexts of songs written many decades ago with the stories that people continue to tell to give shape and sound to these songs in the present. This is thus a (hi)story that, like sound, moves in circles, reverberating around the "voice of love" at the heart of hees jacayl.

"Cilmi Is Our Ka'bah": Love(-Suffering) Finds Voice

Boqorkay huq iyo ciil	O my king among poets!
Hagardaamo lumisow	You who were driven onward to destruction
Hadimada kalgacalka leh	By your sorrows, by your helpless anger
Cilmigii u hoydow	And by the harshness meted out to you—
Heesaha baroorta ah	O Cilmi, you who died from passion's griefs,
Halqabsiga jacaylkow	You are the very paragon of love!

Maxamed Ibraahin Warsame "Hadraawi," "At the Grave of Cilmi Boodhari"
(Translation from Andrzejewski and Andrzejewski 1993, 90)

During the first few weeks of my time in the archives with Hanad, one name seemed to creep into conversation again and again. My notebook from this period contains hastily scribbled reminders to myself on nearly every page: "Who is Cilmi Boodhari?" "Find out more about Cilmi!" "Cilmi = the 'father' of Somali love?" By the time of the conversation with Sada recounted above, I knew immediately that "the most famous Somali love story" she was referring to was the story of Cilmi Boodhari and his ill-fated love for a woman named Hodan. Now Cilmi's voice itself does not exist in any sound archive. A baker reportedly turned poet in the 1930s, Cilmi lived and died before radio and sound-recording technology had arrived in Somaliland. But it was impossible not to hear Cilmi everywhere. In the case of Cumar Dhuule's "Heesti Boodhari," Cilmi's own words are given musical voice.[5] Direct references to Cilmi also abound, as in the song "Hud-hud," which uses the text of the poem by Hadraawi quoted above. And, indirectly, the "voice" ushered in by Cilmi's love poetry as well as the nature of the doomed love experiences captured in his verse reverberate everywhere. "If you want to understand Somali love, Christina, you need to start with Cilmi," one friend put it bluntly. Another poet-friend, Weedhsame, put it like this: "Cilmi is the axis of our love. He is the Ka'bah.[6] Like on the *xaj* [pilgrimage], people surround the Ka'bah in Mecca. He is the Ka'bah of our love." So let us begin with Cilmi, his "voice," and a consideration of the literary-love revolution his verse and love-death set in motion.

Cilmi Boodhari was born to a family of modest means in the rural borderland between Somaliland and Ethiopia, sometime in the early twentieth century. Like many other young men of his generation, in the wake of a twenty-year war—which had pitted British colonial forces against the army led by the poet-warrior Sayyid Maxamed Cabdille Xasan—Cilmi left the countryside looking for work in the city. After first going to Hargeysa, Cilmi eventually settled in Berbera, where he found work in a bakery. The name

"Boodhari" is a Somalization of the word "border" or "powdery," depending on who you ask, a reference either to Cilmi's natal land or eventual profession.[7] As the story usually goes, one day while at work a girl named Hodan entered the bakery. Upon seeing Hodan, Cilmi was immediately smitten and fell hopelessly in love. Preoccupied with thoughts of Hodan, he stopped eating and put little effort into his work; then his health began to fail. Unaccustomed to seeing a man so overpowered by love, Cilmi was mocked, reviled, and accused of feigning illness (Abdillahi and Andrzejewski 1967, 196). While not known to be a poet before, Cilmi began composing poetry that expressed his all-encompassing love. In verse that drew on the pastoral imagery, alliteration, and meter of the prestigious gabay genre, Cilmi produced a body of work that expressed his singular and complete love for Hodan, admonished those who chastised him for his love, and expounded on the virtues and pains of love in terms that often approached the mystical.[8]

Despite this outpouring of poetry—or, indeed, perhaps because of it—Cilmi's love for Hodan was, by most accounts, never returned. Two years after their initial bakery encounter, Hodan married a man named Maxamed Shabeelle. Why Cilmi could not marry Hodan is a matter of debate. Abdillahi and Andrzejewski (1967) suggest that Hodan's family rejected Cilmi because of his lower socioeconomic background and weak affiliation to his own clan. Members of his own Ciidaggale subclan, the Daa'uud Garhajis, were in fact some of the ones who ridiculed him most harshly (as he put it in one poem: "If a man has a wound he is taken to the doctor / But the braves of Daa'uud are ridiculing me!").[9] Laurence (1993) also reports that Cilmi's family only had a few camels (the traditional bridewealth currency) and that he failed to persuade her clan to let him marry her because he was so poor. Gabobe (2014), however, doubts that Cilmi even proposed marriage and instead suggests that Hodan's family was hostile toward him because of the poetry he composed. Not only was being moved entirely by love in the choice of a wife considered to be antisocial, but some of his poetry contained descriptions of Hodan's body that were as scandalous in a literary sense (gabay poems were certainly not known for describing a woman's beauty) as they were socially taboo; as such, they brought shame to Hodan's family through the suggestion of an extramarital affair. One of his poems, for instance, praises Hodan's "magnificent bearing" and "fine-shaped bones" that stand out under her flesh and likens the gloss of her gums to "blackest ink"[10] and the flicker in her eyes to the "clear light of the white spring moon." He also describes how his heart leaps when he sees the "infinite suppleness in her body's sway."[11] Whatever the case may be, Cilmi was so grief stricken that he grew even thinner and weaker. Various interventions to cure Cilmi of his lovesickness failed, including sending a group of girls to present themselves as possible brides. Frail, frustrated, and brokenhearted, by the late 1930s or early 1940s, Cilmi died, reportedly of a broken heart. This death earned him a reputation as the first Somali to have died for love.

While Cilmi met an unfortunate end—or, perhaps, precisely because he did—his poetry and the story of his love-death soon spread like wildfire. His verse was unequivocally a challenge to the status quo, both in a literary and social sense. On the poetry front, while ideas of romantic love and longing exist in some documented poetry from this time—especially in the "miniature genres" (Johnson 1996), including dance songs like *dhaanto*—respectable or "prestigious" genres of poetry like the gabay did not engage the topic of romantic love.[12] When women were the topic of poetry, descriptions tended to focus on the characteristics of the ideal marriageable girl (beautiful, from a good family, naive in matters of sexuality) and the proper wife (obedient, faithful, competent in their housework and child-rearing duties) (Kapteijns 1999, 23–49). Descriptions of the physical features of a woman would have been completely taboo. So too was the very idea of being compelled by love in the choice of a wife, as marriage required the approval and financial support of one's immediate and extended family. But while Cilmi's verse represented a clear "discourse of defiance" (Abu-Lughod 1990, 39), and he was mocked and reviled by many for his predicament, it was precisely his transgressiveness, alongside the indisputably beautiful nature of his poetry, that gained him a devoted following. This was especially true among young, urban men, many of whom similarly wished for greater freedom in marriage "but lacked the ability and courage to defy the established, traditional view of love and marriage" (Abdillahi and Andrzejewski 1967, 205). Unaware of his own eventual influence, Cilmi became "the mouthpiece of a powerful social trend" (Abdillahi and Andrzejewski 1967, 204). Like a religious martyr—whose suffering of an injustice serves to bring into focus two competing belief systems and whose death lends credibility to the marginalized cause for which they were ready to die (Cook 2007, 2)—Cilmi is credited with paving the way for greater acceptance of the ideal of romantic love and companionate marriage. He is also widely esteemed as a poet, both for the beautiful verse he composed and for "breaking the chain of silence," as Weedhsame put it to me, regarding the public expression of love in "serious" poetic verse.

Stories about Cilmi and his legacy could fill many volumes. Indeed, he is the subject of numerous Somali-language books, and his story features in several English accounts of Somali orature.[13] But I would specifically like to highlight the facets of Cilmi's impact that can be heard most forcefully in the love songs and popular love imaginaries that followed his love-death. First and foremost, according to Gabobe (2014), we have Cilmi to thank for the displacement of the "traditional warrior" by the (suffering) lover as the hero of Somali orature. The love-suffering hero, of course, is not unique to Somali orature, and stories of love martyrs abound in literature across the Muslim world (Cook 2007, Giffen 1971). Some of these stories, notably the seventh-century Bedouin story of Qays and Leyla, are also popular among Somalis and bear a striking resemblance to Cilmi's story: a man falls in love with a woman he cannot marry, he is considered crazy by those around him (earning him the nickname "Majnuun," i.e., crazy), he is compelled by love to write verse, and he eventually dies.[14] But Cilmi physically manifested a story of ill-fated love for a Somali audience for the first time, giving powerful witness to the potentially lethal force of love in real life, not just in legend. That Cilmi was a flesh-and-blood individual known to have lived and then died on Somali soil, who composed beautiful poetry in Somali, is absolutely fundamental to his legacy.

This new hero, importantly, is an individual who suffers on two accounts. He suffers, firstly, because of the very force of love—a force conceived to be beyond the control of the individual, catching its host unaware and producing ravaging effects on the body. Its symptoms include loss of sleep, loss of appetite, body aches and pains (notably in the heart, liver, blood, and bones), and general bewilderment. These are symptoms that resonate with local ideas of illness and helplessness caused by spirit possession (Lewis 1989, 64–71). They are also symptoms rooted in an understanding of emotion as residing in both the heart and the liver (which controls the appetite) that are documented in medical and philosophical texts across the Muslim world, as well as in some Hellenistic medical literature.[15] Sada's comments that love songs may be considered "anatomy" lessons attests to the continued prevalence of this conceptualization of love. The second source of the lover-hero's suffering are the structural constraints and attitudes that prohibit him from being with his beloved. These include the social expectations that suitors come from an appropriate clan and financial background and the general view that falling in love is a sign of weakness. As Cilmi put it in the poem "Caashaqa haween" (The love of women), "Evil is the custom of Somalis—otherwise they would not revile me" (in Abdullahi and Andrzejewski 1967, 196–97). While the cultural attitudes and social constraints that thwart love aspirations have evolved since Cilmi's day, this too remains a central theme in love songs up to the present.

Cilmi did more, however, than give witness to the power of love with his death. He also did so in a well-preserved and highly revered body of poetry that gave voice to the effects of love in a particular way. In contrast to the politically and clan-oriented gabay poems that were popular in the early twentieth century, Boodhari's poetry marks a shift toward an inward-looking, self-reflexive subject, a subject at odds with the world in which he lives, and a subject who seems to have no recourse except to voice his frustration in verse (Gabobe 2014). The voice that "breaks the chain of silence" regarding the public expression of intimate sentiments is thus understood as a voice almost compelled by love itself and, at the least, as the unmediated outward expression of deeply felt love-pain. It was the pain of love, after all, that turned Cilmi into a poet. Why else would he risk giving voice to sentiments that would turn him into such an outcast? The voice of love is thus naturalized as the exterior and spontaneous expression of interior sentiments.

How and why this voice took hold as it did and when it did is not an accident of history. There are, to begin, clear resonances here with modern idealizations of the voice as "providing access to a 'pure interiority' that is linked with subjective self-presence" (Sterne 2003, 15). The voicing subject at the center of Cilmi's verse is a subject who desires greater autonomy and freedom and a change to the social status quo. And indeed, Gabobe (2014) suggests that the inward-looking self-reflexive subject of Cilmi's verse points toward an emerging modern subjectivity reflective of the far-reaching sociopolitical changes (and crises) of the late colonial period in which he lived. Elsewhere, this naturalized or "sincere" voice has been linked with notions of autonomy, agency, and freedom (Keane 2002, Haeri 2017, Kunreuther 2014). It is little surprise that this voice also makes an appearance in the anticolonial, proto-nationalist discourse that grew louder in the decades after Cilmi's death.

But there were also antecedents to this voice in Cilmi's religious milieu. More specifically, the voice of Cilmi's poetry also resonates deeply with Sufi conceptions of a self who suffers the pain of separation (from the divine) and for whom suffering is redemptive, perhaps even pleasurable, because "love loves the difficult things" (Farid al-Din al-Attar, in Gabobe 2014, 29). Cilmi's verse details a process of self-discovery and transformation that includes sometimes ecstatic experiences of emotion and devotion that strongly parallel the stages of self-development of the Sufi novice (Gabobe 2014). So strong are these resonances that some have suggested that Cilmi's poetry was in fact about divine love.[16] When it comes to love martyrs, Cook (2007, 98) notes that this is not an uncommon phenomenon: one of the reasons such stories may circulate so widely across the Muslim world is that they may be read as allegorical stories of divine love and Sufi devotion. Now I have been resolutely assured, by sources including Hodan's son, that Cilmi most definitely loved a woman named Hodan and that anyone who suggests Cilmi's poetry was about an otherworldly divine love is neglecting historically established facts and missing the point of the story: that profane love is so powerful it may have mortal consequences. What is important to note is that the voice in Cilmi's poetry resonates with local religious conceptions of selfhood defined

by suffering, self-discovery, and devotion, as well as emergent modern notions of the voice as linked to ideas of autonomy and freedom.

While Cilmi was mocked and ridiculed in his lifetime, in death he has
undoubtedly become an "iconic and uniting figure" (Gabobe 2014, 18),
variously revered as the king (*boqorka*) or father (*aabbaha*) of Somali love,
whose love-voice continues to echo through Somali orature. No other poet
has gained the kind of sympathy that Cilmi has received, and his death has so
preoccupied poets since that Cilmi features in innumerable songs, and his
grave has become a site of pilgrimage. It was in fact a pilgrimage Hadraawi
took to Cilmi's grave that inspired the poem that became the songs "Hud-
hud" and "Haatuf": in "Hud-hud" (named for the hoopoe bird, believed to
be a messenger between the living and the dead), Hadraawi speaks to Cilmi
in the afterlife; Cilmi then responds in "Haatuf" (referring to a voice that is
heard but not seen). Yet Cilmi's story also elicits a complex set of emotions,
ranging from commiseration and sympathy to shame and guilt. Something
about him and his story remains, as Gabobe puts it, "disturbing and unassimilated" (2014, 18). While originally the shame was Cilmi's, in death
a kind of collective shame has also come to envelop his story, as his death
has "metamorphosed" from one of individual responsibility to "a collective
Somali guilt" about a death caused simply because Cilmi's love aspirations
were so at odds with the society in which he lived (Gabobe 2014, 18). On the
one hand, this guilt has softened attitudes toward romantic love, yet it is still
somehow troubling for the constant reminder it serves of the challenge love
continues to pose. Cilmi's story, in this way, produces a sense of what Herzfeld (2005, 3) calls "cultural intimacy," a kind of intimacy that arises from
the shared "recognition of those aspects of a cultural identity that are considered a source of external embarrassment but that nevertheless provide
insiders with their assurance of common sociality." If Cilmi is the "Ka'bah"
of Somali love, this complex mix of reverence, pity, guilt, and shame is also
a critical component of the affective infrastructure that his verse and love-
death continue to provide. We will hear resonances of this complicated intimacy time and again in the songs and stories and voices to follow.

Of Broken Hearts and Broken Lorries: A Genre Is Born

Quraaradayow, dawada quba	Oh bottles, pour out your medicines,
Oo qalfoofyahay, wada dhaantada	And when you have emptied, resound with a love song.

unattributed belwo
(Text and translation from Andrzejewski and Lewis 1964, 148–49)

"You know, Christina, I have met many love viruses," Hanad explained, pensively, as we sipped cappuccinos during a break from our archiving work one day. We had spent the preceding hour listening to some of the older recordings in the center's collection, including some of Hanad's favorite qaraami. This had prompted a reflection on some of the love difficulties he had personally faced and why he is so drawn to these songs: recall from the introduction that Hanad's girlfriend had recently left him, as he did not have the financial stability required to get married (not unlike some of the difficulties that Cilmi faced). "But then I like to sit alone and listen to qaraami," he continued, "then it is like a big rain. The rain is raining with me. I know someone else has met these days too." He paused. "Do you know that poem, by the poet Weedhsame? Barkhad [a mutual friend] he played it on VoA?" "Yes!" I responded. "He says the oud is like an IV drip, right?" "That's the one!" Hanad exclaimed. "'Cusbitaalka boholyowga' [The hospital of longing]. It is a hospital for people suffering from love sickness. Medicine does not work. But the treatment is the oud. And the food of the hospital, it is qaraami."

Love songs' healing powers, especially in relation to qaraami, is a theme that we will see quite clearly reflected in the chapters to come. From the Arabic *gharāmī*, meaning "amorous" or "passionate," these songs hold a particularly special place as the earliest form of hees jacayl. And as Hanad's comments and Weedhsame's poem attest, qaraami continue to circulate widely and remain central to Somali love imaginaries. But these songs are also fundamentally the creation of a particular sociopolitical and technological moment and, I would suggest, mark the solidification of a specific kind of voice. In the years after Cilmi's death, conditions were ripe for the emergence of a new form of orature. The migration of men toward urban areas intensified, leading to the emergence of a new, young, urban elite. The opening of radio stations across the region—including Radio Hargeysa (originally Radio Kudu) in 1943—facilitated the spread of new sounds from abroad and closer to home (alongside rising anticolonial sentiments). But as was the case for love's grand entrance to Somali orature, the birth of qaraami is often narrated in a series of stories of happenstance and misfortune, featuring two key figures: Cabdi Deeqsi "Sinimo" and Cabdullaahi Qarshe.

As the story is usually told, the birth of hees jacayl can be traced to a mechanical failure on a dusty road between Jabuuti and Boorame, sometime between 1943 and 1945.[17] The protagonist of this story is Cabdi Sinimo, a lorry driver also known for his storytelling prowess (hence the nickname "Sinimo," from "cinema"). One day while driving his lorry, Cabdi Sinimo was forced to the side of the road by engine trouble. Frustrated and alone, unable to figure out how to repair his vehicle—and possibly also distracted

by thoughts of a woman, or his friends enjoying themselves back in Boorame—he composed a short verse to air his grievances. Improvising on
the vocative form of the word *belwo* (sometimes written *balwo*), from the
Arabic *belo* (meaning "misfortune" or "calamity"), he reportedly sang some
variation of the following:[18]

Belwooy, belwooy, hoy belwooy	Oh *belwo, belwo,* hey *belwo*!
Waxaa i beeleeyey mooyaane	I'm unaware of what has caused me to suffer
Waxaa i beeleeyey baabuuree	What caused me to suffer was a lorry
Waxaa i beeleeyey Beerguba	She is Beerguba [the "liver-burner"] who made me suffer
Waxaa i beeleeyey Boorame	What caused me to suffer was Boorame

When he finally managed to tow his lorry back to Seylac (a coastal town between Jabuuti and Boorame), he repeated his poetic complaint in public to
instant success. Encouraged by this warm reception, back in Boorame he
and others continued composing similar poems, on themes ranging from
everyday events to descriptions of the women they fancied, often reflecting
on some type of calamity, from the reflexive perspective of the individual
caught in the middle of it. Accompanied by upturned jerry cans and tin
drums (and, later, the oud), belwo borrowed the poetic meter of the dance
genre dhaanto, which uses a midlength-lined meter (shorter than gabay)
that requires two alliterating words in each line. Facilitated by the radio
and the group of artists that gathered around Cabdi Sinimo, who began
touring to perform their new compositions live, belwo quickly spread to
neighboring cities. Before long, belwo had enthusiastic audiences, especially among urban youth, in cities like Jigjiga, Jabuuti, and Hargeysa. The
spread of belwo was even amusingly described in one belwo itself, as recited to me by Rashiid Bullo, a musician who was one of the earliest staff
members at Radio Hargeysa:

Belwadii baxsatoo baraay qabatee	*Belwo* escaped and went to the East
Baabuur ma ku baadi doonnaa?	Should we ride a car after it?

While a beloved art form in its own right, it was the belwo's eventual
encounter with the oud that would lead to the birth of qaraami. Enter here
Cabdullaahi Qarshe, who would bring differentiated melodies and instruments to the poetic expression of love. Born in Tanzania and schooled in
Aden, Qarshe grew up surrounded by the sounds of Sufi praise songs. But

after the opening of Radio Aden he became especially enthralled by the music that featured during the station's Hindi- and Arab-language broadcasts. Hoping to bring instrumental music to Somalis, Qarshe managed to buy an oud, even though his religious family considered music xaaraan. When he moved to Somaliland in 1945, he found an Arab musician who agreed to teach him. By this point the radio had facilitated a shift from shorter belwo to longer *heello*; at first these new heello were formed by stringing together shorter belwo by different authors, but they later evolved into longer single poems with standardized alliteration (Johnson 1996). The introductory formula "belwooy, belwooy, hoy belwooy," which had negative connotations of drinking and promiscuity, was also replaced with "heellooy heelleelloy," borrowed from more culturally accepted dance genres (Qarshe, in Johnson 1996, xiii). Drawing on the melodies of existing hees, Qarshe began experimenting, first attempting to set some of Cilmi Boodhari's love poetry to music; later he composed original music for the texts of belwo and heello, alongside some of his own and others' poetic compositions. His early compositions on the theme of love eventually became known as qaraami.[19] While he himself disavowed the title—emphasizing that Somalis have always had song, they just did not use nonpercussion instruments—Qarshe is fondly known as "the father of Somali music" (see Hassan 2008, 80).

In both subject matter and voice, there are very clear resonances between Cilmi's poetry and the belwo and qaraami that followed. As was the case for Cilmi, belwo and then qaraami offered accounts of frequently unfortunate love experiences from the first-person perspective of those caught in love's path. As in Cilmi's poetry, this included reflections on the social conventions that limited freedom in love and marriage and decried prevailing attitudes that resulted in ridicule:[20]

Maankiyo madaxaa i kala maqanoo,	My mind and my head are apart,
Idinna waygu maadsanaysaan.	And all of you make fun of me!
Dhibtayda dadkaa ka dhuumanayow,	O you people who hid from my problem:
Dhirtoo maqashaa i dhaafteenoo,	While the trees lend an ear, you passed me by;
Dhagaxyaa damqan laa dhibaatada.	[Even] stones would sympathize with my plight.

On occasion, they also ventured into the especially taboo territory of describing the beauty of a woman's body, using veiled pastoral idioms:

Cagaarka ka baxay, caleen-weyniyo,	The growing buds and leaves mature,
Cosob aan cidi daaqin baad tahay.	The fresh and ungrazed grass are you.

But mostly, as in Cilmi's poetry, belwo and qaraami depicted love as an unruly and all-consuming force that affected the sufferer's very anatomy. Take, for example, the following three belwo, the last of which was sung by Cumar Dhuule in the qaraami "Xaafuun":[21]

Cishqigu ma aha cuud la dhaqdee,	Love is not incense to be used sparingly;
Waa cudur ka bilaabma curuqyada.	'Tis a disease which begins in the muscles.
Anigoo buka baahidaada iyo,	While I was still ill with need of you,
Ku baal-maray beerku may go'ay?	I passed you by; did my liver break?
Culayska i saaran ciirciiroo	The burden on me caused me to stagger
Caguhu qaban waaye ciidda dhulkee	My legs cannot move through [grip] the sand of the earth
Calooshani caafimaad qabine	This stomach is ill!

In belwo and qaraami, we clearly see the consolidation of the love-suffering hero as the principal protagonist of a new form of love poetry. Cabdi Siniino and Cabdullaahi Qarshe, however, also ushered in some significant social and sonic innovations. In contrast to other forms of orature that were performed by men or women for audiences of the same gender (including the gabay Cilmi composed), belwo were composed by both men and women for both men and women, who often gathered in homes late in the evening to socialize, compose, and perform for each other. And, critically, women like Khadiija Ciye Dharaar, who became known as Khadiija "Belwo," were among the genre's earliest torchbearers. Belwo thus offered both men *and* women a space to air their grievances and the opportunity to hear about the love tribulations of members of the opposite sex. This feature indelibly shaped their reception. On the one hand, *belwo* proved to be incredibly popular among urban youth, because of both the intimate sentiments they voiced and their mixed-gendered nature. These same things, however, also provoked harsh criticism from other quarters. Established poets critiqued these belwo as frivolous. Timo-Cadde, a well-known mid-twentieth-century poet, reportedly famously quipped "maansada qaraamigan yaree qayliyaa dilaye" (these noisy qaraami are killing poetry). And belwo were especially reviled among elders and religious leaders, who blamed the belwo for "bringing corruption and spreading sin,"[22] even going so far as to ban the fathers of Cabdi Sinimo and Khadiija Belwo from their own mosques. Like Cilmi's love poetry before, belwo elicited a complex set of reactions.

In addition to the belwo movement's mixed-gendered sociality, qaraami marked the emergence of two critical artistic/sonic innovations. The first was the introduction of distinct melodies (laxan). This change set qaraami apart from both maanso and earlier hees (including belwo). At the time, all genres of maanso, including gabay, were sung or chanted to a luuq—a melodic mode that utilizes three or more pitches of an anhemitonic penta-tonic scale, performed syllabically, and guided by the scansion of the po-etry rather than a strict musical meter (Banti and Giannattasio 1996; see figure 1.1).[23] While luuq varied by performer, each genre, like gabay, had a prototypical luuq (Banti and Giannattasio 1996). While a clear voice might have been prized for the clarity it could bring to the recitation of a poem's words, the luuq was not emotionally expressive, and the contribution of the reciter's voice singing the luuq was not an affective one (Orwin 2003, 340; O'Dubhda 2009). Traditional hees also had unattributed, genre-specific melodies, with underlying rhythmic structures related to the activities they accompanied: the rhythm of dance songs facilitated dancing, while work songs provided rhythmic structure for repetitive work activities (like camel watering or millet pounding). These melodies were very repetitive and of-ten featured antiphonal and responsorial singing (Giannattasio 1988, 161). These features allowed for the easy substitution of texts, which were also often unattributed (all written in a genre-specific meter) and simply taken up by individuals as different situations demanded. This was also the case for belwo, which were all sung to the same unattributed melody; as repre-sented in figure 1.2, performances often included a lead singer and chorus, who alternated between a common refrain featuring the invocation "bel-wooy, belwooy, hoy belwooy" and the text of a performer's choosing.[24]

Qaraami, by contrast, are sung to a set of distinct melodies, most of which are named—like Xaafuun, Subcis, Raaxeeye Burcaawi, Laac, Nuu-gal, and Jawhara Luula—and attributed to musicians including Qarshe, Je-biyey, and Maxamed Siciid "Guroonjire." Compared to the luuq of poetry and the melodies of dance and work songs, these melodies are more musi-cally varied and expressive: they make fuller use of a singer's vocal range and the pitches of a scale (though they still use the same anhemitonic pen-tatonic scales as luuq and earlier hees), include more distinct phrases or sections, are sung by a single vocalist (the responsorial/antiphonal features

♩ = approx. 70, with *rubato*

3

A - wal   maan - so waa-taan   gud-boo,   gu-dhi – yey waa-yaa-ye   Waa-taan   gal-beed-kaas   u di-ra-y,

gu-ga   hor – tii – sii – ye   Aan ga-shee – yo tii xa-lay   hur - da – da   ga-ma' - a ii   dii   –   day

Awal maanso wataan gudboo, gudhiyey waayaaye   To begin with, I had neglected poetry and let it dry up
Wataan galbeedkaas u diray, guga hortiisiiye   I had sent it west in the beginning of the spring rains
Aan gasheeyo tii xalay hurdada, gama'a ii diiday   But let me set forth what prevented me from sleeping last night

FIGURE 1.1. Example of a gabay performed to a luuq: an excerpt from the poem "Gudban" (alternatively known as "Gaala-leged") by Sayyid Maxamed Cabdille Xasan and recited by Aw Daahir Afqarshe. The transcription features the poem's opening tercet, with each line comprising two hemi-stiches containing a word beginning with the alliterative sound "g." In Afqarshe's performance, each tercet (totaling 153 lines of poetry) is performed to this luuq, with slight variation. The translation is from Afdub and Kapteijns (1999, 37).

♩ = 80

Lead vocalist 1st time only, group on all others   Group

Bel – wooy!   Bel – wo – oy hoy bel – wo – oy   wa – xaa   i   bel – eey – ey   mo – oy-aa – ne   Bel –

Fine

wooy!   Bel – wo-oy   hoy bel – wo – oy   wa – xaa   i   bel – e – ey-ey   mo – oy-aa – ne

Lead vocalist   Group

I – ya-doo uur-ka   hoo – ya – deed   ku jir – ta   In – dha-cad ar – ki   may – sid   la   yi dhi   ye   Bel
I – ya-doo uur-ka   hoo – ya – deed   ku jir – ta   In – dha-cad ku ay – aan – so   la   yi-dhi – ye   Bel
Ha – dda-na   i – ya-doo   a – dee-ge-y – saa   In – dha-cad ar – ki – may – sid la   yi-dhi – ye   Bel

Belwooy, belwooy hoy belwooy   O belwo, belwo, hey belwo
Waxaa i baleeyey mooyane   I am unaware of what has caused me to suffer

Iyadoo uurka hooyadeed ku jirtaa   While she was in her mother's womb
Indha-cad arki maysid la yidhiye   I was told I will not meet Indho-cad

Iyadoo uurka hooyadeed ku jirtaa   While she was in her mother's womb
Indha-cad ku ayaanso la yidhiye   I was told Indho-cad would be my good luck [I would have her]

Haddana iyadoo adeegeysaa   Then when she was mature
Indha-cad arki maysid la yidhiye   I was informed I will not meet Indho-cad

FIGURE 1.2. Example of a belwo, as performed by Ibraahin Garabyare, a contemporary of Cabdi Sinimo. The melody and the lyrics of the refrain are common to all belwo. The text is in the dhaanto meter, with the stanzas each containing two words that alliterate in the vowels. *Indho-cad* literally means "white eyes," and here refers to a woman.

were dropped), and make extensive use of long melismatic (rather than syllabic) phrases. Like belwo, the poems sung to qaraami melodies all utilize the dhaanto meter. But the sung texts of qaraami also feature nonlexical vocables, repeated syllables, words and phrases, and additional exclamatory words that fall outside the poetic meter. For instance, in the song "Xaafuun," the three lines of belwo text quoted above become six sung phrases (see figure 1.3). The first two lines are sung as written, but the third is repeated three times, with the extra-metrical words "Alla" (O God), "Mahee" (In fact), and "Aabbow" (O Father!) tacked on to the beginning for emphasis; the "caa" in "caafimad" is also repeated the first time it is sung, and an additional melismatic phrase on the nonlexical vocables "haa heellee" precedes the third repetition.[25] Importantly, these features are dictated not by the meter of the poem but rather by the melody and the emotion it carries. Unlike earlier genres, the melody of a qaraami is not just a vehicle for conveying words: the melody itself is central to a song's aesthetic-affective force.

With these increasingly expressive melodies, qaraami also heralded the beginning of a shift in terms of the specificity of the "voice" recalled by a

Culayska i saaran ciirciiroo	The burden on me caused me to stagger
Caguhu qaban waaye ciidda dhulkee	My legs cannot move through [grip] the sand of the earth
Alla calooshani caafimaad qabine	O God, this stomach is ill
Mahee calooshani caafimaad qabine	In fact, this stomach is ill
(Haa heellee)	(Haa heellee)
Aabbow calooshani caafimaad qabine	O father, this stomach is ill

FIGURE 1.3. Example of a qaraami: the first stanza of "Xaafuun," as performed by Cumar Dhuule (transposed up a fifth). The text is in the dhaanto meter, with each line containing two words alliterating in "c." Note the addition of nonlexical vocables and a number of exclamatory words that fall outside the poetic meter, as well as the extensive use of melismatic phrasing.

given song. Whereas the luuq of poetry and melodies of dance and work songs identified the genre alone, the melody of a qaraami always recalls a specific "song." Like belwo, early qaraami allowed for the substitution of different lyrics, and the songwriting process remained somewhat open-ended—poets and performers could add lyrics that reflected on their own experiences. Khadra Daahir's performance of "Xaafuun," for instance, uses different words than Cumar Dhuule's, which itself includes verses contributed by different poets. But the shared melody in these performances make them all renditions of "Xaafuun," rather than qaraami more generally. And while it would be some time before a single set of lyrics by one poet became fixed to a single melody, because of the emotion carried in the melody of qaraami, songs also became increasingly identified with the singers—or *codka* (the voice)—who performed them. Mention the song "Xaafuun" today, and listeners will immediately recall a song popularized first by Cumar Dhuule, then later sung by Khadra Daahir.

Qarshe's second innovation was his use of the oud—a short-necked pear-shaped string instrument fashioned from wood (also known locally as a *kaban/kaman*). While earlier genres may have been accompanied by a drum, no other instruments were involved. Qaraami, however, were fundamentally defined by the oud, which Qarshe endeavored to play in a uniquely Somali way. Qarshe also paved the way for the incorporation of an increasing number of instruments, including the flute and violin. Importantly, in Somali these instruments also possess a *cod* (voice). I give a detailed account of Somali oud playing in chapter 5 but will highlight here that the *cod* of the oud and other instruments adds an additional expressive layer to a song's performance. The oud does this in several distinct ways. Qaraami all feature long instrumental introductions, in which a song's melodic motif is introduced. During vocal sections of the song, the oud either doubles the vocal line, lending support to the vocalist and adding heterophonic texture, or "dialogues" with the singer (and percussionists) in a kind of call and response (replacing the antiphonal/responsorial singing characteristic of dance and work songs). But like a good vocalist, the *kabaniste* (kaban or oud player) also adds their own flavor to the laxan; a good kabaniste plays "from the heart," and their instruments "sing" in their own emotionally expressive voice. This is most clearly audible in the way the kabaniste riffs on the laxan in the instrumental introduction and between vocal stanzas and in the *xawaash* (spice) or ornamentation that the kabaniste adds to his playing.

Given the complex place of music in Islam—especially instrumental music—these innovations gave critics of the belwo even more reasons for criticizing these new artistic developments. But as the IV-line dripping the sounds of the oud in Weedhsame's love hospital suggests, the instrumentation of qaraami is crucial to their affective force and therapeutic potential. Qaraami give voice to deeply held personal love sentiments in words from a unique introspective position. But they also voice these sentiments in *sound*—in their distinct, emotionally expressive, and singularly voiced melodies and in their instrumental accompaniment. For this reason, qaraami were described to me as the "quintessential" Somali love songs: songs that are able to make you "feel love." They are so closely aligned in sound and voice with the experience of love itself that Weedhsame described them to me as "the garden of lovers and beloved ones"—and, more succinctly, as "love incarnate."

By the 1950s, qaraami had taken form as a genre differentiated from other forms of orature by their intimate subject matter, mixed-gendered creation and consumption, the distinct and emotionally expressive melodies to which texts are sung, the self-reflexive personal "voice" in which songs spoke, and their instrumentation. On each account, we might say that these songs represented a "discourse of defiance" (Abu-Lughod 1990, 39): in their expression of deeply felt sentiments of love-suffering individuals, which posed a challenge both to the marriage status quo and norms of acceptable topics for poetic reflection; in their mixed-gender nature, intermingling deemed both "un-Somali" and "un-Islamic"; in the public display of emotion they represented; and in their eventual *musical* incarnations, the Islamic permissibility of which has long been contested. Challenging the status quo in both content and form, these artistic innovations were celebrated and revered by urban youth for giving voice to shared aspirations yet were simultaneously reviled by the prevailing authorities for doing so. In the coming decades, the social and political place of hees would undergo a radical transformation. But as was the case for Cilmi's poetry, the complex mix of reactions and emotions that these early love songs elicited—joy, relief, gratitude, shame, guilt, anger—continues to shape their affective work.

Love and Revolution: Mainstreaming Music and Romance

Anigaba lafiyo jiidh	My flesh and all my bones
Waa kii i laastee	Were completely consumed by love-pain
Liqi waayay oontee	I could not even swallow food
Adigaa lis caanood	Fresh milk
Iyo laas xareediyo,	And pure well-water and
Laydhiyo hadh diidee	Fresh air and rest in the shade, you have rejected

"Leexo," words by Axmed Saleebaan Bidde, vocals by Hibo Nuura

In terms of sheer volume, Hanad and I spent the vast majority of our time cataloguing cassettes from the 1970s and early 1980s, or what is fondly recalled as the golden era of Somali music. The overwhelming number of cassettes from this time is partly a result of certain technological innovations, which made cassette technology widely accessible to the public during this period. But it also fundamentally reflects a marked increase in artistic production following Somali independence (1960) and a massive investment in the arts under Barre's rule. This was a period in which the place of artists—especially singers, including women—was radically refigured and when music and love entered the mainstream. Cassettes from this era are the cassettes that Hanad himself was weaned on in the late 1980s and early to mid-1990s, as he listened alongside his older brother and sisters to the likes of Hibo Nuura, Khadra Daahir, Magool, Axmed Cali Cigaal, and many others. It is also on these cassettes that qaraami gave way to the broader category of hees jacayl, and an aesthetics that privileged performing "from the heart" takes an even fuller form. The fundamental anatomy of hees jacayl, however, remains remarkably familiar—even as their sound and the social status of those who gave them voice evolved in significant ways.

The transformation of what came to be known as modern hees (or popular song) into a respectable genre began in the 1950s, when it was hitched to the anticolonial project of an emerging political elite (Johnson 1996, 83). Cabdullaahi Qarshe was critical in this movement, composing songs about not only love but also the evils of colonialism and the sacrifices to be made in pursuit of independence. Broadly known as *hees siyaasadeed* (political songs), these included both *hees waddani* (nationalist songs) and *hees anti* (songs that were "anti" the powers that be). In 1955, under Qarshe's leadership, artists' efforts were consolidated in Walaalaha Hargeysa (the Hargeysa Brothers), the first artistic collective of its kind. In the immediate wake of independence in 1960, music also played a critical role in fomenting feelings of Soomaalinimo, a clan-transcending pan-Somalist ideology (cf. Hassan 2018). But as disillusionment with the political leadership and distribution of resources in the new polity grew, musicians began critiquing the government. Political songs more or less replaced the gabay as the voice of a new political elite. This would have a knock-on effect for the mainstreaming of love songs. But the political climate of the 1960s also had a more direct link with the genre. While anticolonial songs were written in very direct language, to avoid censorship from the Somali governing authorities, poets took to disguising political critique in love songs (Johnson 1996, 118). By the end of the decade, listeners were so accustomed to hearing veiled "anti" sentiments that the playing of Hibo Nuura's song "Leexo" (Light breeze), quoted above, during the 1967 election is credited with swinging support from the incumbent to his challenger, making it "the poem that overthrew a President" (Johnson 2010, 237). The song's poet maintains that this song was really a hees jacayl about a woman scorned by a man. But listeners heard it as "anti" commentary about the government's deceit and ill-treatment. Whatever its original intent, this case highlights not only songs' interpretive malleability but also the extent to which love songs had entered mainstream consumption.

Although music had begun to circulate with more frequency and acceptability by the late 1960s, Barre's socialist government, brought to power in a bloodless coup in 1969, was to indelibly reshape Somali musical production. Barre saw the arts as a means of educating the population and promoting support for his government; he thus effectively nationalized the entire artistic sphere. This had a number of effects on artistic production. On the one hand, the increasingly repressive regime severely curtailed freedom of speech, and artists who did not toe the line faced imprisonment or exile. Subversive songs and poems banned from the radio began circulating illicitly on cassettes. Yet nationalization also meant artists had financial and human resources at their disposal like never before. National theaters were built in Muqdisho and Hargeysa; artists were organized into collectives associated with or employed by different government agencies; new talent was recruited through school singing competitions and cultivated in youth groups; and musicians had access to an increasing range of instruments, from guitars and saxophones to synthesizers and basses, giving songs an increasingly cosmopolitan sound. Waaberi (Dawn), the principal national collective, had well over a hundred members who regularly performed across the country and represented Somalia abroad. Many members of Waaberi quickly became national icons—and are still revered as such. As was the case with earlier musicians like Cumar Dhuule, the arts continued to offer a route to fame for members of marginalized clans, who became significantly overrepresented in artistic fields.[26] And while playing instruments and composing the lyrics and melodies of songs remained the domain of men, many of the most celebrated singers of this era were women. Encouraged by ideals of gender equality and anticlannism advocated by the quasi-secular socialist government—and encapsulated in the saying *abwaan qabiil ma leh* (a poet has no clan)—artists became celebrated as clan-transcending national heroes, and women singers in particular were treated as the country's "pride and joy" (Khadra Daahir, in Sohonie 2017). Taken together, the status of artists was raised to levels of respectability and recognition never dreamt of before, facilitating an unprecedented amount of new music. Despite near-universal disdain for Barre's rule, nostalgia for this golden era of Somali music continues to shape contemporary listening as well as efforts to reinsert music into public soundscapes—including the opening of Hiddo Dhawr and the Cultural Center's sound archive itself.

The incorporation of musicians into anticolonial, nationalist, and socialist projects served to mainstream previously marginalized forms of popular expression. But music was, of course, not just popular because of its occasional political undertones. The overwhelming majority of songs continued to be about love, and while sometimes disguising political critique, these songs found their primary impetus in broader social transformations in gender relations and marriage aspirations. As Fair (2009, 79) points out, across the continent vocabularies of independence were put to work not only for political purposes but in intimate affairs as well. In the Somali Horn, as elsewhere, music served as a key means of expressing both political and personal aspirations. Indeed, from the 1950s through to the height of socialist rule, Kapteijns credits love songs with helping to mainstream an emerging youth culture, one that advocated for companionate marriage and for the recognition "of the emotions of the individual over the political discipline of the male-dominated family and kin group" (1999, 111). Love songs, and the theatrical productions (plays) in which songs were frequently performed, were critical sites where young people reimagined the nature of courtship, expressed desire for the opposite sex, asserted more forcefully the ideal of companionate marriage, and also pushed an agenda of women's emancipation. Significantly, in a study of 120 songs of this era—mined from the cassette collection of Maryan Omar Ali—Kapteijns highlights that the love and marriage agenda advanced in these songs was based on a delicately balanced appeal to "tradition" and a desire for greater personal freedom in matters of the heart. In some songs, tradition is presented as an impediment to romance and, in particular, to women's freedom. However, the more successful songs were those in which love, romance, and marriage were presented as compatible with traditional norms and ideas, often drawing on pastoral imagery and idioms. The song "Xiisaha kalgacalkeena" (The yearnings of our love), a duet sung by Saado Cali and Maxamed Axmed "Kuluc" as part of the play *Xuskii Jacaylkii* (The celebration of love), for instance, describes the couple's marriage as "written [for us] in heaven": their nuptials were sanctioned by God and the sheikhs and elders who know customary law; they were also blessed by their fathers and deserving of respect, like the union of Adam and Eve.[27] At the same time, it is a union described as one that both parties intentionally chose, guided by their "common star": it will lead not only to a bountiful new home (with children and livestock) but one based on a yearning that makes Saado "shiver" and "bite [her] lips, her fingers." These songs undeniably advanced an agenda of innovation in the sphere of love and marriage but did so by appealing to long-established cultural norms and literary idioms.

While a notable number of songs from this period reflect on the beauty of requited love and companionate marriage, one need not listen long to hear the overwhelming presence of the theme of love-*suffering* in these songs. The causes of this suffering, to be sure, had evolved since the days of Cilmi. The mockery Cilmi received for falling in love does not feature as prominently. These previously challenging attitudes about love began to be overshadowed by new social realities that thwart love aspirations or otherwise complicate relationships—including the financial demands placed on men who wish to marry, the pain of separation caused by increasing labor migration, and evolving gender expectations (including greater freedom for women) that shifted the dynamics of heterosexual desire, courtship, and marriage (see Kapteijns 1999; Kapteijns and Ali 2001). One clear constant, however, is that love itself—which continues to be described as an agentive force in its own right and often linked to fate—is frequently the cause of suffering that leaves individuals confused, unable to eat or sleep, and sometimes in agonizing bodily pain (as in "Leexo" quoted above). The inward-looking love-suffering subject, who uses verse to soothe his or her love wounds, becomes even further entrenched as the primary subject of love songs. Take, for example, another of Hibo Nuura's songs, "Ruuxa gala abaal" (Someone who makes a benevolent act). This is one of Hanad's favorite songs, a song he likes to listen to on days that he is remembering a particular person and wants to rekindle certain feelings. The song begins with familiar images of the physical pain caused by love:

Garkiyo wadnahaad	My aorta and heart
I kala goysoo	Were cut off by you
Gantaalihii jacaylkaagii	The arrows of your love
Bay i ganaayee	Pierce me
Inta aanan go'in	Before I die
Godka aanan galinee	And enter the grave
Ii soo gurmoo	Rescue me
I soo gaadheey	Come help me

The song continues, describing the other effects that love is having on her—including being unable to sleep and being weakened by thoughts of her beloved—while the refrain repeats a plea for her beloved to respect the love she has for him and to build a relationship.

Significantly, the love-suffering subject of this song and others of this era is one whose innermost love-pains are made known to the world through a specific kind of sound and voice. Musically, these songs had evolved from the qaraami that came before. Most notably, they have more distinct verse and refrain sections and much more diverse instrumentation—including full bands in the 1970s, which give these songs quite a different sound. Recordings from this period also bear traces of Somali artists' increasing embeddedness in a cosmopolitan network of musicians (cf. Hassan 2019). But I would also suggest that in these songs we see the consolidation of the "voice" that was precipitated by qaraami. As for qaraami, the melody and instrumentation of a song are key to songs' affective force. By this point, the melody of a song had become completely fixed to one set of lyrics, and melodies were composed specifically for poems penned by a known poet writing about real-world love experiences. Lyrics were also no longer tied to the dhaanto meter, with poets instead choosing a meter according to the emotion of an experience; short-lined meters that require a single al-literative word per line, like the jiifto were (and still are) especially popular (nearly every song quoted in this book uses a short-lined meter). Songs also had uniform alliteration throughout, reflecting the fact that they were composed by a single poet and about singular experiences. These completely individuated songs became universally associated with the singers who performed them, known simply as *codka* (the voice). And the most revered of these singers were those whose voices carry the sentiments expressed in a song's words and emotionally expressive melodies—naturalized voices conceived to provide unmediated access to a singer's innermost interiority.

The consolidation and idealization of this naturalized voice emerges most clearly in listeners' comments about "good" songs and singers from this era. In speaking about "Ruuxa gala abaal," for instance, Hanad explained to me that this a good song because it was made "through feeling" and be-cause Hibo Nuura is "singing her emotions." Huda, another Hibo Nuura fan who we met in the introduction, similarly explained that Hibo "was always talking about someone who broke up with her," and "the way she puts the lyrics, the ways she puts her voice on it, and the emotion, it looked like it happened to her, rather than that she is talking about someone else." All of her favorite songs, she continued, are those in which she can "see and analyze the feelings of the singer, because if there is no feeling for the singer, and he cannot feel the music and the way he sings, he couldn't even take me to the highest place." These sentiments were echoed in comments about other singers as well. One listener described Sahra Axmed as hav-ing a "sweet" voice in which "you can taste her emotions and experiences." Maxamed Nuur Giriig, similarly, was praised for his "emotional voice," and his ability to "make you to feel, to live the moment with him." While Cilmi's seemingly unmediated outpouring of emotion served to worsen his fate, by the time these Waaberi legends took the stage, a naturalized, emotive voice is what listeners had come to respond to—indeed, to expect. This was an expectation no doubt shaped by broader sociopolitical transformations, in which ideas of autonomy and self-determination were reshaping both political and more intimate aspects of people's lives. As Kunreuther (2014) highlights, the "political" and the "intimate" are frequently coconstituted. And in a setting where other forms of speech were heavily censored and where the public discussion of love remained relatively taboo, hees jacayl was one of the few art forms in which unrestrained self-expression was acceptable. The love song, we might say, was a mode of expression in which a person could and should speak the truth (*runta*) and could and should speak from the heart.

By the end of the 1980s, then, we can make the following observations about hees jacayl. As a genre of Somali orature, love songs are defined by their uniquely melodic musical and instrumental form, their mixed-gendered production and consumption, their deeply intimate subject matter (frequently that of love-*suffering*), and the expectation that the "voice" in which they are sung provides unmediated access to a singer's innermost sentiments—and a voice intimately linked with the emergence of a certain kind of postcolonial subject. While the climate in which these songs now move has been radically refigured, songs' basic "anatomy," as well as the affective expectations that have attached themselves to hees jacayl continue to sound in these songs themselves and in the songs produced by a new generation of artists to come.

The Not-Yet-Archived: Love Songs in the Aftermath of War

While most of my conversations about music with Hanad revolved around the tapes we were handling, on occasion he would come into the office humming the tune of a more recently produced song by a member of Xidigaha Geeska. When I asked him about these songs, he often gave a somewhat ambiguous response. On the one hand, his favorite songs were definitely qaraami, and his favorite singers were mainly singers popular in the 1970s and 1980s. New songs, he said, often didn't "taste as sweet" as old ones—especially those produced by diaspora musicians—and he had mixed feelings about the electronic keyboards that new artists use. But at the same time, he acknowledged that the circumstances under which new artists worked were extremely challenging, and, in certain cases, he enjoyed the stories and the feelings that songs put forward. He also liked

singers—such as BK and Yurub Geenyo—who were known to have experienced the love sentiments they were singing about. While the instrumentation and the language in these songs was different from his favorite
qaraami, some new songs, Hanad said, could still make you feel or "taste"
something of another's love(-suffering) experience.

Hanad was not alone in these sentiments. Among the topics that inspired the most heated debate during my research was the relative merits
of old (prewar) versus new (postwar) songs. To be sure, a lot has changed.
While musicians occupied a place of pride in the 1970s and 1980s, musicians' lives were to be radically altered by a war that not only decimated the
artistic sphere but also precipitated the emergence of a new polity, where
shifting political-religious forms continue to make the work of artists exceedingly difficult. The bombing of Hargeysa in 1988 not only decimated
Hargeysa's theater but also left artists, as one singer put it, "like scattered
prayer beads." Many were forced abroad never to return, and those who
did return lacked the state support they once relied upon and did not have
the resources or morale to rebuild their careers. While a number of artists who settled in Europe began producing new music from the mid-1990s
onward—notably Walaalaha Sweden (the Sweden Brothers), whose name
was inspired by Walaalaha Hargeysa—for two decades, virtually no new
music was produced in Somaliland or Somalia. Despite an encroaching religious conservatism, in the last decade there have been some notable signs
of artistic recovery, including the 2012 founding of Xidigaha Geeska, the
2014 opening of Hiddo Dhawr, and the establishment of some smaller music groups and ad hoc music venues. For reasons I will elaborate on in chapter 6, Hiddo Dhawr exclusively performs music from the prewar era, and its
popularity undoubtedly taps into a nostalgia many feel for music from this
time. And for those young artists producing new music, the results have
been songs that, as Hanad noted, somehow "taste" different. Nevertheless,
these new songs are clearly still composed and received as hees jacayl: the
love imaginaries they draw on share themes with earlier songs, and debates
about what makes new songs good (or not) index the enduring presence of
the idealization of a particular kind of voice.

Let me start with what has changed. The most obvious shift in new musical productions is in their instrumentation. Young artists rely heavily on
synthesizers or electronic keyboards. Songs are almost always prerecorded
and when performed "live" rely on playback. Songs continue to use the
same pentatonic scales as before, although they undoubtedly have a different sound, and the programmable percussion lines they utilize also contain
influences from Western pop music. For artists in the Somali regions and,
to an extent, those in the diaspora, this shift is a direct result of decades of

insecurity and the current political-religious climate: instruments are incredibly hard to find in Hargeysa; support for learning an instrument has diminished; and spaces for informal music-making and live performance are now much more limited (more on this in chapter 5). Many young artists I met wish the situation was otherwise, and there are certainly efforts underway to revive a tradition of oud playing and live performance. In the meantime, the instrumental tracks of songs are usually produced by a single musician using an electronic keyboard, with pre-programmed rhythm tracks and various sound effects applied to different instrumental "voices." (This is not unlike the emergence of ragtime after the American Civil War, in which the piano was played to sound like a full band, see Schafer 2008, 115.) For some Somalilanders, especially diaspora returnees, these new sounds are welcome. There is also the acknowledgment that each generation has its own music. Qaraami were also criticized in their time as noise. Yet for many prewar music lovers, this shift to electronic music production has led them to complain that new music sounds fake. Echoing a sentiment I often heard expressed by critics of new music, Sahra Halgan suggested to me that songs produced by "one machine" do not "taste as sweet" as those that feature the oud or live performances of songs when a singer is accompanied by multiple musicians.

A second notable yet predictable shift is the nature of the romantic scenarios that songs describe and, to an extent, the type of language and poetry that songs deploy. As was the case in the 1970s, these shifts reflect changing romantic experiences as well as changing expectations in the spheres of love, marriage, and gender, both in the diaspora and in Somaliland itself. New songs, for instance, give voice to a host of new love grievances, including challenges brought about by the increasing practice of dating before marriage, as well as the high prevalence of divorce. For example, one friend identified the song "Hoteellada" (The hotels) as one that reflects what he described as the negative impact of "culture change on human morality." Penned by Laabsaalax, then the chairman of Xidigaha Geeska, and sung by Hodan Cabdiraxmaan Dheere (the daughter of singers Aamina Cabdullaahi and Cabdiraxmaan Dheere), the singer chastises a man she thought was interested in marriage but seems to have had something else in mind. The song's refrain puts things rather bluntly:

Hay geyn hoteellada	Don't take me to hotels
Hay galaafanoo	Don't influence me badly
Ha i seejin gabadhnimo	And cause me to lose my girlhood
Markaad iga gun-gaadhana	When you quench your need
Durba gooso hay odhan	Don't tell me to go away

Also reflecting on what is seen as a regrettable but common relationship scenario is one of Hanad's favorite new songs, "Nasiib" (Fate/destiny), also penned by Laabsaalax, and sung by Mursal Muuse Cumar. The song describes the plight of a divorced single mother and encourages her not to give up on all men but to select a partner more suitable for her. The song has well-known origins in an encounter a friend of Laabsaalax's had with an old classmate after she had become divorced. According to Hanad, this song was especially "touching" because it was rooted in this real-world experience, and for its words, melody and the way it was sung.

While reflecting new types of love grievances, there is also a notable uptick among recent releases in what listeners described as "romance" songs—that is, songs in which a man or woman praises their partner, often expounding their desirable attributes and the comfort that their relationship brings. Two of the three contemporary songs we will encounter in chapter 4 fall into this category ("Dhakac-dhakac" and "Laba baal"). Also notable here is the preponderance of romance songs sung by women about men, possibly reflecting a shift toward a greater acceptance of women being able to openly express their feelings,[28] though we will see in chapter 2 that this process is heavily mediated, and expectations of women's xishood (modesty/demureness) remain strong. This increase in romance songs, however, reflects not necessarily an increase in people's love and marriage satisfaction—recall the "love gap" my interlocutors complained about earlier—but rather shifting expectations in the realm of expressing affection. As we will see in chapter 4, these songs' popularity rests in part on the fact that they express what women and men wish their partners would say to them but rarely do: the songs serve as vocal stand-ins for those who lack the words to articulate their own desire, as well as providing listeners with the imaginative resources to temporarily inhabit this longed-for feeling of romance.

Although the prevalence of romance songs might reflect shifting love expectations, it is imperative to highlight that the ideal partners and partnerships described in these songs share much with earlier songs that couched demands for companionate marriage in "traditional" terms. Some songs and music videos produced in the diaspora, to be sure, are quite explicit in their descriptions, and the imagery deployed departs from the pastoral metaphors popular in the Somali regions; this is one reason fans of prewar music often dismissed newer productions. Songs produced and popular in Somaliland itself (rather than the diaspora), however, are notably conservative in their descriptions of the opposite sex (possibly even more conservative than in the 1970s and 1980s), and the ideal woman is described much as she was in earlier songs—and, indeed, in poetry from the early twentieth century (cf. Kapteijns 1999, 2009). Two popular BK songs, "Muuna" and

"Aamina Aamisha," describe their namesakes as honorable and obedient, chaste/virginal, slow to anger, bashful, courteous, compassionate, devoted to their children, and religiously blessed. A duet sung by Faraax Murtiile and Farxiya Fiska, "Han iyo dookh" (Desire and taste), similarly begins by likening a woman's beauty and modesty to that of Hodan (i.e., the woman Cilmi fell in love with) and praises her "heritage and culture," while the woman responds by describing their relationship in pastoral idioms as a "tree and its shade" and like that of a "she-camel and her calf." Other romance songs use well-worn anatomical descriptions to reflect on the beauty of love. Lafoole's song "Ruun" (a woman's name) for instance, paints a familiar picture of love's bodily embeddedness, but this time in a celebratory way:

Laf dhabarta adhaxda iyo	The backbone and
Unugyada dhiigee jidhkaa	The blood cells and
Laxaadka intiisa kale	Also the rest of the body
Adimadii celinayaay	You hold them together
Ubucda beerka iyo wadnaha	In the abdomen, liver and heart
Adaa masallaha dhigtoo	You have laid out the prayer mat
	[i.e., you have made yourself at home]
Xubnaha jidkha unugiyo	You have roots in my body
Ruxaad ku abuurantoo	In my organs and cells
Irridda sambabbada degtoo	And you are in the lungs
Cid kale looma ogolaa	No one else is allowed

While contemporary songs are notably different from earlier ones in certain respects—in their instrumentation, in the grievances they voice, and in their language—their affective force still relies on idioms and imaginaries that have animated hees jacayl for many decades (including a continued reliance on anatomy lessons).

On the theme of love songs' anatomy, finally, it is pertinent to note that, despite certain notable changes, both the force of love in these songs and the voice that should (ideally) animate them are consistent with the love and voice that have animated Somali love poetry from Cilmi onward. A proliferation of romance songs notwithstanding, the overwhelming theme in new songs remains the pain and suffering caused by love. As the Cultural Center's founder Dr. Jama Musse Jama put it to me succinctly (echoing a well-known proverb): "One sings for love because they are suffering. This has not changed." *Ciil iyo caashaq ayaa loo gabyaa* (poetry is made from oppression and love). Sometimes the cause of this suffering is structural:

men's marriage aspirations thwarted by financial realities; women expected to marry men approved by their families (not necessarily the men that they love). Sometimes love's problems are caused by individuals caught up in love's changing realities: sometimes women are hurt by men who appear interested but then turn to other women; then there are men given the cold shoulder by women playing the field. And sometimes this suffering is caused by the very force of love itself—a force that still causes lack of sleep and appetite, pierces like arrows, and "shakes" the very core of one's being. One song, "Laxaw" (Harsh pain), penned by Weedhsame about his own early unrequited love experiences (in the ever-popular jiifto meter, alliterating in "l"), puts it in these familiar terms:[29]

Anuun baa lallabayoo	I'm nauseous and
Caashaqu i lulayee	Love shakes me
Shaw jacaylka laabtiyo	But [little did I know] there's no love in your heart
Lubbigaba kumaad hayn	Or on your mind
Kalgacaylkan leebkiyo	This painful infliction, like an arrow
Ila laacay hootadu	Like a small sword
Anuun buu i loodshee	It hurts me alone
Shaw dhankaaga laydhiyo	From your end, no gentle breeze
Leexaba kamuu kicin	Or whirling wind moves your feelings
Anuun baa la liitoo	It weakens only me and
Ladi waayay jiifkee	Disturbs my sleep

Finally, as has been the case from Cilmi onward, this love-suffering continues to be articulated in a self-reflexive, first-person voice that, ideally, should strike listeners as the unmediated outward expression of deeply felt internal sentiments. Accusations of songs sounding "fake," alongside other criticisms sometimes directed at new singers—mainly, that they "just sing" for the sake of money or fame rather than because of some duty or impulse to give voice to certain sentiments—on the one hand may seem to suggest a shift in this regard. But I would contend that these types of accusations, and the continued concern for songs' "authenticity" among artists and listeners alike in fact index the enduring force of an aesthetics that privileges a naturalized voice. "Good" songs and singers are described much as they were before: as speaking or singing "from the heart" and as successfully conveying the "truth" of a real-world love experience in word, melody, and voice. Not all songs and singers succeed in this task. And new songs are inevitably inflected by the changing romantic predicaments of their protagonists, as well as the constraints of contemporary music production. But when songs do succeed, the results are textual-musical-vocal articulations that allow you to "taste" the love(-suffering) of another, as Hanad put it, to "feel as another feels." Chapter 2 is devoted to documenting the collaborative process by which this "voice" continues to be produced.

The Anatomy of an Archive . . . and Beyond

When Hanad and I began our archiving work, there were approximately three thousand cassettes in the center's collection. The contents of these cassettes contained echoes of a form of love poetry that predate recording technology's arrival in the Somali regions, as well as records of a half-century of Somali musical production, including a sometimes-dizzying array of examples of the genre now known as hees jacayl. As a genre forged in the turmoil of the late colonial era that came into its own in the equally volatile decades of Somalia's early independence and then socialist experiment, love songs have been shaped by (and have themselves helped to shape) both the political and personal aspirations of an emerging urban middle class, proving themselves to be malleable and adaptable to diverse purposes. Yet I have also suggested that hees jacayl have a discernible "anatomy" of sorts: their differentiated melodies and instrumentation, their mixed-gendered production and consumption, and their intimate subject matter set them apart from other genres of oral poetry. These features have frequently led to love songs' and artists' ambiguous and unassimilated status, by turns—and often simultaneously—both revered and reviled. And guided by an unfortunate baker-turned-poet-turned-love-martyr, hees jacayl are also animated by a certain kind of love and voice. The "love" of hees jacayl is an unruly, all-consuming, and transformative kind of love: this is a love often thwarted by social expectations and other unfortunate circumstances and one that frequently shakes, squeezes, and pierces the very anatomy of those caught in its path. Moved, and sometimes even compelled by this love, the voice of hees jacayl is a deeply personal, self-reflexive voice of an individual who has personally experienced love. This self is revealed not only in the words of the poetry of love songs but also in their individuated, singularly voiced melodies. And shaped both by Sufi conceptions of a self that suffers in pursuit of divine union and an emerging postcolonial "modern" subjectivity, the voice of hees jacayl is a voice expected to speak from the heart. Across a range of incredibly diverse sociopolitical contexts, this "anatomy" gives love songs their unique affective-aesthetic force and guides the processes of envocalization that I document in the rest of this book.

FIGURE 1.4. Some of the catalogued cassettes in the archives at the Hargeysa Cultural Center. These cassettes were part of a secondary wave of donations and were being stored in a temporary location while more cabinets were being purchased. Photograph by the author.

Alongside a half-dozen other ad hoc volunteers, Hanad and I did our best to catalogue, label, and organize the cassettes that the center had acquired. But before long cassettes seemed to beget new cassettes, and the cabinets bought to house the collection were full. Three thousand cassettes became five thousand, then eight thousand, then fifteen thousand, and so on. Word had got out. While the bulk of the initial collection had been purchased from a former owner of a music studio in Djibouti, soon enough music lovers with their own personal cassette collections were turning up at the center with donations and with ever-multiplying stories about their encounters with these songs: these were stories of the sometimes-epic journeys that cassettes had been on, animated by a shared hope that the intimacies expressed in these songs might be preserved for others, shared and heard into an uncertain future. In one sense, they need not have worried: many of the songs contained on these cassettes are already in wide circulation, turned into digital files and shared across the globe via YouTube and a multitude of Somali music-sharing websites. But the more crowded our workspace became with cassettes that did not fit in their designated cabinets, the more I also realized that the donations that kept pouring in pointed to something about love songs that was equally fundamental to their anatomy: as they document the most intimate of love sentiments and give voice to experiences that affect one's very anatomy, love songs exist to be shared. Recalling the genre's connection to older work songs, one Aamina Cabdullaahi song puts it like this: "Waa shubaaleh, ila qabo" (This is a watering song, join in with me).[30]

CHAPTER TWO

Lie Down in the Love Hospital

(Or, How Love Finds Its Voice)

"They come to me," Weedhsame quipped, smiling somewhat mischievously, "because I am their doctor." Showing measured patience with my line of inquiry, he continued: "Somali poets have a different role than the poets of Western people. We are doctors. There are so many people who come to you and tell you their love problems. You, the poet, are a boon of experience, because you have the stories of a lot of people. So, you listen, and you consult them. And if they have very serious . . . what we call 'serious serious' love problems, then you *must* make a poem. So, you see, I am their love doctor, isn't it?"

Weedhsame and I were sitting in our usual corner on the first floor of the Sun Hotel, our habitual haunt on Jigjigayar Road, sipping papaya juice with lime and spiced tea respectively. Xasan Daahir Ismaaciil, or "Weedhsame," as he is more commonly known—a nickname that roughly translates as "[the one who] makes good words"—is a young poet who had graciously offered me informal lessons on the ins and outs of Somali poetry. Mentored and pronounced an *abwaan* (poet) by Maxamed Xaashi Dhamac "Gaarriye," a widely revered Somali poet who passed away in 2012, Weedhsame is a torchbearer of sorts of the Somali oral arts for the postcollapse generation, whose body of work includes everything from poetry on social and political themes, like youth emigration (*tahriib*) and government corruption, to an impressive repertoire of love songs, many performed by the leading voices of Xidigaha Geeska. Between his wordsmithing activities, Weedhsame had recently taken over the University of Hargeysa's course on Somali literature that Gaarriye himself used to teach and, as a kind of outreach side project, had taken it upon himself to get me up to speed on the bewildering technical aspects of Somali poetry.

Usually accustomed to teaching students with a more intuitive understanding of Somali verse, we had a notebook spread open between us that contained what looked like a cross between a language and mathematics lesson: words and numbers and graphs, penned in Weedhsame's distinctive scrawl, illustrated the strict scansion rules of Somali verse. A series of ones and twos arranged in various patterns marked the unique combinations of short and long vowels that rhythmically define various genres and that differentiate jiifto from gabay and buraanbur from dhaanto. Alongside the use of alliteration, it is these scansion rules that differentiate poetry from prose and that give Somali verse its taste. As I scanned the page I could hear Weedhsame's smooth, steady voice counting out the melodic and rhythmically punctuated phrases. For most lay listeners, these patterns simply sound "right." The breaching of these metric rules would frustrate poetically attuned Somali ears. For novices and nonnative speakers like me, the rules were bewildering.

While the book between us recalled the primary purpose of our meeting, I had side-tracked our lesson by inquiring about one of Weedhsame's recent poems, "Cusbitaalka boholyowga" (The hospital of longing), which went viral after airing on an online Voice of America (VoA) broadcast. This poem had come up in conversations with various friends—including Hanad, in the archives—and I was curious about how the poem had come about. In the poem, Weedhsame imagines a hospital where love-sufferers can gather when all other remedies fail: a place where staying awake all night pining for absent lovers is the norm ("Cusbitaal boholyowga / Saamaleelku waa caadi"); where IV-lines drip the melancholic sound of the oud ("Sayloonku waa cuudka"); where patients thin as toothbrush sticks, due to their love-induced lack of appetite, are principally nourished by qaraami ("Duul caday ka dhuudhuubaan / Cuntadduna qaraam weeyi"). The poem struck a chord, and in the days after it aired Weedhsame and the VoA reporter who had reported the story were inundated with calls—from Muqdisho to London to New Zealand—from lovesick listeners keen to be admitted, inquiring about the location of this "love hospital" (as it came to be called in English, a subtle yet telling semantic slip). Weedhsame had to clarify that this hospital existed only in his imagination. But his inspiration for the poem, he explained on air, had been his desire to offer some kind of collective relief to the droves of people who seek his love counsel "in the middle of the night," a time when love-sufferers are known to be particularly restless. Intrigued by the poem's origins, not to mention the diagnostic of Somali youth's love-suffering its reception provided, I had asked Weedhsame why so many people came to him, a married man approaching forty, for such advice. The answer, I was to learn, lay in the particular social role occupied by poets in this setting, and the expectation—or even duty—that a poet has to "give voice," or at least words, to the fears, aspirations, and anxieties of his peers. For a poet attuned to the concerns of youth, Weedhsame explained, he is particularly obliged to lend a listening ear and

then his *weedh*-making or wordsmithing skills to the cause of love. Pucker-
ing at the bitter lime in his drink, and straightening up with a certain pride,
he told me that it is his duty as a love-doctor-poet to help relieve the pain
of bottled-up love emotions by forming them into words, to "give voice to
the voiceless," to facilitate a process by which (silent) intimate experience
becomes publicly audible in song.

In a setting that has long and fondly been termed a "nation of poets,"
Weedhsame's reflections on his *abwaan* duties were in some ways unsurprising. This is, after all, a place where a poet's words offer unparalleled
insight into the "pulse" of a community. As Said Samatar put it: "As Somalis
feel, so do their oral poets sing" (1989, 49). It follows naturally, then, that
poets may be love doctors whose duties include giving words to otherwise
inexpressible sentiments. And yet, in my many conversations with love-
sufferers and love song listeners up to this point, I had been told time and
again that the best songs are those in which the *singer* "makes you feel what
she feels." Good love songs are conceived to be the sonic-textual embodiment of love sentiments that sound from the depths of a singer's lovestruck
soul, striking the listener as an unmediated outpouring of emotion. Borrowing an English term used colloquially as an adjective in Somali, the best
songs were frequently described to me as "really" songs: that is, songs that
reveal *runta* (the truth) in which you can "taste" (*dhadhami/dhadhanso*)
the emotion of an experience—in contrast to songs that may disdainfully
be referred to as "fiction" or "fake" (again, borrowing from English). As we
saw in the introduction and chapter 1, Somali love songs are defined by an
aesthetics that privileges singing from the heart—"at times so insistent as
to occasion pain" (Middleton 2000, 28). Love is conceived here, after all,
as a personal and embodied emotion that affects one's very anatomy. How,
then, can the responsibility for expressing something so intimate be tasked
to another? How can a singer make you feel what she feels if singing about
strained internal organs that may not belong to her? How can the truth of a
deeply personal interior experience be maintained if a song requires input
from a poet, a musician, and a singer, each of whom lend their voice to an
experience that may not be strictly their own?

This chapter explores these questions by tracing the process by which
personal love experiences become song. In short, this chapter documents the initial process of envocalization by considering, to borrow from
Amanda Weidman, how love "come[s] into voice" (2003, 195, paraphrasing
Sinha 1996). Like Weidman, I take the notion of "com[ing] into voice" in a
literal and sonic sense, to explore the conditions by which love comes to be
vocally tangible and publicly audible. Yet whereas Weidman is interested in
the sociopolitical conditions that allowed female Indian singers to "come

into voice" at a particular historical moment, I am concerned here with the more immediate, intimate, and collaborative process by which experiences of love move from the realm of embodied, individual, and often unspeakable experience to finding words, melody, and vocal expression. In Karin Barber's (2007a) terms, how do words, sound, and voice come to congeal into a text that will outlast the moment? What kind of intimacies and subjectivities are indexed and arise concomitantly with love's journey into song? And how might this process help us to understand how a collaboratively produced song can move listeners to experience a singer's voice as the unmediated outpouring of emotion, sprung from the depths of her lovestruck soul?

In answering these questions, this chapter tells a story about the collaborative and intersubjective making of a love song. For reasons I will elaborate below, I anchor this discussion in an account of the song "Qirasho" (Confession), for which Weedhsame wrote the words. Guided by Weedhsame and the song's other contributors, we will see how love comes into voice via a process that is deeply multivocal, yet that nevertheless sounds from the heart. This is a process that reveals envocalization to be about much more than technical text-making skill: it also rests on the possibility of *feeling with others*, and the ability to combine feeling with imagination in order to give voice to another's love perspective. Indeed, I will argue that without this process, songs would not stick. This is, then, a story about the kind of dareen-wadaag or "feeling-sharing" that allows love experiences to congeal into love songs in the first place—and that, we will see in chapters to come, seems to open infinitely outward into new moments of intimacy wherever songs travel.

Some Preliminary Notes on Love's Journey into Song

This chapter documents the making of one specific song, "Qirasho." I have chosen this song, first and foremost because it has been a particularly compelling example to discuss in my conversations with Weedhsame. This is a song that Weedhsame identified as exemplary in its effectiveness in conveying the emotion and sentiment of the original love(-suffering) experience that it represents in words, sound, and voice—and that provided significant relief to its unnamed and otherwise mute love-suffering protagonist. It is little wonder that it continues to stand out in Weedhsame's mind as a "very beautiful" song (and, to be sure, a testament to his love-doctor skills). Additionally, I was also able to speak with Xuseen Aadan "Karoone," the song's melody writer (*laxamiste*), and Ubax Daahir "Fahmo," the song's vocalist or "voice" (*codka*); each offered me further insight into the process by which feeling is translated into sound.

I have also chosen "Qirasho" because it typifies a number of song features that surfaced in conversations with a range of artists and listeners both about how a song comes into being, *and* what makes a song good. The feeling aesthetics that it abides, the collaborative process by which it was made, and the gendered division of labor that it reveals are common to almost all Somali love songs. To begin, this song follows the general formula that I was frequently told is required for a song to come about. "Those poets will tell you that a song needs two things," one friend explained, "the first is the experience of love. The second is the fear that you will end up alone." Songs, in short, are expected to be rooted in real-world experiences of love and, more often than not, some kind of love grievance. Recall that at least since Cilmi Boodhari was compelled by love to give voice to his ill-fated and eventually fatal love for Hodan, love has been conceived as a kind of force that wills itself into words through inhabiting unfortunate bodies and compelling voice. And while Somali love songs are not universally about painful love experiences, the trope of the love-suffering hero still looms large. Like many songs before it (and many more to come), the origins of "Qirasho" are a real-life love experience, an experience that included the fear of being alone; its final voiced form thus joins a large body of songs that begin from the premise of suffering in/for love.

Additionally, "Qirasho" demonstrates an ideology of voice that privileges sounding from the heart. Choosing a postwar song to demonstrate this aesthetics may strike some connoisseurs of Somali music as odd. As discussed in chapter 1, one of the frequent criticisms leveled against "new" music, after all, is that it is "fake": not only in its use of digital editing software but also because singers are sometimes seen to be "only acting" and "only interested in money"; thus, they are not sincerely reflecting the original love experiences they sing about.[1] Such criticisms are, to be sure, sometimes warranted, and the ease with which songs can now be recorded, digitally edited, and uploaded to Facebook and YouTube has surely lowered the standard of entry. There are artists who just "sing and sing," unable to effectively move their audiences because they themselves have not sufficiently experienced pain (cf. Schafers 2015, 51). And yet, as will become abundantly clear in the accounts below, the expectation of authenticity—that words, sound, and voice *should* accurately reflect the emotion of the original love experience, should "provide access to a 'pure interiority' linked with subjective self-presence" (Sterne 2003, 14)—remains at the heart of the (ideal) composition process. Love songs, after all, are one of the few spaces in which emotion may be freely expressed and, in contrast to other genres of orature that speak about collective sociopolitical concerns, love songs continue to be composed from the perspective of a self-reflexive, inward-looking subject. While themselves sometimes critical of their own lack of musical training, young artists nonetheless continue to aspire to the same ideal of singing from the heart that defined the giants of prewar musical production and the perfect unity of emotion, words, melody, and voice that lead to, as Weedhsame put it, "songs that never die."

"Qirasho" is also representative of nearly all Somali love songs in that it came into the world through a process in which various creative tasks were distributed to different people, and each of these contributors is known. This sets love songs apart from both maanso poems, which are composed and performed by a single poet in response to specific real-world situations, and from older genres of hees (including many belwo), which may have involved multiple contributors, but the lyrics and melodies remain unattributed and the specific context of composition unknown (see Orwin 2021). Despite their idealization as unmediated emotional outpourings, Somali love songs are almost always produced in this collaborative manner. With very few exceptions, there are no Somali singer-songwriters. At a minimum, any given song usually involves a poet, a musician, and a singer; it may express the experiences of one of these three individuals or another person entirely. And while changes to recording technology mean that the various collaborators of a song may be geographically dispersed, and the instrumentation, in particular, may be concentrated in "one person and one machine," the necessary interdependence of different artists was emphasized by both young and older artists alike. In the words of Xasan Xaaji Cabdillaahi (Xasan "Ganey"), a poet-playwright and former member of General Daa'uud: "The poet is the one making the words, another makes the music, another is singing, another makes the rhythm. All of these things are related. You can't do it by yourself. If you just compose it and put it up it's just useless. Just like the human body, there is a relationship between them." These sentiments were echoed nearly identically by a young FanSan vocalist: "In my view, if there is no poet there will be no singer. If there is no musician, then there will not be a singer either. And if there is no singer, there will be neither a composer nor a musician. They are all interdependent." This situation is not unlike what Socrates described as the "divine distribution" of creative tasks in the making of classical Greek poetry, one in which a poet serves as the messenger of the mute muse, with the rhapsode then delivering this message to an audience in what Cavarero describes as "rings" of "vocal transmission" (2005, 88). I will return later to a reflection on the audibility of different voices in any given song, though suffice it to say for now that I think we have much to gain from considering the nature of this collaboration. Indeed, this is what lies at the heart of this chapter.

Significantly, while love songs as a genre have been both revered and reviled for their mixed-gendered characteristics—and Khadiija Belwo wrote and performed her own verse—since belwo gave way to qaraami, the distribution of creative tasks in the making of love songs has been highly gendered. As is the case in "Qirasho," while songs that give voice to love experiences unique to women are always sung by women, the poet who gives words to these experiences, and the musician who gives them melody, are nearly always men.[2] In the early years of the development of love songs the absence of women could be explained by the extremely taboo and shameful nature of voicing love in public—as a result, Cumar Dhuule became especially well-known for his ability to perform as a woman, facilitated by his high vocal range. But even at the height of socialism, when female performers were particularly adored, women did not write words nor play instruments. This is particularly interesting considering that female poets certainly exist. There are entire genres of poetry reserved only for women (see Adan 1996, Kapteijns 1999), and in recent decades women have increasingly been composing historically male genres, like the gabay. When I asked why this was the case, I was usually met with answers such as "Women just don't/can't write love lyrics"—not because of a lack of poetic skill but rather because of gendered expectations about showing emotion. As we will see below, expectations of women's xishood (modesty/shyness) remain incredibly high and, indeed, women's expected silence on matters of the heart are in fact often the cause of women's love-suffering—and a frequent condition that male love-doctor-poets are expected to treat. In her exploration of the presence of women's voices in Somali orature, Kapteijns (1999, 156–57) sees the absence of women wordsmiths as limiting the emancipatory potential of the genre, suggesting that love songs did little to challenge patriarchal gender norms. While the gendered distribution of love songs' production does offer us an interesting diagnostic of the gendered power dynamics and expectations at play here, I think we miss something if we see this as only a case of men speaking for women. Following Weidman (2014a, 43), I would suggest that attending to practices of voicing, and singing in particular, serves to trouble "the dichotomy often drawn between 'having a voice' and being 'silent' or 'silenced,'" and provides us with the interpretive resources to make sense of "voices that are highly audible and public but not agentive in the classic sense . . . including voices that sing rather than speak." While women do not make words, not unlike the audibility of the mute muse in classical Greek poetry, love songs *do* provide a platform for the (rare) public audition of female voices—of singers, and of otherwise silent love-sufferers—in a setting where women's public voices are highly curtailed, and the private expression of love remains difficult.

Finally, it is worth noting that Weedhsame himself was, at the time of the incident recounted below, known to be a "lonely lover." In 2007, Weedhsame fell in love. But the woman who had captured his heart moved abroad abruptly with her family, and Weedhsame found himself alone. "It was the opposite of 'out of sight, out of mind,'" he explained to me, "the saying should be 'out of sight, on the mind!'" Provoked by her sudden absence, he realized how deeply in love he was, an experience he described as "one of the most beautiful of my life." She, however, did not return these feelings. Overcome with emotion, Weedhsame began to write verse—both maanso poems and lyrics that described being overcome by love, the fateful inevitability of love/longing, and the difficulties that arise when love is not reciprocated.[3] Although he dabbled in poetry as a schoolboy and began to turn heads with his lyrical sociopolitical commentary—evidence that he likely possessed the "poet gene"—this was a different kind of poetic experience: one that he says was caused by love itself. In a setting where the "Ka'bah" of literary (and everyday) love imaginaries is a baker-turned-poet by the overwhelming force of love, it is unsurprising that love itself is frequently credited as a force responsible for making poets. As one friend put it, "You can't write a poem without the experience of loving a woman!" I have yet to meet a poet who does not credit his own love(-suffering) experience as the impetus for his love verse, in some way or another. That he himself had suffered from love, earning him a reputation as a "lonely lover" adept at putting love-suffering experiences into verse is a critical component of how it is that Weedhsame is able to give words to the love experiences of others. His status as a "lonely lover" also featured in the making of "Qirasho," to which I now turn.

Where Lonely Lovers Meet: Intimate Disclosures

After the call for afternoon prayers has sounded, artists, friends and other well-wishers gather in homes across Hargeysa. Bodies and bundles of qaad fill lavishly carpeted though sparsely furnished spaces, settling against cushions that line the rooms' perimeters. Thermoses of sweet tea and soft drinks form a kind of inner circle, laid out strategically to cut the bitterness of a leafy qaad-chewing pastime. Conversations meander from politics to music to everyday ailments, to the difficulties of finding a paycheck, or finding a woman. These are spaces defined by an intimate conviviality, where guards are let down, where filters are removed, where both men and women come to get everyday stresses off their chests. As we will see in chapters to come, such spaces serve as "treatment centers" of a sort for brokenhearted lovers, artists, and others who are drawn to the warmth and companionship of other hearts similarly broken by love, seeking comfort in the knowledge that they do not suffer alone. In my own time in such spaces I have discussed whether or not diabetics should chew qaad and listened to musings about how to live with that "number-one incurable disease" (i.e., love). I have been asked for outsider advice on how to win over (or get over) women who seem uninterested and have waded into debates about whether Facebook is an appropriate venue to profess one's love (the general consensus: this suggests desperation and might cause the woman shame, so it is best avoided). I have heard older men wistfully reminisce about loves won and lost, and women vent about husbands who do not pay enough attention. And I have been cautiously queried about my own love health, including offers of admission to Weedhsame's love hospital— despite my own confusion as to why being in a relationship might require hospitalization.

As the afternoon turns into evening, songs both old and new are streamed via YouTube on smartphones, sometimes prompting debate about a song's origin, sometimes group singing, and sometimes contemplative silence. Women slip out into more private side rooms to discuss boyfriends and husbands, pregnancies and children, vocal technique, and the vagaries of negotiating public transit when music videos on social media now mean that people know your face. As the *mirqaan* (the "high" one gets from chewing qaad) sets in, instruments appear. Musicians experiment on keyboards plugged into precarious power sources, and singers practice vocal lines. Sometimes an oud circulates, tarrying in both well-accomplished and aspiring hands. Lyrics scribbled on napkins are passed from poet to musician, singers study words typed into WhatsApp, and melodies-in-progress are hummed into smartphones to be circulated to singers and musicians at a distance. As evening turns to night, and eventually early morning, restless love-sufferers arrive to unburden themselves, hopeful (or desperate) for their heavy hearts to be healed, or at least to relieve the pressure of their love wounds.

On a cool and fateful autumn evening in 2010, Weedhsame found himself in one such space. He had come to the home of Ubax Fahmo, one of the many singers "in his network." It was here that he encountered the story of a desperately lovesick woman. In Weedhsame's telling, sometime after he arrived, with other guests by now well settled into a pleasant *mirqaan*, a woman in her midtwenties arrived. At first, she sat silently in the corner, listening and observing, yet hesitant to speak. (It should be noted that

Weedhsame takes his love-doctor obligations of patient confidentiality very seriously and has consistently refused to disclose even this woman's first name.) Weedhsame explained that the flow of intimate conversation seemed to agitate her, and he suspected she had something to say, even though it caused her discomfort. While the woman had not previously met Weedhsame, she knew herself to be in the presence of a poet and, perhaps equally important, in the presence of another "lonely lover." Reflecting on what eventually prompted her disclosure, Weedhsame was quick to highlight that he "cannot know inside her head"—and, indeed, he is adamant that his poetic process does *not* involve mind reading. However, he noted that when she finally began to timidly narrate what was on her heart, she prefaced her remarks by saying that she was speaking "from one lonely lover to another." As we saw at the opening of this chapter, that poets are seen to be a "boon of experience" when it comes to matters of the heart explains, in part, why they are sought out for their love counsel. It also helps to explain why such spaces are seen to be places where one may unburden oneself, perhaps even without planning such confessions in advance. And, Weedhsame also clarified, sometimes you just *need* to get things off your chest. "Psychologically," he said, "in order to get relief, you must express your pains. Expressing your emotions uplifts your soul, and it frees you from the stress, isn't it?" Braced by the presence of another lonely lover, she was no longer able to keep what she had kept hidden for nearly a decade inside, and she began to tell her story.

Nine years before her intimate disclosure, that evening's lovesick patient had realized herself to be deeply in love with her *ina-abtiyo* (cross-cousin).[4] While her cousin normally lived abroad, he had come to Hargeysa one summer on holiday and stayed in her family home. She dutifully cared for him for the duration of his stay, ironing his shirts and bringing him food, all while concealing a love that grew deeper by the day. When he left at the end of the summer, she continued to keep in touch, though always taking care to inquire only as an attentive extended family member and nothing else. In Ubax's account of this song's origins, she also added that the woman had told her that she had been so overcome by this love that she used to shake and faint every time she heard her cousin's voice on the phone. This persisted for years, and her behavior became such that her family believed her to be possessed by a *jin* and even proposed taking her to a mental institution.

Despite being overcome by intense longing, this woman had been unable to share her feelings. On multiple occasions, she explained sheepishly, she had attempted to confess her love, beginning emails with "my dear *hebel-hebel* [so-and-so]," yet invariably erasing "my dear" before she pressed send, too shy and afraid of the potential shame such a confession might bring. On one visit, concerned about his sister's health, her brother approached their cousin and suggested that she may be in love with him. But she vigorously denied such claims and contented herself with being in his presence only as a caring member of the household. As Weedhsame explained matter-of-factly when I queried about her silence: "Shyness makes her silent. Our ladies are too shy. They are nurtured not to talk about their love or sexual needs. They are too shy to express their feelings." The founding principal poet and chairman of Xidigaha Geeska, Laabsaalax, similarly suggested to me that such expectations are a frequent cause of women's love-suffering and in turn a frequent impetus for a love song. "Women hide their sentiments," he said, "so we have to produce a lot of love songs to take their place." In a setting where it remains shameful for women, in particular, to say "I love you," even to their husbands, our unnamed lovesick protagonist resigned herself simply to suffer this unsayable love in silence. This changed, however, when she found herself in the presence of another lonely lover, and long-bottled-up emotions finally came out. Ubax also suggested that "before she was forgotten in a mental institution" she had decided to "visit the artists" to seek another kind of therapy.

This woman's story had a profound effect. By Ubax's account, her experiences touched and changed everyone who heard it. Ubax also told me that Weedhsame was especially shaken, and he appeared as though "he had felt all the emotions." In Weedhsame's telling, he recalled that he could "feel that she was silently crying and dying inside." And although she did not specifically ask him to put words to her experiences (as some of his lovesick patients do), Weedhsame knew immediately that this was a "serious serious" case that would require intervention. "She did not ask us to make a song," he told me, but "when one has a story that is deeply touching your heart, it's *compulsory* to make a song about it." In Weedhsame's reckoning, songs are not so much created as they are the natural and necessary result of being *moved* by an experience of love, including the love-suffering experiences of another. "We can't hold our feelings!" he exclaimed, when I asked about his use of the word "compulsory." "Poetry expresses our inner feelings, and words are derived from emotions. . . . And we cannot control our emotions, because we are emotional creatures. Emotions are reflexive. They are a reflex . . . so it is compulsory to make words to express these emotions." On hearing this woman's story, he explained, "words started raining down in my head." He simply knew that he needed "to give voice to this voiceless human being." In this moment of intimate disclosure, one that *moved* or compelled Weedhsame to feel something of the pain of this other lonely lover, "Qirasho" began to take form.

Giving Love Words: Affectively Attuned Imaginings

As is the case for nearly all Somali love songs, "Qirasho" began as a poem. Hours later, in the quiet solitude of his own home, Weedhsame sat down to put words to paper, to document what had "rained down in his head." Before we look at these words, however, it is worth briefly considering how it is that Weedhsame might be able to represent the experiences of another on the page. The first thing to note is that the possibility that Weedhsame might successfully represent the *run* (truth) of another's love-pain begins from the premise that it is possible to know something of another's feelings—and that it is possible to *feeling-share*. Now one need not have experienced the precise love situation of another—and, indeed, Weedhsame is adamant he cannot get inside other people's heads. Nor is he a woman. He was, however, himself a lonely lover who knew something of what it means to suffer from lovesickness. And furthermore, he says, "because we are human beings, we can feel as others are feeling." In phenomenological terms, we might say that it is the intersubjective possibility of trading places with another—and the possibility of empathy—that sets the stage for a "really" poem to emerge at all.[5] Put another way, Weedhsame's compulsion to respond in verse began not in "an *aspiration* for . . . something shared" (Berlant 1998, 281, emphasis mine) but in the real-life unfolding of this sharing. This simple possibility has profound implications for what love songs are and how it is that they seem to open out into an infinite number of intimate possibilities as they travel.

The second thing to highlight is that this possibility for feeling something of another's experience must be actualized. Not all intimate disclosures lead to poems. In short, the poet must *feel* or *empathize* with another. A particular experience or disclosure must resonate—at least if a song is to stick. Empathy, of course, has long been linked to aesthetic appreciation, as a condition that arises spontaneously in viewers/listeners/readers when they engage with a visual, aural, or narrative work of art (cf. Lipps 1979, Englund 2015). But here we have a case where empathic-like modes of feeling-sharing are a precondition for the very *emergence* of a love song. Indeed, one young poet who writes for Xidigaha Geeska told me that he sometimes struggles with what to do when stories are brought to him secondhand. Like Weedhsame, his early poems had come from his own love experiences, and he had gained a reputation as a competent love poet. This prompted a number of people to bring him different love stories that they wanted made into song. But as these had been recounted to him secondhand, and he did not always fully understand the nature of the love(-suffering) they contained, they did not resonate very deeply. He tried to write a few poems, but they did not "feel" right, either to him or to his listeners. "I can feel the difference," he explained, "between poems based on real emotions, and those that are made up. And the people [your audience], they know the difference too." In order to write words in which listeners can "taste the emotion" of the original experience, one first has to *feel*. This is of utmost importance for love songs. As Weedhsame further explained to me: "When I write about politics, I can write about people's circumstances [in general]. But when it comes to love, if I don't have a feeling, I can't compose anything at all. I *must* feel something. Something must drive me to compose."[6]

In the case of "Qirasho," Weedhsame could quite clearly *feel* that this woman was in a great deal of pain—and, in feeling something of her pain himself, that this was the sort of "serious serious" love problem that would require a poetic intervention.[7] Yet the feelings of others do not simply become words, especially when these are the feelings of a woman. In addition to feeling, they also require a poet to "stand in the shoes of a woman," as Weedhsame put it. Or, as Laabsaalax explained, you must learn "to let a woman's voice speak from within." Both poets suggested that this is a task that requires what they described as empathy *and* imagination. In short, this is a process that requires the poet to move from a more responsive and spontaneous form of feeling to an active and intentional form of perspective-taking (cf. Halpern 2001, Hollan and Throop 2008, 2011).[8] Rooted in the "coordinated emotional context" (Halpern 2001, 92) provided by the initial experience of resonance, the empathetic love doctor works to intentionally imagine the perspective of a song's eventual protagonist before representing this in verse. After "standing where she stands," the poet "lets [another's] voice speak from within," imagining not only how their love-patient feels but also what they might say and how they might give voice to otherwise inarticulable love feelings.

Sufficiently moved by the "silent crying" of our unnamed lovesick protagonist, and able to imagine her perspective, Weedhsame sat down and tried to imagine what he might say if he was a woman who had concealed her "so-long love" for nearly a decade. Alliterating on the letter "q," and in the pulses of *baarcadde* verse (a meter he said was "decided by the emotion" of the story, not his own poetic preferences), Weedhsame began by describing the woman's lovesick state but also her inability to let her feelings show. He ruminates in the first person, yet without disclosing any revealing details, on the expectations of modesty that kept her silent, her fear that expressing her sentiments would potentially cause more grief, and her decision to stay quiet:[9]

Qof baan ahay aawadaa	I am a person, who
Qandhada caashaqa qabtoo	Has caught the fever of love
Haddana waan kaa qarshaa	And yet conceal it
Xishood igu qaydan baa	This deep-rooted shyness I carry
Afkii qufuloo xidhoo	Has sealed the mouth shut
Runtaan ka qaloonayaa	[Discovering] the truth [his response] worries me
Markaan warkaa qeex idhaa	As I attempt to bring clarity to my feelings
Dhambaalkana aan qoraa	The letter I wrote
Billee uu qoonsadaa	Perhaps it will cause him grief
Qorshaha ku gunaanadaa	I conclude the matter

After reflecting on her inhibitions and inability to express her feelings, finally, her long-held love sentiments erupt, in straightforward speech:

Maantaba aan kuu qirtoo	Let me confess today my wishes
Qasdiga soo jeediyee	And suggest my feelings
Qareenkii ila dhashoow	My close relative, born of my kin
Adoo qoys iga dhigtoo	Make me your spouse [lit. "family"]
I qaabila baan rabaa!	I want you to receive me!

Truth now spoken, however, he further reflects on the pained state this love has caused and the persistent conflicted feelings about expressing this love. He represents this conflict as a battle between the self and the heart. By Weedhsame's reckoning, after all, the heart "sometimes forces you to do things that otherwise you would not do" (like reveal long-concealed love sentiments):

Qoonkayga intaan damqaan	I reopen my wound
Ilmada dhaayuhu qubaan	Tears spill from my eyes
Haddana ku qaboojiyaa	And I use them as a balm to my wound
Wadnaha qiiroonayaa	This sad heart says to me:
"Qiruu caashaqa" i yidhi	"Reveal your love plight"
Qudhuna way maagaysaa	Though my inner voice warns me otherwise
Duruufaha igu qasbaa	And circumstances say to me:
"Indhaha isku qabo" i lee	"Shut your eyes" [i.e., accept your situation]
Miyaan qawl iyo dhawaaq	With words or speech
Qummaatiya odhan karaa	I can't express it clearly

In what became the song's refrain, he plainly restates her confession and plea for a relationship:

Maantaba aan kuu qirtoo	Let me confess today my wishes
Qasdiga soo jeediyee	And suggest my feelings
Qareenkii ila dhashoow	My close relative, born of my kin
Adoo qoys iga dhigtoo	Make me your spouse [lit. "family"]
I qaabila baan rabaa!	I want you to receive me

What we have here, then, is the textual representation of love sentiments first experienced by another, then given words via a poet's emotionally resonant, imaginative, perspective-taking abilities—combined, of course, with his technical skill as a poet. While neither spontaneous nor unmediated, and abiding by the strict metrical and alliterative rules that govern Somali verse, a poet is guided by "feeling" to represent the deeply felt interior sentiments of another in a way that maintains their truth (*run*). In this manner, love takes its first step to finding voice.

Sounded Emotion: Words Find Melody

While love nearly always begins its journey toward voice with words, words alone do not make a song. Indeed, since Cabdullaahi Qarshe first began setting love poetry to music, as a genre of poetry, love songs are defined by their distinctive sonic form—not only their use of instruments but also their unique melodies. Love songs' semiotic force is both linguistic *and* sonic. As Weedhsame put it: "Music is another language, even if you can't express your inner feelings in words, you can feel what the melody tells you. If it's angry, if it's sorrow, if it's sad, if it's a song which is very happy, all these things must be tasted from the melody." As one music lover explained, "The laxan [melody] is what makes a song a hit or a flop"; the laxan is "what makes a song sensational and breath-taking . . . because it shapes the music and the rhythm, it exposes the drama and the emotion which the song contains. . . . It is the laxan that can make you happy or sad, show you hope or take you to a place where you were before."

While Weedhsame is sometimes inspired to write his own melodies, which he hums into his smartphone and circulates for feedback, in the case of this particular song, as is the norm for most songs, the melody-making task fell to another artist. Our love doctor is, after all, a (word) specialist, not a GP. When he had completed his poem, Weedhsame passed the lyrics he had penned to Karoone, an accomplished oud player and regular performer at Hiddo Dhawr, who is known locally to create particularly beautiful melodies. How does a love experience, by now represented in words, sound? If, as Weedhsame suggested to me, the emotion must drive the laxan, just as it compelled words, how does the laxamiste (melody writer) put the emotional experiences of another to melody? In chapter 5 I will give more detail on the figure of the musician and the process by which one learns the embodied skills required to produce sounds-as-sonic-emotion that in turn enable singing about love. For now, let us visit Karoone to get a preliminary sense of how a love experience is given melody.

First thing first, Karoone explained to me, sitting cross-legged in a more private room of the home-majlis where I had found him, with an air of seriousness and importance, "If three songs are brought to you, and one is about a love experience, not everyone can write its melody. [First] you must know the words and their interpretation. . . . The person who does not know the words and their objectives cannot make the music." The laxamiste, importantly, rarely interacts with the original love-sufferer and may or may not be told anything of the original encounter that produced the poem they have been given. He may even not know the poet's "agenda" in creating a song (i.e., whether it is an *anti* song or not). In this case, Weedhsame simply gave Karoone the words and mentioned the person he had in mind to sing the song, so he would know what kind of vocal range the melody should take. As the Xidigaha Geeska musician Maxamed Miyir explained to me, the first task of the laxamiste is thus to sit with the words and "fully absorb their content," whether the song is a love song or a nationalist song. In the case of love songs, Karoone explained, you must be particularly attentive to the song's *bad* (sea, or genre)—that is, you must understand the type of love a song professes. "There are many different love feelings," he said, "such as crying, or longing to see a person who is far away, or sometimes it is a hallucination and you do not know what you long for but you have a painful love feeling." When you receive a song, therefore, "you must be capable of figuring out the type [*bad*] of love experience that the song is about. When you know the type of love, you can understand its behavior, and when you know the behavior of this type of love, then you can suggest your views on it."

As is the case for the poet, the laxamiste can only start to compose if and when he has a sense of the "taste" of the original love experience. If the poet has done his job well, then this is something that he may glean from the words. Conversely, "If the words aren't good, it won't affect you," one member of FanSan explained, and the song won't get very far. It also helps, Karoone added, to reflect on one's own love experiences. "You cannot taste it," he explained, "if you have not yourself gone through the experience of love." As was the case for the poet, the laxamiste need not have experienced the precise situation a song describes—Karoone is not a woman who is too shy to express her feelings—but one must have a sense of the feeling of love-pain. And as we saw in the case of the poet who had trouble articulating secondhand accounts of love, if the laxamiste does not fully understand the experience to which he gives sound, the song will flop. Karoone likewise suggested that this is the problem with some young artists who try to make songs "but do not know what the song is about, and a song's true objectives." They do not sufficiently understand, he said, that love may behave in many different ways and are too quick to assume that all love songs are calaacal or foorjo. Instead, they contrive situations, leading to songs that do not sound *real*. "Reality is different from fiction," he explained, "you can pretend a 'fiction' love song, but you can't pretend a real one. You can only make a real song when you have tasted the love. If you taste what love is, you can imagine it." As is the case for the poet, the first step of sounding love is "tasting" or tuning into the experience the song represents.

Having sufficiently absorbed the content of the lyrics and contemplated the behavior of the type of love that a song is about, the laxamiste may then set to work giving melody to words. While I have been told that sometimes melodies simply "float in on the breeze," or "come to you in a dream," just like the poet is bound by the rhythmic and alliterative conventions of the poetic genre in which he composes, so too is there a formula to follow in putting together the melody. And while Karoone told me that music is, on the one hand, a "God-given talent," it is also something that one must learn—becoming acquainted with the *bad* of different songs means learning how it behaves in words and sound. All melodies, for instance, make use of either a major or minor anhemitonic pentatonic scale. In Somali, Karoone explained, this is known as a song's *waddo* (road). As it is for the lyrics, it is the emotion of the song rather than a composer's preference that should drive decisions about the scale in which to compose. In the case of "Qirasho," the wad is built around an F# minor pentatonic scale. The rhythm, similarly, must match the "taste" of the love experience at its root, and the rise and fall of pitches must work both with the rhythmic qualities of the words *and* their referential content (and sometimes adjusting words so they fit the flow of the music, in consultation with the poet).

As there was in the word-making process, there is an element here of "standing in the shoes" of another in order to imagine the experience and flow of the music. As Maxamed Miyir explained, if he is composing the melody for a song in which a man is singing for a woman then "you should

imagine the girl to be right in front of you, and you assume you are addressing the words directly to her." Similarly, if one is giving sound to a song
about longing for someone at a distance, you should imagine that you are
"calling to someone far away." In such instances, he says, "there is a specific
tone. . . . I must raise my voice because of the distance." Karoone similarly explained his composition process as one of matching the emotion
of the original love-sufferer, represented in words, with particular sounds,
so that the "emotion [can] exist in all of you"—from the song's protagonist
to vocalist to future listening ears. The best laxamiste are those who are
technically skilled *and* able to affectively attune themselves to the original
love-suffering experience to which they give sound.

"Standing where she stands," Karoone set to work melodizing our unnamed protagonist's longing (see figure 2.1). Matching the difficulty of her
confession, the song begins timidly, the words "Qof baan" (I am a person)
repeating at the outset in a hesitant descending phrase. The melody then
rises with some confidence as the lyrics reveal the catching of love's fever
then again hesitates as she resigns herself to concealing this love. This hesitation is expressed in the repeating of the phrase "Haddana waan" (And
yet I), first in a descending phrase, then dwelling on a single note. After
repeating the opening lines, the next section consists of the twice-repeated
phrase "Xishood igu qaydan baa / Afkii qufuloo xidhoo" (this deep-rooted
shyness I carry, has sealed the mouth shut), followed by the phrase "Run-
taan ka qaloonayaa" ([discovering] the truth worries me), repeated three
times with different musical phrasing. Karoone explained to me that these
repetitions add "taste" and keep things moving along. "If you do not repeat
words and phrases," he said, "the song loses its taste and the emotional objective of the poet gets lost." These repetitions also make the song "richer"
and serve to make the poem unfold in a way that "doesn't feel squeezed
awkwardly together"—and in this case serve to underscore the difficulty
of the confession to follow. The song then reaches its highest pitch in the
repeated phrase that broods over whether she should confess her feelings,
"Markaan warkaa qeex idhaa" (As I attempt to bring clarity to my feelings).
Just as you might raise your voice as if calling from a distance, the effect
of this phrasing is one of calling out for help, almost in desperation. This
desperation is then tempered slightly, moving toward resignation, with
the phrase "Billee uu qoonsadaa / Qorshaha ku gunaanadaa" (Perhaps it
will cause him grief / I conclude the matter) repeated twice in descending
phrases, each starting on a note that moves toward the middle of the singer's range. Finally, in the refrain where the protagonist at last clearly states
her confession, the mood is again more contemplative as it returns to a
lower register. The hesitation of the lyrics is mirrored in the melody, with

FIGURE 2.1. The first stanza and refrain of "Qirasho," with words by Xasan Daahir Ismaaciil "Weedhsame" and melody (laxan) by Xuseen Aadan "Karoone." The words and melody are notated as sung by Ubax Daahir "Fahmo" to show the vocal embellishments she uses to convey pain and longing.

an entry that is a half beat later than the earlier stanzas and the addition of a 2/4 bar of rests immediately before she finally exclaims in a kind of whisper "I qaabila baan rabaa" (I want you to take me).

The music then repeats with the second set of lyrics, ending with a repeated refrain. Throughout the song, alternating ascending and descending phrases, and the melisma they each end with, work together to "open the door," in Karoone's words, and provide an answer to the sounds that come before. "Each sound," Karoone explained, "must have an answer" if the song is to be balanced. Taken together, the sonic effect is one that moves between hesitation and confidence—or, at least, a desire for confidence—before returning back to a more measured, contemplative statement of longing. By first tuning into the affective experience reflected in a song's words and then standing in the shoes of a song's protagonist and imagining how her longing might affectively sound—all the while working within the genre's musical and rhythmic confines, and established ideas about the sonic qualities of particular emotions—Karoone transformed worded-emotions into sound.

Words and Sound Find Voice

When the melody of a song is ready, it is finally time for unspeakable love experiences to be *voiced*. In the final instance, it is a singer's ability to effectively convey the "taste" of a song in their voice that, as one listener put it to me, "determines whether he can take you to that highest place." It is also in the voice that words and melody finally come together. The way a singer "puts their voice on the words" in a way that convinces listeners "that they are talking about something that happened to them"—or, in Butterworth's (2014, 106) formulation, that they have "lived the song"—plays a crucial final role in a song's success. In Weedhsame's reckoning, songs should have a singer who is "real"—that is, a singer who does not just sing for money or fame but "sings because they need to sing" and who is able to "get inside the song." Yet while the best songs seem to spring unmediated from the depths of a singer's lovestruck soul, the final recording or live performance of a song is preceded by a process that combines technical skill, emotional attunement and an element of imagination—in short, an intentional process of feeling-sharing and artistry similar to what we have seen for poets and musicians.

The first step in this final process requires choosing an appropriate singer. In some cases, a poet or musician may have a vocalist in mind from the beginning of the composition process. Occasionally, the vocalist is the love-suffering individual who inspired the song's text. But more often than not, the singer is not acquainted with the specific origins of a song and is chosen by the poet or laxamiste because they believe them to be an appropriate "fit." Technically, a singer's vocal range—and whether their vocal character is suited to a song's experience—is considered. Emotionally, a singer's own love biography and personal circumstances that are known to the poet, laxamiste, or the general public may also be a factor—that is, whether a singer may need to sing a certain kind of song to relieve their own love-suffering, or be particularly suited to convey a certain kind of story. Additional logistical considerations, like who is available within a specific timeframe, might also come into play. This was partly the case for "Qirasho," as the serious nature of this case precipitated a quick turnaround. Ubax Fahmo was available and understood the urgency of the situation. It also helped that she herself had witnessed the woman's confession and had been deeply moved by her painful situation.

Just as the laxamiste begins by sitting with the words, once a vocalist has been selected they must spend time with the words and melody in order to understand their objective. Before a singer can sing, Ubax explained, they must "listen and get immersed in the love experience," to ascertain whether it is a song about pain and suffering, happiness, or anger and rebuke. They must then also decide if they are able to appropriately convey this experience. The singer need not have experienced the precise love experience that a song represents; what is important is that the experience represented by a song's text and melody resonates, and they are able to empathically imagine themselves in the position of a song's protagonist. One singer, Ruun Xaadi, explained that she "can see through the words and the laxan if it is a happiness or a sorrow song." But if she cannot "feel" a song's objectives, or if the melody is inappropriate for her voice, she will tell the poet or laxamiste to find someone else. "If I am not touched by the experience, I would not sing about it," she said. "I need to be in her shoes. I can't sing if it does not have meaning for me." Ubax echoed this sentiment, explaining that a singer's job is to "interpret" another's emotions. But to do this you have to be able to "cry with them and show empathy. You have to imagine that it happened to you." And beyond "standing in the shoes" of another, Ubax suggested an even more immersive and embodied form of imaginative perspective-taking: "You and the sufferer become one."

The importance of this stage cannot be overstated because if a singer does not or cannot sufficiently feel a song, or an experience does not resonate appropriately, then they will inevitably fail to convey the *run* (truth) of the love experience it represents. Sahra Halgan put it to me simply: "If you

are not feeling a song, you cannot transmit [the emotion] to the people."
Like the poet who struggled to put words to secondhand experiences, one
young singer at Hiddo Dhawr was honest with me about his struggles to
convincingly perform covers of some prewar love songs. He explained that
he tries to "imitate" and "match" the emotion of a song in his voice, but
sometimes he does not fully understand what a song is about. He was still
young, he explained, and had not yet experienced profound love-suffering.
As a consequence, he said that he "could not make the audience feel the
song as deeply" as more experienced singers could. But he was hopeful
that with more practice, and with more personal experiences of love under
his belt, in time this would come. Sahra Halgan similarly suggested that
"pretend" songs might circulate briefly, but they "only last a month." We
might say that songs that lack sufficient feeling have difficulty sticking. But
when *real* singers perform, and "the voice as musical instrument" and "the
voice as self-expression" (Bicknell 2015, 49–50) are perceived to seamlessly
align, then you get, as Weedhsame put it, "a song that will never die."

Once a singer has decided that a song is appropriate for them to sing,
the next step involves memorizing the lyrics and working on achieving
the right "voice" for the song. As was the case for the poet and the laxamiste, this involves combining feeling and imagination with technical skill.
In a singer's case, this involves vocal control and an artistic sense of the
relationship between emotion, comportment, and vocal sound. Ruun,
for instance, explained that once she feels a song, and if the melody goes
beautifully with her voice, she then goes about preparing to sing by "going where she stands" (*hal ku tagana ayaan tagaye*) to find the right voice.
"The lyrics, melody, and voice must all match," she continued, so "going
where she stands" means using her voice in a particular way to enhance
the emotion conveyed by a song's words and melody. Ruun explained that
every song has a *turuko* (trick), and she often starts by playing with the
vocal line to help her find the right tone. Different vocal techniques, which
are both consciously learned and unconsciously absorbed (more on this in
chap. 5), are used to enhance the melody and convey the emotion required
of a song: sliding into a pitch, embellishing a melisma, or letting one's voice
crack or warble. These are also accompanied by appropriate gestures and
facial expressions: "I look like what I am singing about. If it's about sorrow,
I cry. [If it's about happiness] I have to show the audience. You must look
like someone who is in love when you are singing."

Ubax echoed these sentiments in a demonstration of the tone, vocal
techniques, and facial expressions that she uses to sing about different
types of love experiences. Using the opening section of "Qirasho" as an example, she showed me how three different types of love might sound. As

an angry/frustrated foorjo, she sang in clipped phrases with her brow furrowed and a sharp edge in her tone and suggested that the main expression must be one of *huruuftan* (a woman's expression of rebuke/scolding). In a *faraxsan* (happy) mode, she sang with a brighter tone and lighter movement through the melismas (which she described as more "patient"), with her eyes wide open and the corners of her lips curled into a smile. And in its proper rendering as a song about longing (calaacal), she sang in a heavier, almost pleading tone that she described as "stretched" (*jiid*), with an expression of deep sorrow on her face; emulating the sound of someone wailing, she also periodically let her voice slide into pitches and "wobble." "A deaf person should be able to tell the type of song from your face," she explained—and a blind person can know "from your voice."

After their somewhat accelerated preparations were complete, Ubax spent an afternoon recording the vocals for "Qirasho," and her husband Yusuf "Subxaanyo" set it to music. A number of the vocal techniques she and Ruun demonstrated for me are audible in this recording (and represented in figure 2.1). Ubax sings the opening descending phrases in a tone that sounds as if she is crying, partly accomplished by singing the melismas on a closed "n," and partly by singing with the "stretched" heaviness she demonstrated to me. Enhancing what is suggested by the shape of the melody, her voice seems to disappear or contemplatively trail off at the end of certain phrases. A palpable longing is audible as a tiny crack when she reaches for the higher notes in her register, yet her voice returns back to a more tentative color, almost like a whisper, when the melody settles back into the lower part of her range. As she demonstrated for me in her calaacal (complaint) voice, throughout the song she frequently slides into pitches rather than hitting them dead on, wanders around notes that are held for long periods, and otherwise lets her voice "wobble" (represented as mordents in figure 2.1). At various points, the hesitancy of the melody is doubled in the hesitancy of her tone—and sometimes by entries that are intentionally delayed and slightly out of time. And in the refrain where she finally lets her feelings be known, she mirrors the xishood (shyness) of the song's protagonist, reflected in the words and the melody, by eliding the "i" (me) into "qaabila" so much so that it is barely audible.

Only time will tell if "Qirasho" will be "a song that never dies." But I can say that after its release, it did attract attention from various news outlets that were especially interested in having its contributing artists recount the song's real-world origins. For their part, listeners have described this song as tasting of "deep sadness" and "painful feeling" (*dareen xanuun badan*). And perhaps most importantly of all, when they gifted the song to the woman who had inspired it, Ubax said that she was brought to tears as she listened to the feelings that she had been unable to express, now finally given voice.

Feeling, Tasting, Translating the Truth

When I interrupted my poetry lesson to ask Weedhsame about his love hospital poem, I was at first perplexed by his reflections on his "love doctor" duties. Since songs seem to spring from the depths of an individual's lovestruck soul, how could the task of giving experience voice be delegated to another? Yet in listening further to his account of "Qirasho" and more broadly exploring the process by which private, often unspeakable, and long-concealed experiences of love "come into voice," we have seen how the *run* (truth) of a love experience may be translated into song. We have also seen that the initial process of envocalization is far more than a technical process of turning discourse into text (i.e., entextualization). It is also more than a process of creating text that is then revocalized to music. Songs become songs through a collaborative and intersubjective process of feeling-sharing that requires multiple contributors to "taste" the love experience of another, and then use their respective artistic abilities to translate this experience into song. Not all contributors successfully manage these responsibilities all the time. A failure to feel and taste the experience about which one writes/makes melody/sings may lead a song to flop, or to sound fake. Yet when all collaborators succeed in conveying the taste of an experience, the affective power of songs is so great that it can cause listeners to feel and taste the original love experience as well. These are also songs about which one might say, in the highest praise: *Runta ayeey ka turjumayeey* (the truth has been translated).

In addition to contextualizing Weedhsame's love-doctor duties, this collaborative and intersubjective process by which love comes into voice has a number of implications for how we think about the voice of love songs— and what this voice affords listeners once released into the world. The first implication is that love songs are quite clearly *multivocal* from their initial inception. As Weedhsame put it to me, although you only physically hear the singer's voice, when you dissect any given song you can hear the languages of many hidden stakeholders (including an otherwise mute love-suffering individual). "Songs are a combination of different languages," he explained, "the language of emotion, which is derived from the experience of love, [the] poetic language created by the poet, and the musical language created by the musician. All these languages must be combined in a way that must match the lover's original emotional experience." For those who know how to listen, multiple voices are thus always audible in any given song; while people very often associate a song first with its singer, they also often know the poet and the musician who were involved in bringing it to fruition. This is different from other genres of Somali orature. The "voice" that listeners hear in maanso poetry, for instance, is always the poet who has composed the specific poem (Orwin 2021). And while work and dance songs are multivocal in their own way (most audibly in their antiphonal/ responsorial components), given that their lyrics and melodies are unattributed, the "I" of a song is the physical voice of whoever is singing/performing (Orwin 2021). The nature of love songs' multivocality, by contrast, means that the voice is malleable. Listeners physically hear the singer. But they may also hear the laxamiste or the poet—and, indeed, the otherwise mute love-sufferer whose "serious serious" love problem necessitated a song in the first place. We will see in chapters to come how this malleability opens out into a number of possible voicing-listening arrangements.

The multivocality of love songs, however, is not the kind of multivocality that the term usually evokes. It is not a form of speech that gains its power by ordering or representing distinct voices and perspectives into a single narrative account (cf. Englund 2015, 2018, Hill 1995). Nor is it some utopic public/democratic forum where multiple voices are simultaneously audible. The multivocally produced voice of love songs gains its power by condensing felt experiences of multiple contributors into a singular sonic-textual voice—a deeply personal and naturalized voice that is conceived to provide unmediated access to the lovestruck soul of another. But given this voice is neither spontaneous nor unmediated, another thing this process demonstrates is that a song may sound from the heart *and* be heavily mediated. Put another way, a message can be heard as *runta* (the truth) even when delivered in a voice created and sounded by (multiple) others— and the voice may even be all the more powerful for its malleability and its subtle multivocal inflections. We will see in chapter 3 that this has implications for how singers' voices circulate and are storied. And we will see in chapter 4 that this also has profound implications for listeners who lack the words and voice to express their own love feelings yet wish to feeling-share with others.

What might this mean for the lives that love songs lead once they are released into the world? I will suggest, finally, that the initial multivocal process of envocalization by which love songs turn intimate experiences into public expression points the way to understanding their affective power, the forms of intimacy that they facilitate, and the kinds of intimate imaginings that songs afford. We will see in the coming chapters how love songs become indefinitely entangled in a variety of relationships and aspirations, opening space for dareen-wadaag (feeling-sharing) wherever they travel and providing relief to otherwise lonely love-sufferers. The voice seems to multiply outward yet resonates more deeply inward with each subsequent envocalization. If, like Berlant (1998, 281) we take intimacy as being about an "aspiration for . . . something shared," and if like Barber (2007b, 41) we see genres as "bearer[s] of social relations," then I would suggest that love songs' intimacy-opening potential is present in the very form itself. Songs do not only aspire to feeling-sharing, or dareen-wadaag. They are, in their very multivocal sonic-textual-vocal substance, a *distillation* of it. At the time they come into the world, love songs already represent a love experience twice or thrice (or more) contemplated, imagined, "tasted," and shared with or by another—and given "voice." Love songs model the very possibility of feeling-sharing, of opening oneself up to others, via the voices of others. Love songs, or at least the "really" ones, contain the seeds of their own intimate unfolding.

CHAPTER THREE

Storied Voices, Storied Songs

(Or, I Am Calaacal)

A voice means this: there is a living person, throat, chest, feelings, who sends into the air this voice, different from all other voices.

Italo Calvino, "A King Listens"

Of the many evenings I spent at Hiddo Dhawr over the course of my research, one of my earliest visits stands out as particularly memorable. Sahra Halgan, the venue's founder, had taken the stage early in the evening. Sahra knows how to command a stage and captivate an audience. But her performance that evening somehow seemed more personal and intimate. With her gaze cast slightly upward, she sang about "a soul thirsty for love" ("Naftii jacayl la ooman") that cries out like a she-camel for its missing calf ("Sida igadh maqaaray / Olol reemay goortaan"). In a deep undulating voice, she sang about a love that had caused wounds deep in the womb and stomach ("Uurkiyo calooshay / Aramidu l jiftaa"), a love that was tormenting its host with its persistence. But constrained by expectations of women's modesty and shyness (xishood), this love could not be properly expressed. At one point, Mustafe, the evening's emcee, made his way to the stage, exclaiming, "*Ya salaam!* Sahra is hot tonight!" Sahra acknowledged him with a slight nod of her head but remained consumed in her own performance. The audience sat enraptured, at first in complete silence, soaking up each phrase. But each time the familiar refrain came around, audience members joined Sahra in singing about the impossibility of expressing love. And feeling the raw emotion in Sahra's voice, women in the audience periodically let out cries of commiserative solidarity, voiced as ululating whoops. My friend Warsame, who had been unusually captivated by Sahra's performance, finally leaned over and explained: "Sahra is really on fire! She must be sad or upset with a man. Tonight, she is singing Khadra Daahir. These are the songs of women who have been hurt by love."

While on the evening of this performance the name "Khadra Daahir" was relatively unfamiliar to me, I soon learned that this was a woman whose songs, voice, and story held a special place in the pantheon of Somali music giants. As a member of Somalia's flagship musical collective Waaberi, Khadra could boast of an exceptionally successful singing career. But she was especially beloved for her voicing of calaacal—a subgenre of songs that document the pain and regret of failed relationships and that literally translates as "complaint" or "wailing." Indeed, so touching were Khadra's calaacal, and so entangled had they become in her own well-known love journey, that she had earned the esteemed yet somehow also pitiable title *hooyada jacaylka* (the mother of love). More than four decades after recording her first song, her plaintive melodies continue to weave their way through the urban soundscape, inviting listeners to contemplate the vagaries of love-suffering. "Oh Khadra Daahir, she is our mother of love!" one friend mused. "Listen," another said, "and you will learn what it means to suffer from love." Or, as Huda once explained: "When she is singing, what happens is the song comes from deep, deep, deep inside her soul, it makes you to feel what she feels. Why did he act that way? Why did he cause her that pain? Why is she suffering? You ask a lot of questions of yourself, and you feel sick and you can't eat anymore." And as the commiserative whoops of the women listening to Sahra sing Khadra's song suggest, this is a woman who continues to pull people in, drawing love-sufferers together and animating conversations of love, longing, and loss decades after her voice was first set into circulation.

This chapter documents the making of hooyada jacaylka, the esteemed mother of love. This is a story about the ongoing making of the voice and the intimate work of songs as they move across space and generation. Anchored in a story about Khadra and her voice, I ask: What happens to songs when they enter public circulation? What happens to the voice when it detaches itself from the body that first gives it breath? To whom does that voice belong? How are songs and singers made familiar and intimate as they travel? And how might exploring these questions help us to make sense of the instant affinity and sense of familiarity felt by the women who, upon hearing Sahra sing Khadra's songs, called out in commiserative solidarity, decades after she initially voiced the pain of unspeakable love?

At the heart of this chapter is a simple observation, yet one with profound effects. People like to *talk* about voices. The voice, after all, is fundamentally social (Feld et al. 2004, 341). Indeed, one reason it took me so little time to familiarize myself with Khadra's story is that considerable "sociable energies" are often devoted to this talk (Stokes 2010, 7). Separated by recording technology from the bodies that gave them breath, singers' voices elicit all manner of conversation, appreciation, and speculation. Listeners poetically describe the emotional quality of a given voice, its ability to transport and transform. Music lovers lose themselves reminiscing about their encounters with particular songs. Fans delight in speculating about the lived experiences (thought to be) reflected in songs, talk that sometimes slips between myth and reality, fantasy and fact.[1] In the first instance, we will see that this often intimate talk is guided and enabled by the sonic-textual-vocal form of love songs and a particular ideology of voice—that is, one that figures the voice as a deeply personal mode of individual self-expression. Yet this talk, I will show, is not only an *effect* of how people conceptualize the voice: it is in fact *constitutive of* the voice itself.[2] This talk is itself an act of envocalization and is fundamental to the kind of intimate public that sticky songs summon.

Approaching voices in this way demands a recognition that songs (and singers) are never just a single instantiation of vocal expression but are rather "complex and collective discursive constructions" that are constantly emerging and taking shape (Stokes 2010, 7). What follows is thus a necessarily *multivocal* account of the life and music of Khadra Daahir: a story about the relationship between lived experience, song, singer, and audience that weaves together the stories people tell about her and that she herself told, the texts of her songs and listeners' reflections about her voice. Whereas in chapter 2 we saw how multiple voices are collapsed into a single singing voice, in this chapter we see songs to be multivocal collaborations of a different sort: collaborations that reveal the "inherently dialogic and embodied qualities of speaking and hearing" (Feld 1998, 471), where each new listening and vocalization recalls the memory of past auditions and voicings. These are collaborations that unfold across time and space, in which a singer's voice is constantly in the making.

As a quintessential love-victim-songstress, Khadra and her story provide a compelling entry into thinking about the voice in circulation. Yet my reasons for focusing on Khadra are also more personal. As a daughter of Hargeysa, stories about Khadra's songs were often accompanied by stories of encounters with the vocal legend herself. Stories of boyhood crushes on Khadra, the teenage basketball star. Memories of sharing a room on the *xaj*. Accounts of chance meetings at Gollis restaurant, known for its sweet, succulent camel meat. Some especially lucky individuals also tell stories about invitations to her home, and Khadra's soul-soothing presence. Indeed, Khadra is beloved not only for daring to publicly voice love-suffering but also for the magnetic *qalbi-furan* (open heart) such experiences seem to have produced. Khadra's was a love-pain that "open[ed] [her] to the outside" (Seremetakis 1991, 116). Early in my research, I was fortunate to be introduced to Khadra. And over the course of my stay, she became one of my closest confidantes, a surrogate mother of sorts. It was over many afternoons in Khadra's living room—where a revolving crowd of friends, fans, and politicians constantly passed through the semipublic, semiprivate, and somehow still intimate space of her home—that I came to appreciate the importance of artists as living, breathing, persons, not just disembodied voices, in the way that love songs and singers are storied and move across space and time. It was from this vantage point that I gained insight into the relationship of a singer to her own voice and the simultaneously detached-yet-present role singers play in shaping the stories others tell about them. And as will become evident below, Khadra and her qalbi-furan made an impression on *me*. While a feature of our own intimate relationship, this impression is not dissimilar to the one Khadra and her voice and her songs have had on her Somali audiences, and the subsequent stories that her fans like to tell.

While my focus here is on one singer, two emergent themes speak more broadly to the ways that the voice of love lends itself to certain forms of envocalization. The first has to do with the *type* of talk that hees jacayl elicit: talk that is often preoccupied with the real-world origins of songs and that construes singers in particularly intimate terms. Indeed, I was intrigued from my earliest encounters with listeners by the lore-like origins stories that seemed to travel with songs and the gossip that songs elicited about singers' love lives. The story of Magool's Sudanese admirer and Hadraawi's role in interpreting his blood-inked love letter, recorded in the song "Jacayl dhiig ma lagu qoray?" (Has love been blood-written?), was recounted to me more times than I can recall.[3] Hibo Nuura's rocky breakups and Cumar Dhuule's use of songs to plead with his wife to come home (rather than send a delegation of elders to negotiate on his behalf) are the stuff of legend. Stories of Axmed Gacayte's vagabond lifestyle, living in Hargeysa's riverbed dependent on fans' gifts of food, wove their way through conversations about his music. Speculation about which members of Xidigaha Geeska might be in love with whom, and whose love story might be reflected in any given song, flared up with each new release. Yurub Geenyo's divorces and Maxamed BK's tender relationship with his wife endeared them to their fans. The expectation that some flesh-and-blood experience of love(-suffering) lies behind each voice precipitates an especially intimate person-centered discourse about songs. This talk in turn influences how audiences listen and the sense of familiarity they feel toward their favorite singers.

That fans construe their favorite singers in particularly intimate terms is of course not unique to the Somali context. But scholarship on vocal celebrities elsewhere has highlighted a paradox in star culture; while fans may think of celebrities in very intimate terms, these celebrities usually remain distant and inaccessible (Butterworth 214, 46; Rojek 2001). In Somaliland, however, celebrity artists are surprisingly available. Want to talk to Hadraawi? Turn up at the Plaza Hotel in Burco after afternoon prayers. Looking to reminisce with Cabdi Qays? Stop by his favorite majlis in Hargeysa's Jigjigayar neighborhood. Need to speak with Ruun Xaadi or Aamina Cabdullaahi? The neighborhood kids will be glad to direct you to their houses. (Indeed, on a trip to Boorame to meet Aamina, I was sent in hopeless circles when I asked about the location of a specific mosque that Aamina had given as a landmark; when I changed tack and asked where *she* lived, I was guided to her home with ease.) Voices may live animated lives detached from the bodies that first gave them breath. But in Somaliland, they are also shaped by the presence and living memories of the flesh-and-blood love-sufferers who dared to publicly express their love (sorrows)—people who may be a neighbor, a friend's mother, a fellow passenger on the bus. And artists' real and potential familiarity is critical to the way that voices are storied and continually made intimate. Whereas work on mass mediation elsewhere has highlighted the importance of stranger sociability to the making of publics (even intimate ones), the public summoned by hees jacayl is rooted in a far more familiar kind of sociality (cf. Habermas 1989, Warner 2002, Berlant 2008).[4]

This intimacy and familiarity is acutely audible in the voices that circulate and story Khadra's voice—including, I think, in my own voice, which is inevitably part of the multivocal process I describe. Let's take a listen.

Intimate Encounters with the Mother of Love

I first met Khadra Daahir Ciige on a Thursday afternoon in mid-November 2015. A few weeks earlier, I had interviewed Cabdi Aadan "Qays"—a poet and musician known for his *anti* poetry, affable wit, and titular role in the play *Leyla iyo Qays* (a Somali take on the centuries-old Arabic love story). During a conversation about the artists Qays had worked with in the heyday of his career in the 1970s–1980s, he suggested to me that I come along the next time he went to chew with his old friend Khadra. That morning he had called Warsame, a mutual friend, announcing that today was the day. Himself a Khadra fan, Warsame excitedly passed on the news. By early afternoon, I was sitting in the passenger seat of Warsame's old Toyota as we made our way through the quieter early afternoon streets toward the Masalaha neighborhood by the airport. Before long we arrived at Khadra's home. I would later learn that this was one of the first houses built on this land after the civil war in the mid-1990s. We were let in the front gate and shown to the house but cautioned to be as quiet as possible. We had arrived, it turned out, just after a documentary film crew similarly set on finding Khadra and Qays together had arrived and begun filming. We removed our shoes at the back door, entered a heavily curtained sitting room, and settled on the floor around the room's perimeter. The film crew, we learned, had come to question the two artists about their role in sheltering a political dissident in the 1980s, effectively saving him from execution by Barre's regime. While Qays's anti-pan-Somalist and anti-Barre poetry had already drawn the ire of the powers that be—leading to his temporary exile and imprisonment—as an iconic Muqdisho-based member of the regime's flagship band Waaberi, Khadra's artistic career had mostly remained politically neutral. For Khadra, I would learn, speaking of such a politically charged incident was a rare disclosure. Yet by this point in the regime's deterioration in the late 1980s, political neutrality was no longer an option. To the camera, they spoke cautiously and with reverence, as the situation they were recounting seemed to demand, though their speech was often punctuated with Qays's boisterous laugh. To each other, they smiled and gestured in the familiar way that old friends do, privy to their own set of jokes and memories, both happy and painful.

When the cameras stopped rolling, Qays jovially introduced Khadra to the peculiar caddan (white) woman who had come all this way to study love songs. Khadra was dressed in a green *dirac* with a pink *shalmad*—a large headscarf that covers the head, neck, and most of the shoulders. Her shalmad framed a kind and wise-looking face that appeared younger than her nearly sixty years. Now off-camera, she removed the shalmad, exposing a black *masar*—a smaller kerchief tied behind her hair—and settled back into what I would learn was her usual corner at the top of the room. She greeted us warmly, though with cautious curiosity, demanding that we be served tea and brought extra pillows, and then offering us a bundle of qaad. The half-dozen others present in the room were already well settled into their own qaad piles. Warsame politely declined, excusing me by joking that a white woman surely could not be expected to handle the bitter leaf. Instead, we sipped sweet tea, chatted with those seated around us, and answered Khadra's inquiries about how we were finding Hargeysa. Sufficiently vouched for by Qays, Khadra agreed to sit down with me for an interview in a few days' time. We said our goodbyes and set out for the long drive back across the city, with Warsame gushing excitedly the whole way home.

A few days later we were back in the car en route to Khadra's home.

We arrived and were let in the main gate to find a house still asleep. A few men were gathered in the room attached to the outside kitchen, which functioned as a kind of local majlis for politicians who lived and worked in the area and needed a semiprivate/semipublic afternoon chewing space. Ministers and mayors, politicians of the ruling party, and the opposition gathered here almost daily, drawn both by the availability of space and the prestige of chewing at the house of a national musical legend. Warsame joined the men outside, while I, suffering from a rather bad case of laryngitis, took the welcome time to lie down on the couch. Soon thereafter I was greeted by Khadra's live-in caregiver/housekeeper (and distant relative), who suggested that perhaps I wanted somewhere more comfortable to sleep. Khadra was waking up, she explained, and upon learning that I was lying on the couch, invited me to sleep in her bed. I was shown inside the bedroom as Khadra was dressing after her nap, urged to change into more comfortable clothes, given one of Khadra's *shiid* (a light, loose-fitting cotton dress worn by women at home), and tucked into bed. They left me alone to sleep and to ponder this disarming show of hospitality.

When I groggily came into the living room about an hour later, Khadra immediately sent for some cardamom-laced coffee and a bottle of local honey—her prescribed remedy for my laryngitis. We sat on the living-room floor and chatted, eventually rejoined by Warsame, who had volunteered to help with the interview. He suggested we begin. Somewhat hesitantly, though with an air of professionalism, Khadra consented, suggesting we return to her bedroom to avoid the noise of the afternoon chewing crowd that would soon trickle in. After settling onto the floor, I turned the recorder on and launched into the standard set of questions I had been asking artists. She told us of being discovered by her Form 5 teacher, of afternoons after school recording songs at Radio Hargeysa, her recruitment into Waaberi after a school singing competition, and the first time she was cast in a play across from her eventual husband and fellow singer, Axmed Cali Cigaal. She described joining the artistic scene in the mid-1970s, a time when there was "something in the air" musically—something that, compared to the path-blazing and frequently disparaged women of a slightly earlier generation, made it easier and more acceptable for a woman to become a singer. In those postrevolution years, the arts had been elevated, hitched to a project of pan-Somalist nationalism and the spread of *cilmiga hantiwadaagga* (scientific socialism), and artists' public role and reputations were taken to new heights (even as their freedom of expression was severely curtailed). She explained her own popularity as a consequence of her songs' authenticity. Her songs were rooted in her own love experiences, she said, and people connected to that. She laughed at the title hooyada jacaylka, explaining that she keeps telling people, apparently to no avail, that she was now too old to be called such things.

In what turned out to be a rather short interview, Khadra responded graciously though with brevity, narrating her artistic career in a way I imagined she, and others, had narrated it before, providing biographical snippets already in circulation—details of her life I would hear repeated about her by others during my stay. When I turned the microphone off, her posture visibly relaxed. We returned to the main sitting room to join the assorted guests arriving for an afternoon of qaad and conversation. Those assembling included some of Khadra's friends, some politicians, and the guests they had brought along. I would soon learn that those who came here, inside the house, were drawn not only by the prestige of chewing at Khadra's but by Khadra's own presence. "This is where we come for our therapy," one guest later quipped. "It's like our asylum center! Or our mental health hospital!" When you are around Khadra, they explained, you can just be yourself. You can forget about all the other things bothering you. You need not necessarily speak out loud of your own love-pains or those of Khadra. In fact, these were often off limits. Khadra's love-pains preceded her, her voice long ago reaching innumerable ears. Simply being in the presence of the mother of love—being near someone who has been broken by love—does something to you, her regular visitors would tell me. Khadra's simple presence, her love-suffering-induced qalbi-furan (open heart), brings relief.

As the afternoon wore on, Warsame and I excused ourselves to head for home. But as we negotiated our departure, Khadra's generous qalbi-furan revealed itself in another gesture of disarming hospitality. She insisted that I leave with her bottle of honey and while still wearing her *shiid*. This departure ritual repeated itself in the coming months: gifts of clothes, food, perfumes, incense, and a *girgire* (incense-burning pot) were to follow. At first, these offerings made me uncomfortable, and I vehemently resisted. I even made a point of wearing clothes that Khadra would deem suitably comfortable for relaxing in her home to avoid being persuaded to change into hers. Eventually, I relented, partly because I learned that many of these things had been gifted to her in the first place—locally sewn *dirac*, incense from Dubai, a laptop from Denmark—brought to her by adoring fans from near and far. Khadra's singing career had not made her exceptionally wealthy, and she had also spent two decades as a refugee living in council housing in southwest London. But in the land of her birth, the land where she is the mother of love, she was kept in good stead.

Material gifts aside, the sentiment that simply being in Khadra's presence seems to have an effect on people is something that I would come to understand more fully over the next year. The interview now behind us, Khadra extended an open invitation to me to visit her. I soon took her up on the offer and showed up alone a few weeks later. She was already seated on the floor, surrounded by some friends, in a characteristically jovial mood. "*Naayaa* Christina! *Kaalay* [come], sit, *qayil* [chew]!" she demanded, in a mixed Somali-English hybrid that would become our common language. With no laryngitis or otherwise valid excuse, I finally accepted. She arranged a pile of branches beside me and began picking off the most tender leaves from her own collection, passing them to me on her outstretched palm. I tentatively put a few in my mouth, immediately repulsed by their bitter juices. Khadra laughed in great amusement at the expression on my face and passed me a cup of sweet tea. After some small talk with the other guests, seemingly out of nowhere Khadra then demanded: "Tell me the happiest moment of your life! I want to know who you are." As I fumbled to come up with something meaningful, she responded without hesitation: "Mine was when my youngest son was born." After not being pregnant for over fifteen years, the child born to her by her second husband brought her immense joy.

Disarmed by Khadra's warmth and motherly curiosity in me, like those who flock to Khadra for mental relief, I too soon let down my usual guard, forgetting the reflexive cautiousness I inhabited as a caddan (white) ethnographer, constantly assessing the implications of my relationships and actions. We would pass many afternoons together like this, sitting on her floor, Khadra teasing me for chewing qaad "like salad," while conspiratorially passing me handfuls of the best leaves. She habitually chastised me for not learning Somali quickly enough and for not strumming my oud properly—then bragged to others about her caddan friend, her dumaashi (sister-in-law), who could speak Somali and even play some Somali songs! Over the course of many afternoons spent in the company of a rotating assortment of friends, retired and aspiring artists—and, sometimes, when the outside majlis overflowed into her sitting room, retreating to her bedroom floor—our conversations wandered through all manner of topics. I learned of her love for Turkish soap operas, Sudanese music, and Lionel Richie. I listened as she proudly recounted stories of her children's and grandchildren's lives. I heard stories of her days as one of Waaberi's leading divas, touring across Somalia, North Africa, the Gulf—and that one time she performed for Saddam Hussein at a private party for Baghdad's political elite. I listened as she recounted the profound impact going on the *xaj* had had on her. So transformative was this experience that she decided to make the journey a second time. (My friend Farxiya later shared her own *xaj* experience with me, which included her surprise and delight at being billeted

FIGURE 3.1. Khadra and friends sing together at a picnic celebrating Eid, near Arabsiyo. Photograph by the author.

to a room shared with the mother of love.) I learned of Khadra's distaste for London weather and her bill-paying lifestyle as a refugee-housewife, and her decision to finally return to the land of her birth. And when she was occasionally in the mood, I heard her sing—sing in that rich, magnificently vulnerable voice, now deepened slightly by age, that has soothed the wounds of Somali love-sufferers for decades. At an Eid picnic gathering in the countryside with a group of friends and musicians, I also quite literally witnessed the continued magnetism of this voice. Unencumbered by the crowds that frequented her home, Khadra decided to sing. Within minutes the local women who had prepared our food had unobtrusively made their way from a makeshift kitchen set off at a distance to the shade of a nearby mango tree to watch and listen. They had been drawn by the presence and the naked singing voice of the woman they knew to be the mother of love.

While I heard Khadra speak of many things, I soon learned that certain topics were best left alone. Even though fans spent copious hours speculating about the experiences that had inspired her songs, prying for details about aspects of her personal relationships was decidedly off limits in her home. I had been warned of this early on by a friend who had once been in a majlis with Khadra. When a guest asked her a pointed question about the intimate origins of a song, her mood immediately changed. In her own home, personal questions from guests yet unacquainted with the etiquette of respecting certain privacies were usually met with a gentle though sufficiently aggravated glance to prompt a glimmer of shame on the questioner's face, then a quick change of subject. Compared to others I met in similar spaces, Khadra was particularly guarded in this regard, as if afraid that broaching such subjects would reopen wounds never properly healed. I wondered periodically that perhaps Khadra felt safe with me in part because, compared to those more versed in her repertoire, I was relatively naive to the details of her love life. While the pain of her love had necessitated song, its voicing in public seems to have created a secondary wound. Rendering her pain audible had both made Khadra vulnerable and endeared her to the hearts of many. But this public voicing also entailed a relinquishing of control over her own story—an alienation of sorts from her own voice, an "uncanniness" that is as intimate as it is strange, well-documented in studies of the effects of sound-recording technology.

Yet rather than correcting rumors or feeding others' thirst for information, Khadra usually stayed quiet, leaving her voice, recorded decades ago, to speak for itself. That fans may embellish stories or slip between fact and fiction did not seem of great concern. She seemed to have accepted long ago that her voice in recorded song was not entirely her own. As one playwright put it to me, "if somebody loves someone and he puts his voice up there, then it belongs to everyone else." Khadra seemed to intuitively understand that her voice would live a life of its own, a life suited to the needs of its listeners in different times and places. In a sense, Khadra was perhaps even most fully herself in this voice given over to others—or, at least, most fully a singer, a vocal medium of sorts for love-pains past, present, and future. And yet it was this giving-over of voice, of life, that ultimately drew people back to this space, to her, the esteemed mother of love in the flesh, drawn by the magnetism of her qalbi-furan, the woman who had dared to bare her broken heart to the world.

While I rarely heard Khadra speak of her own love experiences, they were not difficult to hear. Variations of her story of love-suffering floated through conversations with friends. Hearing one of her songs playing often prompted long forays into her difficult love history, reflections on the circumstances that led to particular songs, or expressions of pity for her predicament. "Pass our sympathies to Khadra," one artist-friend noted when learning I was going from his house to hers, "she really suffered from love." Let's take a closer listen, then, at the stories that circulate about Khadra, the relationship between Khadra's own intimate experiences and her songs, and the implicit ideologies of voice that account for her popularity and animate a particular kind of talk about her voice—in other words, the everyday acts of envocalization by which voices of love circulate, and that make voices increasingly sticky.

Pushed by the Winds of Love: Finding First Voice

Khadra Daahir Ciige was born in Hargeysa in 1957, during the dying days of Britain's colonial rule, and raised during Somalia's optimistic first decade of independence. By most accounts, she was destined to become a singer. But for her Hargeysa fans, she first found fame as an athlete, excelling in basketball and athletics. "Did you know Khadra was a basketball player?" friends queried, on learning I had been spending time with the singer. "She used to be a really good runner!" While such endeavors seem unthinkable in contemporary Hargeysa, where sporting opportunities for women are almost nonexistent, this was "a different Hargeysa," one middle-aged friend reminisced. This memory had been elicited by the sounds of Khadra singing "Xaafuun," one of the few qaraami Khadra had recorded. "Women could wear shorts and play basketball then." He continued, nostalgically, to explain that he had become personally invested in Khadra's sporting career when, as a young boy, he and his friends had fashioned themselves into Khadra's personal team of seven-year-old bodyguards. They would wait outside the Timo-Cadde basketball court—named for the esteemed mid-twentieth-century poet—and when Khadra had finished her practices, they would escort her home.

But basketball was not Khadra's only youthful talent. As a Form 5 student in the early 1970s, shortly after Barre's rise to power, Khadra sang her first song. In line with the nationalist fervor of the day, the song was a patriotic anthem, written by her Arabic teacher. Soon thereafter, a group of artists and musicians visited Hargeysa as part of Barre's *heesahaga hirgalay* talent-scouting activities. Among this group was the musician Saalax Qaasim. To Qaasim's oud accompaniment, Khadra performed a popular Sahra Axmed song. Upon hearing her voice, Qaasim declared that Khadra would be a singer. Qaasim's opinion, and continued involvement in her musical development, would prove vital to launching Khadra's singing career.

While already identified as a young rising talent, it was Khadra's love, voiced in song, that was to make her famous. As a tender Form 7 student, she was cast in the lead role of the play *Dab Jacayl Kariwaa* (Burning fire can't kill love), across from Axmed Cali Cigaal, a much older man and well-established Waaberi singer. This was a well-known story recounted to me often, a story which cast Khadra as a young woman to be commiserated for falling in love at such a young age, with a man whose circumstances were bound to cause problems. In a rare moment of intimate disclosure when at her home with only a few close friends, Khadra explained to me that this was a love that just "happened." This was a love that simply "struck" her. And even though in retrospect she can see his many flaws, when you fall in love, she said, you are blind to any possible complications, because "jacaylku indho ma la ha" (love has no eyes). Articulated in Somali, "to fall in love" is an event that places the lovestruck individual as a passive recipient. Grammatically, "love" (*jacayl*) is the agentive/focused subject, "I" is the passive direct object. *Jacayl baa i hayaa.* "Love has me." The best way Khadra could think of explaining this to me was by reciting the lines of a qaraami:

> *Jacaylku waa dabayl duufaani waddo*   Love is a heavy hurricane wind
> *Dibnaha iyo saaran daymada*   It is in the eyes [gaze] and the lips
>   [speech]

Hearing Khadra voice these words, one of her friends quickly explained their origin. These words were first uttered by a woman in Boorame known to be "mad" because she was in love with a local teacher. Walking down the street one day, "Allah put the words in her mouth." Although she was considered "mad," in this instance, he explained, "she had made meaning." A local poet, Timo-Cadde, eventually composed a poem built around these utterances that was later set to music and became a qaraami (likely to Timo-Cadde's chagrin, given his well-known opinion that qaraami were turning poetry into useless "noise").

Not unlike the way Timo-Cadde heard of the "mad" woman's utterances, Khadra's first song came into being through a process that involved others putting words into her mouth. Even before I had met Khadra in person, a friend of a friend who had heard of my research was eager to meet to tell me about his father, a poet, who played a part in "making Khadra famous," because he had "given Khadra her first love song." As he recounted it, encouraged by others at the local majlis where we had met (who I suspect had heard this story many times), some men concerned with Khadra's lovesick state approached his father, Maxamed Cali Weyrax, and explained Khadra's love predicament. Moved by what he was told, he wrote a poem, "Afka lagama sheegtoo" (You cannot speak about it). The poem was taken to Saalax Qaasim, the musician who had first discovered Khadra, who set it to music. The song was then gifted to Khadra to sing. The poem is composed in the jiifto meter and alliterates using vowels (which count as a single alliterative sound). After an instrumental accompaniment that sets out the melodic motif, the song opens with a pair of repeating lines, the second ending on an unresolved pitch, then a third line that takes Khadra into her lower register to express the impossibility of speaking about love without having experienced it oneself:

Afka lagama sheegtoo	You cannot speak about it
Adigoon jacayl arag	If you have never lived through love
Looma uur xumaadee	And do not hold ill-feeling [against something you have not experienced]

The instruments then guide Khadra through a depiction of the suddenness with which love takes hold. In the bridge, she then gives an initial assessment of the pain love is causing her, dwelling in her lower range on the exclamatory "sowtan" (which translates roughly as "there it is"), staking a personal claim of sorts to the possibility of discussing love, announcing that love-pain—and she—is here:

Aniguu i helayoo	Me, it [love] found me
Intuu soo abraaruu	It was sudden
Xadhig igu adkeeyee	Tied me with rope
Sowtan aramidiisii	Its wound, there it is
Igu sii fidaysee	Still spreading [through my body]
Aan ka jiifsan waayee	I could not sleep

In the refrain, Khadra shifts from describing the effects of love, to pleading with the one who has caused this pain to come and save her:

Kii igu abuuree	He who sowed the seed of love
U ilmaynayow	I'm still shedding tears for him
Haygu eeginee ii imaw	Don't just watch, come save me

In looping phrases, Khadra continues to describe love's effects, in language reminiscent of Cilmi:

Anfacadii ka go'ayoo	I lost my appetite
Eedaadka caashaqa	The unbearable pain of love
U adkaysan waayee	I cannot endure it
Intuu igu itaalsaday	It got stronger
Iimana tudhaayoo	It's not merciful towards me
Anfariir ka qaadee	It frightens me

In the second bridge, Khadra replaces "pain" with "afflictions," again announcing her experiences, this time with a poignant image of the ravaging effects of love on the body:

Sowtan alhuumadiisii	Its afflictions
Oofaha dhexdoodiyo	Cut through my ribs
Adhaxduu i gooyee	And broke my backbone in two

Finally, she pleads once more with the one who has set alight this feeling in her to come:

Kii igu abuuree	He who sowed the seed of love
U ilmaynayow	I'm still shedding tears for him
Haygu eeginee ii imaw	Don't just watch, come save me

Barely sixteen, Khadra recorded her first song at Radio Hargeysa, sending into the world a song that remains a fan-favorite, and a song I saw performed frequently at Hiddo Dhawr by various lovesick women. Curiously, while I was first told that this song was specifically gifted to Khadra by a poet concerned with *her* condition, and the song is almost always heard as a reflection of Khadra's own love woes, Khadra's account of the song's origins differed. Rather than being autobiographical, she suggested the song reflected the poet's "preoccupation with something," and that he gifted it to her as a rising talent who he thought could best give the song voice. Her own love predicament, she conceded, may have influenced this choice, his belief that she could adequately convey the song's *run* (truth). On first hearing of this discrepancy, I was initially perplexed. The poet's son had recounted with such pride his father's role in giving Khadra her love-voice. I *wanted* the song to be autobiographical. Like many other listeners, I expected the song to be "true." I have since come to see this rather as an incredibly powerful testament to three distinct but related features of the voice of hees jacayl. The first is that, as we saw in chapter 2, a singer may sing "the truth," even if a song begins in another's love experiences—songs, after all, emerge from the premise that feeling-sharing is possible, and that feeling-sharing is enabled by the voice. But this elision also speaks, secondly, to the way that songs become attached to the biographies, and (gendered) bodies of those who give them voice (Gracyk 2001, 181)—and here I mean "voice" in a very literal sense, as sound produced in the throat of a specific body. This is unsurprising for a genre in which listeners expect a seamless alignment between "the voice as musical instrument" and "the voice as instrument of self-expression" (Bicknell 2015, 49–50). Once we know something about the lives of our favorite singers, we hear these histories in their songs (Bicknell 2015, 45–50). As we will see below, it was the frequency with which Khadra's biography *did* align seamlessly with her songs—even songs that were not strictly biographical—that accounts in part for her celebrity.

And yet, in this instance, I think there was also a third thing at play, something about the pull of familiarity that animates stories about Khadra. Something revealed in the eagerness with which the poet's son sought me out to tell this story, the incredible pride he felt in being connected to Khadra in this way. He was the son of the man who had given the mother of love her voice, who had opened the floodgates to a life of voicing love-pain. His father had told him this story, and in turn he himself had joyously shared it with others—in a manner not dissimilar to my recounting of my own intimate encounters with Khadra. He wanted to be part of a story, he *was* a part of a story, part of the making of a voice—a voice that calls out for others to participate in its ongoing animation as it is propelled across time and space.

Becoming Calaacal

Whether or not the origins of this first song were strictly biographical or not, Khadra's longing for Axmed Cali Cigaal quickly became public knowledge. News spread among the tight-knit artistic community, as well as in the teashops, homes, and cars where her songs aired over the radio. Soon enough, more words to express this love-suffering were brought her way—not "put in her mouth by Allah," but given to her by poets so moved by witnessing her love-pain that they attempted to represent these sentiments in words. Or, in Weedhsame's reckoning, poets were *compelled* by the "serious serious" nature of Khadra's love problems to give her remedy in verse. As Khadra explained it: "Poets create out of what they observe and see around them. They don't make songs out of nothing. They used to write songs about me as soon as they saw how I was suffering because of love." Laughing, she added, "they bothered me a lot!" Singing about one's pain, after all, can be a painful and tiring job—even if it simultaneously brings a sort of relief. She thus became a sort of muse, an embodiment of longing, a woman whose love-suffering inspired others to attempt to represent the pain she was feeling and to help her release painful bottled-up emotions. At other times poets sought her out for her voice and an ability to authentically convey the emotion of love-suffering expressed in songs that did not necessarily begin in her own experiences. But these songs too would become so associated with her voice and her story that few can distinguish between what is strictly biographical and what started as another's experience. Whatever a song's origins, Khadra captured the "truth" (*run*) of the love experience she communicated; listeners could "taste" in her voice that she herself had suffered from love.

Consider, for example, the song "Isha sacabka mari" (Wipe away your tears): a song that exemplifies the intertwining of biography, the taste of love carried in Khadra's voice, and lyrics that emerged from another's experience. This song's origins are in fact like those of "Qirasho" as they emerged from an encounter between the song's lyricist, Cabdulqaadir Xirsi "YamYam" and a lovesick "patient." YamYam has explained that a man came to him in a desperate lovesick state, and as he listened to him recount a difficult tale of as-yet-unrequited love, he could visualize a tear running down the man's face, into his torso to envelop his heart. Moved by this encounter, he wrote a poem in the *maqal* meter (which is used by girls herding sheep and goats), alliterating with vowels. The lyrics were then given to Axmed Gacayte, who set it to music, then finally to Khadra to sing. Friends tell me this song was an instant hit when it was released in the mid-1970s, playing in teashops and taxis across the country. While it began in another's experience, one reason for this song's success was undoubtedly Khadra's ability to sing from the heart—*and* listeners' knowledge that the feelings the song represents aligned so neatly with Khadra's own love experiences.

Like many of her early songs, this song expresses the pain of loving someone who has yet to return the love, crying out for recognition. The song opens with a statement on the singular nature of her love. Then, in a long melismatic ascending phrase, Khadra muses that others should be made aware of the pain that love may cause:

Dadkoo ururayoo	If all people assemble and
Isu tagay dhammaan	Come together
Ma ogaan karaan	Only he [the one I love]
Mooyee isaga!	Can understand my feelings
Yaa uga warrama	I wish they were informed that
Aramidu inay	The wound of love
Eel dheer taqaan	Always brings side effects

The song continues to describe a predicament of intense loneliness and longing, drawing on well-known pastoral motifs, with the cry of a she-camel mimicked in a drawn-out final vowel:

Hadba waxan arkaa	I always find myself
Anoo ay cidla ah	In an uninhabited forest and
Eri-dhaban sidiisii	Like a she-camel crying to its young baby
Kuu ololayee	I cry to you

In syncopated phrases, she then directly addresses the object of her desire, and pleads with him to come rescue her from her situation:

Ubax baan sidaa	I brought a flower
Kuula soo ordee!	And rushed it to you
Maad iga aqbali?	Will you take it?

Eedaad kalgacal	You have ignited
Adaa igu unkaye	A painful affection
Dhibtan mayga bixin?	Will you save me from [love's] hardships?

As the refrain rolls around, she declares herself in full submission. Here the melody begins low in Khadra's range, as she repeats the word "Naftan" (this soul) multiple times, rising in volume and pitch with each repetition as if building up the courage to make her declaration. The refrain reaches its musical climax in the twice-repeated phrase "Kugu indha la'" (blinded by your love), each time preceded by a long, ascending melismatic phrase on the nonlexical vocables hee and haa. Finally, using another pastoral idiom (i.e., holding the end of a walking stick), she suggests marriage as a solution, repeating this invitation multiple times with different musical phrasing:

Naftan, naftan	This soul, this soul [that]
Ku oggolee	Submitted to you
Kuu abaajidee	Longs for you
Kuu abaydinka ah	And is your baby [i.e., depends on you]

Hee hee hee hee	Hee hee hee hee
Kugu indha la	Is blinded by your love
Haa haa haa haa	Haa haa haa haa
Kugu indha la	Is blinded by your love
Usha maad u qaban?	Would you take the other end of a walking stick?

In the second stanza, she begins by describing the durability of her predicament, again drawing on pastoral imagery and likening her state to that of an oracle with heightened sensations:

Ifo faalo iyo	Predictions and
Saad aragti dheer	[Good] omens
Sida awliyaan	Like an oracle
Ku oddorosayaa	I sense you
Ayaa way haa	Oh! Ah! [in the sense of a painful cry]
Ilo biyo leh	Water sources
Ku ag meerayoo	I moved around
Oonku ka ba'ayn	But thirst did not go away

She continues, however, to suggest that the situation is so serious that elders should be consulted, explains that tears will not solve the problem, then pleads again for her beloved to save her:

Garta odayada	The elder's verdict
La ajooday baa	Ought to decide
Xasuus iyo aqoon	Wise decisions and knowledge
Afti ka baxshee	Should be the only referendum
Yey ku dhicin ilmadu	Tears should not fall
Dhir abaarsatee	Drought-stricken trees
Isha sacabka mari	Wipe away your tears
	[lit. pass your palm across your eyes]
Eedaad kalgacal	You have ignited
Adaa igu unkaye	A painful affection
Dhibtan mayga bixin?	Will you save me from [love's] hardships?

Finally, she circles back to the refrain, again suggesting marriage as the solution to their problems. In one popular recording of this song, Khadra's performance of the final refrain (represented in figure 3.2) demonstrates some of the ways that "feeling" is made tangible via the voice.[5] For instance, she begins the ascending phrases that start on hee and haa close to a whisper, but as the melody rises so does her own volume, straining as she reaches the climatic "Kugu indha la'," and ending with a "wobble" or mordent. Then during the repetition of the phrase "Usha maad u qaban," she interrupts herself midway through the word "qaban" to let out what sounds like an exasperated sigh, spoken on the word "usha." She does this a second time with an even more drawn-out descending groanlike "usha." While aware of the song's origins, one listener described Khadra's vocalization of "usha" to me as arising spontaneously "through feeling." "It goes outside the laxan [melody]," he said, "because when she is singing, she was feeling that it was

FIGURE 3.2. Excerpt of the final stanza of "Isha sacabka mari" as sung by Khadra Daahir Ciige.

about her experiences, and the words just came out like that." While I did not confirm with Khadra whether these vocalizations were spontaneous, they clearly help listeners to taste the love-suffering of the protagonist's experiences and to imbricate this song into Khadra's own biography.

While "Isha sacabka mari" began in another's experience, it also helped Khadra to voice otherwise unspeakable sentiments—whose unspeakableness was causing her a great deal of pain. But this was only the beginning of her love woes. Axmed Cali Cigaal himself did take note, in a way taking up the plea represented in this song. When Khadra was eighteen, the pair were wed. Khadra's family, however, vehemently opposed this match. Axmed Cali Cigaal was an older man, and he was from a different clan in the south. He had also previously been married to Maryan Mursal, a singer who is *midgaan*—that is, a member of the most marginalized and stigmatized of Somali subclans. By one account I was given (the veracity of which I am unsure of), her family was so opposed to the marriage that some men were sent to beat up Cigaal to persuade him not to pursue Khadra. Despite efforts by the socialist government to purge Somalia of its "clannish" mentality—including Siyaad Barre reportedly personally paying for Cigaal's earlier wedding to Maryan Mursal as a show of support for clan-transcending love—Khadra's family was unmoved. They never excepted Cigaal as a match.

Young and married, despite her family's wishes, to the person she would tell me was her one and only true love, Khadra moved with her new husband to Muqdisho and joined Waaberi. Or, as one friend recounted it, somewhat disapprovingly yet with a kind of affection: "She fell in love, ran away to Muqdisho, got married, and joined a band!" There were happy times. They toured the country, the region, and beyond—from Russia to Sudan to Iraq—often appearing as leads opposite each other in plays. He composed for her. She bore him four children. They sang songs together, sometimes playing parts, sometimes singing of their own love. Sometimes the songs were happy—other times less so. But eventually the marriage, which many saw as doomed from the start, began to crack. By one friend's account (and speculation like this seems to be a frequent pastime among her fans), the age difference was too much, Khadra had been too young and naive, and things were bound to fall apart. These disappointments, too, were reflected in Khadra's songs. This became the period during which she produced what she described to me as her "deepest calaacal," songs in which she expressed her frustration and deep sorrow that her soon-to-be ex-husband was not putting in the effort required to make their relationship work. Alliterating on the letter "y"—a letter especially associated with complaining and anxiety—"Yabaal" (Worry/frustration) is mournfully illustrative of the sentiments that accompanied her relationship's demise. Written by Xasan Ganey, the song documents the downward spiral of her marriage, betraying a woman still in love yet aware of her own mistreatment.[6] The song begins with a depiction of the tension in her heart, in the jiifto meter:

Adigaan ku yeedshaa	I look for you
Ku yaboohiyaa weli	Still trace you
Yuuskana aday baray	You who forced me to nag
Yablas-ciille igu riday	And wail with resentment
Aa aa	Aa aa
Adiguna yaqiintii,	The certainty
Qalbigeenni wada yiil	In our hearts
Ayaad yeelaha u goysee	You breached the contract

The refrain queries the source of her frustration, and somewhat unusually switches into a different poetic meter (*maqal*):

Xaggee buu yabaal?	Where does this worry come from?
Kaaga yeedhayood?	Where is it calling you from?
U yahoonsan tahay?	Why are you upset?
Iga yaabsatee?	Why do you frustrate me?

After an instrumental restatement of her sentiments, the second stanza begins by placing the blame of their relationship's demise at Cigaal's feet. Yet rather than anger, the phrases present a striking image of resignation and despair, a woman forlorn in a place so desolate even the birds have vanished. Playing with words beginning with "y," this stanza also includes a striking image of a woman sitting: *yaxoob* is a position people sit in when they want to sit for long periods, by wrapping a cloth around their legs to maintain balance; *yuruurid* is a downcast position associated with sorrow/anxiety.

Adigaan ku yeeshoo	I have found you
Kuna yeelan waayoo	And failed to have you
Adiguna yuhuuntii	And you destroyed
Yacaygeedii dumisaye	The hope of good will
Hayaa, Alle wey!	O, my God!
Anna waxaan yaxoobaa	And I am sitting
Wali yuururaa meel	Sitting [downcast] in a [desolate] place
Shimbiruhu ka yaaceen	From which even the birds have flown

The song concludes with a repetition of the refrain. Her embellishment of the vowels in the repeated cry, "iga yaabsatee," give the impression that she may at any moment dissolve into tears or give herself over completely to the utter despair represented in this song. Despite the deep pain reflected in this song—or, perhaps, because of it—Khadra told me that of the many dozens of songs she voiced in her career, this was in fact her favorite song to sing.

However painful these songs were to sing, and however more painful the experiences they document were for Khadra, it was precisely Khadra's ability to voice this pain that endeared her to her fans—and the fact that, as one listener put it, "Khadra has a song for every type of painful love experience." From her first song of unspeakable love to songs that document the breakdown of a marriage, throughout her career Khadra came to voice and embody a broad range of the love-suffering experiences that typically give rise to calaacal, painful love experiences to which many women could relate and from which men, too, could learn something about love: a woman in love unable to voice her desires, confined by social conventions and expectations of female modesty; a woman whose marriage was challenged from the start by familial and clan expectations of appropriate marriage partners; a young woman naive to the challenges of love, who grows up to learn that love is not all it is made out to be; a woman treated badly, disappointed by an older man. Many of her songs, to be sure, did not originate from her own experiences. But the way in which Khadra's story effectively merged with others' in her songs, and her ability to get inside the song and feeling-share in her voice, seems to have multiplied their intimacy-opening powers. "Khadra's songs," another friend simply explained, "they show *reality*." They reveal a woman who did not just sing but "lived the song" (Butterworth 2014, 106). Hers was a pain you could taste in her voice, and that coincided seamlessly with the stories of Khadra's personal love-suffering that circulated alongside her songs.

And for her part, Khadra herself explained her success to me in precisely these terms. "There are two types of loves," she once told me, "one is inauthentic, make-believe love and the other is true love." Listeners could tell when the emotion in a song was authentic or inauthentic, when a singer was singing about real lived pain or was just putting on a show. Her songs were *real*. Even when songs were not strictly biographical, she explained: "When I was in love, songs had meaning for me . . . my songs are about my own true love. When a woman listens to my songs, she really loves the man, desires to have a long-term relationship with him, and ultimately wants to build a family." Poets gave her songs, she says, because the love-suffering they described "reflected [her] true being." Indeed, when I asked her one day what defines a calaacal she simply quipped: "What is calaacal? *Waa aniga* [it's me]! I am calaacal."

Departures and Returns

As the sentiments expressed in "Yabaal" foreshadow, and her more recent comments that she herself is the very embodiment of calaacal confirm, Khadra's marriage to Axmed Cali Cigaal came to a painful end. Ten years after they were married, the couple separated. Two years later Khadra was remarried to another musician, but by then the country was starting to unravel. In 1988, while she was still based in Muqdisho, her hometown was razed to the ground. The theater where her career began was turned to a pile of rubble by the regime on which she, as a national artist, depended for her livelihood. Fearing the worst was yet to come, in 1990—a year before Barre was eventually overthrown, and the south descended into full-blown civil war—Khadra traveled to London with a group of nineteen artists originally from Somaliland, where they claimed asylum. Eventually, she managed to arrange for her children to join her.

From the UK, Khadra and her fellow displaced artists watched as Muqdisho descended into anarchy and many of their colleagues fled to refugee camps. In London, Khadra attempted to adjust to a different life, caring for her children in a country where she could not speak the language, cooking, cleaning, and finding ways to pass the time. For the first few years, she continued to sing for refugee audiences in the UK and North America thirsty for the sounds of home. Indeed, Warsame proudly told me about a concert he helped organize for Khadra in Ottawa, where she performed alongside Xasan Aadan Samatar. In the mid-1990s she even recorded an album in London's Peter Gabriel studio, a kind of reunion compilation with fellow Waaberi members Saalax Qaasim, and Cigaal's other ex-wife, Maryan Mursal.[7] But eventually even singing became too much. Watching her country tear itself apart, she told me, did something to her soul. Somaliland's own descent into civil war in the mid-1990s, which pitted Isaaq against Isaaq, broke her heart in a different way, a brokenness much harder to overcome in song. Yet she found joy in the birth of another son and solace in religion. Her new husband, too, turned to Islam, although his newfound rather strict religiosity and total renouncement of his previous career placed demands on Khadra that she did not want to bear. Islam, she told me, can bring you peace, but it should encourage a qalbi-furan (open heart), not close one off to others. They too eventually went their separate ways.

The civil wars in Somalia and Somaliland radically refigured Khadra's singing career, eventually bringing it to an end. But as Somalis were displaced across the globe, her songs also traveled far and wide. And perhaps because the music industry was an early casualty of political instability, the popularity of Khadra's songs has since only increased. Not only are her songs still beloved by her original fans, but she is now also revered by a younger generation of music lovers who have few musicians of their own. And the farther her songs have traveled—temporally, geographically, generationally—and the more they have become entangled in listeners' own lives, the more stories they have accumulated: memories of encounters, recollections of journeys, reminisces of people, places, and feelings. For a community that has been indelibly marked by war and forced migration, the voices of singers like Khadra seems to work as a kind of sonic thread used to weave together fragments of disrupted lives, personal and collective. But as Khadra and her voice have entered the storied lives of others, she is also still construed in the most intimate of terms. The familiarity with which people speak about Khadra has somehow redoubled the farther her voice travels.

For many listeners, Khadra's voice is deeply entangled in prewar childhood memories of people and early listening encounters. One friend from Boorame, for instance, lovingly recounted how Khadra's songs always made him think of his mother. Born in the early 1980s, he was too young to have been exposed to Khadra's career in real time. But he reminisced about helping his mother prepare tea for patrons of the teashop attached to their home. In the cold of the morning, his mother would always listen to Khadra's songs as she worked. Another friend recalled stealthily sitting outside his sister's room whenever she was listening to Khadra. While these were songs of *women's* love-suffering, he strained to hear Khadra's voice from his sister's well-worn cassette player through her bedroom door. An acquaintance now living in the US similarly told me about his sister's love for Khadra. He also recounted a memorable moment from his childhood in Muqdisho when he returned home from school to find the mother of love herself in his home. Khadra was receiving medical treatment at a nearby hospital, and his sister had convinced their parents to let Khadra—a friend of her sister's friend—stay with them for the week. Yet another friend grew up listening to Khadra as she helped her mother with chores around the home. She was doubly exposed to the singer's living legacy as she attended elementary school with Khadra's son, the child of not one but two famous singers, whom she remembers enthusiastically volunteering to sing for the class. When she herself was old enough to understand the weight of Khadra's songs, she told me that this early exposure made her especially keen to "listen deeply" to Khadra, "to understand the exact feeling and emotion in her voice." She is particularly fond of one song that recounts the way that love seemed to follow Khadra wherever she went, from Benaadir to Berbera to Boorame. Hearing this story, I could not help but visualize a trail of loving *stories* that have similarly followed Khadra and her voice, wherever they have traveled.

For other Khadra fans, her music is imbricated in their own travels—and the physical movement of Khadra's voice via cassette tape. Indeed, throughout the 1980s and 1990s, one of the most frequent requests of Somalis living in the diaspora to relatives at home was for cassette tapes (some of which have since made their way back to the archives at the Hargeysa Cultural Center). My friend who had been one of Khadra's seven-year-old bodyguard-admirers, for example, eventually settled in the US, where he and his two brothers amassed a collection of nearly a thousand cassettes. To avoid having music-loving visitors walk off with their prized possessions, they hid the cassettes in their basement. But in the late 1990s, the trio created a website to share the fruits of their amateur archiving work. Here they posted essays about their favorite artists and uploaded the lyrics of their favorite songs, transcribed from their collection. Among these were two of the songs featured in this chapter: "Isha sacabka mari" and "Caashaqu ogeysiis ma leeyahay." Another friend in his late forties also told me an amusing story of a roommate he had in Sweden in the 1990s. As a young adult, his roommate had been so enamored by Khadra that he requested cassettes from every person he knew traveling from Hargeysa. He amassed an impressive collection of nearly one hundred cassettes featuring Khadra's songs, which he would listen to on his cassette player protectively tucked under his pillow at night. Laughing, he explained: "We listened to so much Khadra Daahir I told my roommate 'Our ears are bleeding of Khadra!'" When he discovered that Khadra was in fact his roommate's aunt, the teasing only increased: "She was his close relative, but still he loved her songs so much!"

These types of stories and recollections also abound in the virtual sphere. As cassettes gave way to CDs, then to digital media, Somali music fans shifted from uploading lyrics to sharing digitized versions of songs themselves—most from cassette tapes, some from video recordings of live performances, converted from VHS. As a result, a significant amount of Somali music is now readily available for instant listening anywhere. YouTube abounds with fan compilations of Khadra's music: some from live recordings, most from audio files that have been transformed into videos featuring fan transcriptions of song lyrics set to eclectic landscapes, kitschy romantic images, and pictures of a young Khadra and Axmed Cali Cigaal. And the comments section on YouTube is a lively space for geographically dispersed listeners to converse and reminisce, debate the origins of songs, and reflect on their own listening encounters.[8] Many comments work to place listeners and songs in time and space: "This song takes me back to my teens in the 70s! I wish I could turn the clock back"; "I listened to this song every day the first semester of college"; "I played this song on repeat during a road trip up the East Coast [of the US]!"; "Mama Khadra, *walaahi* [by God]! In 2017 I am listening from the heart"; "It's 2019 and I'm still listening to this song, who else is listening with me?" Some simply thank the people who have made these songs available: "Praise God! Thank you [the video uploader] for giving us this song!" Others reflect on the feelings that songs elicit, addressing Khadra herself: "You trigger some sense of love in our minds any time we hear one of your songs." And yet others simply pay tribute to Khadra and her beloved soul-soothing voice: "Oh, our Khadra, the woman with a voice of gold!"; "Khadra, my aunt, we love you!"; "Long live mama Khadra, we will never forget the legend!"

Whether it is attachment to childhood memories, nostalgia for prewar music, or the ease with which Khadra's songs remain available to a younger generation, Khadra's songs remain as popular today as forty years ago. Indeed, one female singer once quipped to me: "There are places in Somaliland where Khadra is known but Siilaanyo [the then-president] is not!" Perhaps it was this sense of familiarity, of being known, that eventually drew Khadra back to the land of her birth. Two decades after she had watched her country implode from a distance, and now estranged from her second husband, Khadra moved back to Hargeysa—the city where, over half a century earlier, she began her recording career. While she returned to a city radically different from the one she had left, Khadra also returned to a place where *she* remains intimately familiar: a city where her voice still wafts onto the street from roadside teashops or cars tuned to Radio Hargeysa, where her songs still soothe lonely listeners who stream music on smartphones via YouTube. She returned to a city where friends still swap stories of listening to her songs and recount with pride and affection encounters with the mother of love herself. She came back to a city where old poet friends, fellow *xaj* pilgrims, former childhood admirers, the classmates of her children, and a new generation of YouTube fans converge. Preceded by the stories of her life and love, she returned to a city where her songs, even when voiced by another, can cause her listeners to feel what she feels. Back in the land of her birth, Khadra spent her final decade surrounded by family, friends, and fans—and the odd caddan-dumaashi ethnographer—who continued to flock to the woman known to them as hooyada jacaylka, drawn by the mental relief offered by Khadra's magnanimous qalbi-furan. And as per her wishes, in early July 2022 it was also in Hargeysa that she was finally laid to rest.

Remembering and Revoicing the Mother of Love

Like Somali music lovers across the globe, I awoke one morning in early July 2022 to the devastating news that Khadra had passed away. I also awoke to an outpouring of collective grief. My Facebook feed was flooded with Khadra's songs, tributes to the singer, condolences to her family, and well-wishes for Khadra in the afterlife: "May her soul rest in peace, and her grave be visited by a cool breeze"; "May Allah have mercy on our precious Khadra Daahir"; "We belong to Allah and to Him we shall return." The comments section of Khadra's songs on YouTube became a place to mark her death, and for listeners to pay their respects: "3/7/2022 she was buried in Hargeysa—may Allah show her mercy and grant her paradise"; "Hooyada jacaylka, God bless you"; "Rest in peace, my queen." Traditional media sites, including the BBC Somali Service, published extended obituaries.[9] And in private messages, friends shared their own recollections and grief, compelled by the reality of her absence to reflect again on her magnetic presence. In death, as in life, Khadra inspired a particularly intimate kind of talk and an outpouring of dareen-wadaag (feeling-sharing).

But the grief brought about by Khadra's death was also personal: I had lost a friend. Khadra died just weeks before I was due to see her again after a long covid-induced absence from Somaliland. I had so been looking forward to introducing her to my young daughter, born during the pandemic, and somehow conveying to her that the experience of new motherhood had helped me to finally understand how love can be filled so profoundly with both pain and joy. And the stories I have assembled in this chapter—written when Khadra was alive—have inevitably taken on new weight. But I have ultimately found a kind of solace in the insights these stories reveal about Khadra, her life, her voice, and the intimate public her voice in circulation has created—and will continue to sustain. I understand these lessons, these comforts, as follows.

Khadra Daahir Ciige, hooyada jacaylka, lived a remarkable and storied life during which she undoubtedly knew love: a heart-bursting, spine-breaking, transformative kind of love that radiated outward, touching all who were lucky to know her—in the flesh *and* via her voice. Hers is a voice especially beloved for its authenticity of emotion and the experiences of love(-pain) it conveys: a voice understood to emerge from "deep, deep, deep inside the soul." Yet Khadra's voice is also a voice that was long ago given over to others, a love-suffering voice that "belongs to everyone," as my playwright-interlocutor put it. And the longer and farther this voice has circulated, the more stories and voices it has gathered to it: talk about the origins of songs that slips between fantasy and fact; memories of feelings, of people, of place; stories of encounters with Khadra's voice, and with Khadra herself; acts of envocalization that constantly remade (and remake) Khadra and her voice in the most intimate of terms. These are ultimately stories that demonstrate the snowballing stickiness of songs in motion and that reveal songs and singers to be collaborative, *multivocal* constructions. But Khadra was not only a singer. She was also a neighbor, a roommate's aunt, a hospital patient in search of a more comfortable bed: a woman beloved not only for her voice but also for her soul-soothing presence. Her accessibility fundamentally shaped—and will continue to form—the type of intimate public that her songs in motion stitch together: one based not on stranger sociability but on the possibility of familiarity. And her magnetic qalbi-furan sings not only in her songs but also in the stories that people tell about her—including, I hope, in the stories that I myself have told.

By way of conclusion, I would like to return to the story with which this chapter began—an instance of Khadra's voice brought to life by another in the (physical) absence of Khadra herself. How might we make sense of the ability of Khadra's song, voiced by another, to move an audience to vocal solidarity, forty years after it was first released into the world? We should acknowledge that this reaction depended, in part, on Sahra Halgan's skilled vocal delivery and her ability to effectively convey the song's emotion. Comments like "Sahra is really hot tonight!" and "She must be upset with a man, she is singing Khadra Daahir" also betray the audience's awareness that these songs reflected something of Sahra's own emotional state on that night and her own experiences of love. Sahra, in short, could "feel" the song and transmit this feeling to her audience. In chapter 2, Sahra herself told us that this is critical to a performance's success: "When you are singing, if you are not feeling it, you cannot transmit [the emotion] to other people." The audience's reaction also surely depended on the fact that these songs *personally* resonated with listeners. As I will explore more fully in chapter 4, love songs are especially powerful when they give voice to feelings that listeners otherwise might not know how to express. In Sahra's emotionally expressive voice, then, the women who called out in commiserative solidarity heard something of their *own* experiences.

And yet, in this instance, the audience immediately knew this to be Khadra's song. I later learned that the song Sahra sang that night, "Caashaqu ogeysiis ma leeyahay?" (Can love be publicly expressed/announced?), was from the play *Xishood iyo Jacayl* (Shyness/modesty and love), and thus was most likely not strictly biographical. Nevertheless, the song was immediately identified with Khadra and with the love-suffering experiences of the mother of love—a woman whose celebrity rests squarely on the fact that her songs "show *reality*" and that she was known to have personally "lived the song" (Butterworth 2014, 106). But the reality conveyed in Khadra's songs is not only a feature of the quality of her recorded voice. It has always also been produced by the *stories* that have circulated with this voice—stories of Khadra's love-suffering, of encounters with Khadra's songs, and of meeting the mother of love herself: a woman with a notoriously open heart and soothing presence who was incredibly accessible to her fans. Sahra's audience on that evening at Hiddo Dhawr, then, did not simply hear Sahra's voice, nor did they simply hear Khadra's song through her. They heard the intimately familiar voice of a woman who has suffered from love, a voice shaped over time and across space *that they themselves continually help to create*. A voice animated by an entire symphony of voices drawn together by the life and songs of the mother of love.

CHAPTER FOUR

Listening to Love

The hard task is to love, and music is a skill that prepares [us] for this most difficult task.

John Blacking, *How Musical Is Man?*

"If you feel these things Christina—if you feel *love*—then you must listen to music!" Amran responded to my query about what she was doing, as if the answer was obvious. I had just returned home and come into the room we were sharing to find Amran curled up on the floor, cradling her phone. The voice of Nimcaan Hillaac, a young member of Xidigaha Geeska, sang from her phone via YouTube:

Jirradiyo dhibkaan qabo	The pain and problems I have
Tolow ruux la jaar ahi	I wonder, is there another in the world
Miyuu dunida joogaa?	Who has them too?

Amran closed her eyes, lost in her own thoughts, temporarily ignoring my presence. As the refrain started playing, she sang along achingly:

Jamashadan i haysee	This passion that has me
Jiidatee naftaydii	It attracts me to you
Ay ka jeesan weydaa	I can't turn away from you
Ma adigaa, hoy, ma anigaa?	Is it you, hey, is it me?
Ma anigaa? Ma anigaa u jeel qaba?	Is it me? Does longing have me?
Hoy! Hoy! Ma adigaa?	Hey! Hey! Is it you?
Ma adigaa u jeel qaba?	Does longing have you?

As the song came to an end, Amran put down her phone, though she did not yet seem ready to speak. She eventually looked up long enough to explain that these songs helped her to cope with being away from her beloved. A few weeks before I had come to stay with her, Amran had married a man from southern Somalia. A twice-divorced mother of five, Amran explained to me that her previous marriages had been "for her family." This one, she said, was for love. But this was a love with complicated political implications for both parties involved. As an employee of the Federal Government of Somalia, her new husband would not be especially welcome or employable in Somaliland. To be with him, Amran would need to leave Somaliland for Muqdisho. In the short term, she would also need to leave her children behind. But for now, as she pined for her husband from afar, she found solace in these songs.

Over the coming weeks that I spent in her home, variations on this scene were common. I regularly found Amran curled up with her phone in the dark, listening to fellow love-sufferers or whispering to her husband over the phone, sometimes sending him songs or listening intently to the ones he had sent her. Sometimes these listenings were more social: in the evenings after their favorite Turkish soap opera finished, Amran, her children and the other adult women of the household would flip to Horn Cable TV's twenty-four-hour music channel to watch music videos and discuss the songs, chastising men behaving badly, commiserating with scorned women, wondering what it would be like to have a man serenade you with such tender affection. But mostly when she listened, Amran disappeared into her own love ruminations, somehow soothed by the knowledge that she was not alone and that the answer to Nimcaan Hillaac's rhetorical lyrical query—"Is there another in the world who has [love problems] too?"—was a resounding *yes*! Others too had felt this longing and had known the pain and problems of love.

Amran was indeed not alone—both in her love-suffering, and in the solace she found in *listening* to love songs. Over the course of my research, I was frequently struck by the intensity with which many interlocutors listened to love songs, almost always in solitude, and by the central nature of love songs to listeners' negotiations of their own love lives. Despite the religiously and culturally contested nature of both music and speaking about love in this setting—or, perhaps, because of it—listening to love songs emerged as a critical means through which many people prepared themselves for romance, recovered from heartbreak, and fostered intimacy in their own relationships. Here were listeners who intentionally tuned into the voices of love-sufferers in song for the uniquely intimate feeling-sharing opportunities these voices seemed to afford, strategically taking up a variety of voicing-listening arrangements as their love situations demanded. Here I found people who listened with a keen sense of the effect that songs could have on them and who understood that there was something in the way the words, melody, and voice came together that, as one listener put it, could "make you feel as [others] feel"—or even "make you feel love." And against Adorno's (2000) view that listening to popular music is "effortless" and "passive," these were listeners who listened with devotion-like attention and intention, whose listening was clearly a kind of "doing" (Hirschkind 2006, 34) that refigured love songs in often profound ways.

This chapter seeks to make sense of this listening through a series of accounts of listeners listening to love (songs). More specifically, this chapter explores the intimacies that love songs afford attentive listeners, the work of listeners' ears and voices in refiguring and reanimating love songs, and the deep entanglement of love songs in individual listeners' intimate lives. In the first instance, this is a reflection on the fundamentally dialogic relationship between voices and ears, between speaking (or singing) and listening (Feld 1998, 471). As Cavarero (2005, 169) reminds us, "The voice is always *for* the ear, it is always relational." On the side of the voice, we will see how the deeply personal yet multivocal voice of love songs *affords* listeners certain feeling-sharing opportunities and opens into a range of voicing-listening arrangements we have yet to encounter. And as collaborations that sound the possibility of feeling-sharing in their textual-sonic-vocal substance, we will also see how songs may even model intimacy to listeners, working as sonic-affective "diagrams" that help listeners actualize love in their own lives.[1] Yet these intimacies ultimately depend on the work of ears. The accounts of listening I give also reveal that the voice of love songs is itself made intimate by listeners who, like Amran, listen from the heart. Shaped in sometimes unexpected ways by the broader auditory culture in which it occurs, listening here emerges as an "act" in the Austinian speech-act sense, a kind of work that "actively performs something in the world" (Kapchan 2017, 277). Each "listening act" we will encounter is also an act of envocalization, one that is indispensable to the snowballing stickiness of love songs in motion.

This chapter is also about more than voices and ears. It is ultimately a story about aspirations of love and an even deeper and abiding desire to feeling-share—to feel with others. Perhaps naively, this is not a story I initially set out to tell. The listening accounts I document in this chapter come from what I first conceived of as "listening sessions," during which I asked friends to bring me their favorite songs. I thought this might be a good way to learn more about specific songs and about individuals' music-listening habits. I did learn about these things, and I document these more general findings in the first part of this chapter. But without exception, listeners brought me songs that had played a critical part in their own love lives in one way or another. Our sessions thus invariably moved on to conversations about individuals' love hopes and struggles. These conversations

were incredibly revealing of the sociopolitical, financial, and familial constraints that shape Hargeysa's lovescapes, both for unmarried youth and
married couples. But more than this, they were profoundly intimate. And
I was initially caught off guard, not only because this incredibly personal
sharing was usually out of bounds but also because there seemed to be an
expectation of reciprocity. In time, I learned to think of these spaces not as
"listening sessions" but rather as a kind of "love therapy"—spaces during
which my interlocutors seemed especially open and comfortable sharing
intimate pieces of their lives with me and during which they found relief of
sorts in having space to narrate how songs had helped them make sense of
their sometimes very challenging love journeys. I also learned that recip-
rocating this intimate sharing deepened a sense of dareen-wadaag for all
parties involved. I remain humbled by the vulnerability with which people
shared their stories, and also deeply indebted to love songs themselves for
opening space for these conversations to occur.

Lonely Listeners, Attentive Ears: Aural Attention in Hargeysa's Contested Soundscapes

When I began to speak with listeners and more closely attend to their listening practices, I was struck early on by two things. The first was that love
song listening mostly occurs in solitude. Love songs, to be sure, feature in
a number of social settings that are documented elsewhere in this book:
listening to qaraami is popular at some majlisyo, especially when artists are
present (as in chapters 3 and 5); love songs that praise women and marriage
are popular at women's wedding celebrations; families like Amran's may
periodically tune into Horn Cable TV's music channel together; and something quite special happens when love songs are performed to a live audience (as we will see in chap. 6). But the vast majority of love song listening
in Hargeysa occurs behind closed doors, usually in the privacy of individuals' homes. I was also struck, secondly, by the attention and intention that
listeners brought to their solitary listening work: a type of attention and
intention that I had not encountered among lay listeners of popular music
elsewhere, including in my own music listening. Accounting for why this
was the case, however, was not always straightforward. Love song listening in Hargeysa is circumscribed by several intersecting and sometimes
contradictory forces—some political and/or religious, some technological,
and some deeply personal. But when I probed listeners further and began
to attend to Somaliland's broader (Islamic) auditory culture more fully, a

picture of listening as "a doing," and as a potentially transformative and affectively charged "act" began to take form.

Perhaps the most glaring reason for these listening preferences—or at least a proclivity for solitary listening—is the contested nature of Hargeysa's public soundscapes and the conspicuous absence of music. While music is played on Radio Hargeysa (recall that the government has a curiously ambiguous relationship with artists), the political and moral clout of Salafist leaders is such that the city's public and semipublic speakers have effectively been silenced of music. Opportunities for what Kassabian (2013) calls "ubiquitous" listening are basically nonexistent. Many individuals certainly refute Salafism's categorical prohibition of music. But most of these people are nevertheless careful about listening in public, as you never know who within earshot might not approve. More commonly, however, listeners sometimes expressed a kind of "listening guilt." This sentiment was most clearly pronounced in listeners of the postcollapse generation who were largely schooled in Salafist-funded institutions. I heard this guilt tempered in a number of creative ways: "Music is only a small sin and it helps me relax, so it must be okay sometimes," one friend mused. "Music is only bad if it distracts from your prayers, so if you listen a little bit and don't let it distract you, it's okay," another listener explained. Another put it thus: "Music is forbidden in Islam, but I feel rest when I listen, so maybe we can take different meanings from this prohibition." Whatever one's stance, listening is rarely an activity just passively undertaken—it is an activity that listeners consciously and intentionally take up, often against their own or others' religious judgment.

As opportunities for public music listening are curtailed, it is perhaps a godsend for music lovers that recent technological innovations have opened up a range of new listening opportunities that facilitate private, on-demand listening. As we saw with Amran, by far the most popular means of accessing music is to listen on one's phone, either by listening to music files shared among friends and saved on the phone's "memory" (i.e., an external memory card that increases storage capacity) or by streaming songs from YouTube or a Somali music site. (Luckily for music lovers, Somaliland has some of the best and most affordable internet coverage on the continent; I once came across a news article that noted that 4G internet is more readily accessible in parts of the country than clean drinking water.) The "praexeology of listening" (Sterne 2006, 828) these technologies afford includes the ability to listen "alone" even in the company of others (thanks to headphones), and the ability to curate music as one's love situation demands. Scholars elsewhere have noted that individually curated listening has an especially pronounced therapeutic potential and makes listening a compelling "technology of the self" (DeNora 2000, 46; Hirschkind 2006).

This penchant for private listening, however, is not simply a reaction to Salafist prohibitions. And indeed, listeners were more likely to explain their listening practices as a result of the fact that love is a private affair. Indeed, so personal are these experiences that one long-time friend refused to share his favorite songs with me, saying they were "too personal," and "for him only." As issues of love, romance, and marriage remain overwhelmingly private, so too is listening to love songs. As one listener explained, "You listen to love songs when you are feeling lonely"—and given the difficulty of speaking openly about love or finding the words to express what one is feeling, loneliness in love is an inevitability. Continuing to explain that in his family there were probably lots of people who, like Cilmi, had died for love, these cases were "backstage" and not really discussed. But you could (should) instead listen to love songs so you won't feel alone. In a setting where issues of romance, dating, and the ups and downs of marriage remain topics that are largely taboo—difficult to discuss in public, often too painful and private to share with friends—it is in love songs that individuals find assurance that they are not alone in their suffering or love aspirations.

Crucially, listeners also explained that love song listening is best done in solitude because this enables you to give songs the undivided attention they demand. "You need to deeply understand the meaning of the song," one friend said, "so it's better to listen alone, with no one to distract you." Another mused, "I like to feel the music. I like to listen deeply and feel the words. So I go into hypnosis. I dream as I am awake. I dream, and I don't like to talk. I don't like any disturbances. That's why I listen alone." An especially popular time and place for music listening is thus late at night in the quiet of one's own home when there are no distractions. In short, listening to love (songs) is an activity for lonely lovers with particularly attentive ears, and their work is best accomplished in solitude.

While Salafism prohibits music and undoubtedly shapes attitudes among some listeners about appropriate music-listening practices (or lack thereof), the attention and intention that listeners bring to their love song listening work are deeply entangled in Islamic ideas about the ear, sound, and voice. Coupled with Somalis' deep tradition of oral poetry, the "listening literacies" (Kapchan 2009) cultivated by Islam provide the listening scaffolding required for this lonely listening work. Islamic approaches to listening start from a recognition of the unique power of sound, especially the singing or reciting voice, to affect individuals' moods and inculcate different states of knowing God, oneself, or others. This is why, for instance,

Qur'anic recitation is privileged as a way of knowing God's will and guiding acts of devotion. This same recognition also animates centuries' worth of debate on music's permissibility—or what Nelson (1985) refers to as the *sama'* polemic (sama' variously referring to the verb "to listen," as well as a form of "spiritual audition," including devotional singing/dancing). Those who view music as xaaraan rest their argument on the notion that music can bypass rational faculties and directly affect the heart; music is thus best avoided lest it detracts from one's spiritual discipline and stirs listeners to sinful activities. On the other side are interpretive traditions, notably those found in Sufism, that view music as a potential path to the divine, sound serving as a medium through which devotees can orient their hearts toward God. In these traditions, sama' (spiritual audition) enables devotees to enter into a shared affective state and in a sense dissolves the distinction between listening subject and object (cf. Hirschkind 2006, Racy 1998, Kapchan 2009, Eisenlohr 2018a/b). *Both* traditions share a belief in the unique capacity of the human voice and sound to move listeners, to stir bodies and hearts toward particular affective dispositions (Salois 2014).

On the surface, the recognition of the unique capacity of sound to produce specific affective states parallels arguments made by scholars of both affect and sound studies who privilege sound as a material phenomenon that precedes signification and who suggest sound is agentive in its own right. Yet in recognizing the power of sound, Islamic approaches also highlight the importance of the attention and intention that are brought to the work of listening. In any sonic-human interaction—listening to the Qur'an or a sermon, or to music—it is ultimately the listener who is held accountable. This is equally the case for interpretive traditions that reject or embrace music. In the (contested) hadith often cited by those who see music as xaaraan, it is listeners, not singers, who are chastised—for "music does not provoke in the heart that which is not there" (al-Darani, in Hirschkind 2006, 35). And in Arab-Islamic musical traditions that center around the concept of *tarab*, the "affective melding" made possible in sonic-human events (including sama') critically rests on the performer *and listener* existing in an interdependent dyad: a performer must have "soul" (*ruh*) and "feeling" (*ihsas*) for a performance to be effective, but ultimately performances are dependent on *listeners* (Hirschkind 2006, 35–36; cf. Racy 1998). As Hirschkind puts it, "The agency of music to either corrupt or edify, to distract from moral duty or incline the soul towards its performance lies not in the sound itself but in the moral disposition of the heart of the listener" (2006, 35). Approaching listening with the right intention and with a clean heart is thus critical for those who see music as a devotional practice and for those who reject music altogether. Cultivating proper auditory discipline—learning to listen with attention and intention—is fundamental to Muslim spiritual life across all interpretive traditions. It is not a coincidence that accounts of listening in diverse Muslim contexts reveal listening to be deeply entangled in ethical and religious projects of self- and public-making.[2]

This kind of auditory discipline is, importantly, likewise demanded by Somalis' deep tradition of oral poetry—a tradition that conceives of both speaking and listening as a form of action in the Austinian speech-act sense. Poetry has, after all, been known to incite wars and bring them to an end (see Laitin 1977, Samatar 1982). The centrality of poetry to sociopolitical life indexes a fundamental belief in speech as a form of action, and the power of the human voice and language to move people to action. This is also a tradition that fundamentally values the interpretive responsibility of listeners, as myriad proverbs attest, and the possibility that listeners may "mis-hear" a poem always provides the option for listener and speaker to save face. Listeners listen with a keen sensitivity to the technical features of a genre and the interpretive possibilities that poetry affords. And as for listening in Islam, listeners retain a great deal of agency in shaping the nature of a poetic event. As the late poet Gaarriye put it: "Whether a poem brings forth seeds / depends on how it's tended and by whom / the spot in which it's planted / who needs it and for what / its husk is hulled or boiled."[3]

The auditory discipline cultivated by Islam and a deep tradition of oral poetry provide a starting point for understanding the kind of attention and intention that listeners bring to the work of love song listening—and, alongside the personal, technological, and political-religious forces outlined above, the proclivity for listening *alone*. And indeed, there are resonances between how listeners describe listening to love songs and a range of different listening acts, such as the undivided attention required to make sense of a good poem, the intention one must bring to listening to recorded *duco* (religious supplications), and the kind of meditative state that might be achieved by listening to *qasaa'id* (religious songs). Yet listening to love songs is not the same as listening to a sermon or Sufi praise song, and listeners most certainly would not put them in the same category. As we have seen, the love at the heart of love songs is a deeply personal experience, often of suffering, which is distinct from the emotions and obligations elicited by religious poetry or religious texts. Moreover, as we have seen in the preceding chapters, this love is given voice in a specific way, affording listeners unique feeling-sharing opportunities. Rather, I want to highlight how the auditory culture learned and cultivated in Islam carries over into other listening and musicking practices (cf. Salois 2014).[4] Above all, this is an auditory culture that understands listening to be an intersubjective process, one that emphasizes listening with attention and intention, as well as from the heart—listening as "a doing" (Hirschkind 2006, 34) that has ethical and transformational import for its practitioners. This is a kind of listening both highly attuned to the affordances of the voice and that refigures and remakes the voice in fundamental ways.

What happens, then, when listeners who listen with heart encounter the words, melody, and voice that are the product of a deeply intimate and intersubjective process of feeling-sharing, voices that come from "deep, deep, within the soul"? And what happens to these voices when they are taken up by the ears (and sometimes voices) of lonely lovers in their own lives? The best way to answer these questions is to consider how love song listening enters into the intimate worlds of specific listeners. In what follows, I explore specific love song listening practices in the lives of five listeners, ranging in age from their twenties to their fifties, at distinct moments in their love lives. I have chosen these listeners to demonstrate the range of love situations that love song listening typically enters into (dating, marriage, breakups, and divorce), as well as the types of love-pains that are soothed by this listening—whether such pains are caused by cultural expectations about love and its expression, by unattainable or ill-fated relationships, or by love itself. While we will meet listeners with varied love biographies, they all listen with intentional and affectively attuned attention to make sense of love, cultivate a qalbi-furan (open heart), and, ultimately, realize intimacy in their own lives.

Preparing for and Articulating Love

"If you want to feel what love is like," Gahayr explained, "listen to a love song." There are not many places in Somaliland where you can learn about love, he said. Somalis have a culture that rejects love—it is this attitude that led to Cilmi Boodhari's death. And children do not see their parents' relationships as romantic models, like he figures they do in Western countries, where he suspects people understand romance better. So, if you want to learn about love, he said, if you want to *feel what love is like*, then your best bet is to listen to a love song.

Gahayr and I were sitting in a quiet corner of a restaurant on his day off, clicking through songs on YouTube. I had asked Gahayr, a young teacher originally from rural eastern Somaliland, if he would meet with me to tell me about some of his favorite songs. It became immediately clear that I was in for more than I had planned. The pages of prepared notes spread between us were an early clue to the seriousness with which Gahayr takes his love song listening. So too was his insistence that qaraami can help you make sense of just about any love problem—and may very well offer a solution to that problem. So confident was he in the power of love songs that just that day he had advised a lovesick colleague to go home and listen to Axmed Gacayte. But his faith in the power of listening to love songs took more coherent shape as he began to make his way through his notes and recount the story of his own first love.

Gahayr first fell in love when he was a high school student. The young woman who captured his heart was one of his classmates. As such, he explained, she had "become like a sister," and he dared not share his feelings. For two full years he hid his longing. To make sense of the feeling growing in his heart, he explained, he took to listening to love songs late in the evening. If you want the songs to "make the most sense," he said, then you should listen "when you are calm and clear your mind of other things." When you are alone in your room, from ten to midnight is the very best time to "let the meaning of the music really sink in." Alongside watching Bollywood films, for two years this is how Gahayr made sense of the hurricane force of love that had entered his life—listening to give shape and sound to his feelings, to learn from others who had felt these feelings too, and to imagine a future in which he, like the singers, might be able to share this love.

This worked for two years. But things came to a head when he took a trip to Ethiopia. Being apart from this woman was so painful that he cut the trip short and returned to Hargeysa. As a preliminary gesture of interest, he bought the girl a phone card. On June 27 at 8 p.m.—a time and date he recounted without skipping a beat—he worked up the courage to call her. But upon hearing her voice he was tongue-tied. He hung up to gather his thoughts and muster some courage. In that moment, a song he had listened to many times in the preceding months came into his head. The song was a duet by Aamina Cabdullaahi and Maxamed Axmed Kuluc called "Hadal ii daboolnaa" (My secret), a song about the difficulty of expressing one's feelings and the fundamentally difficult task of giving voice to love. These sentiments are expressed in the song's lyrics as well as in the melody, instrumentation, and vocal delivery. After an instrumental introduction that establishes the song's mood, the first stanza opens with a long melismatic phrase that lingers on the preposition "ii" (for me) in a slightly shaky voice that hints of pain, singing of a long-concealed secret that can no longer be kept silent:

Hadal ii daboolnaa	My secret
Dadka aan ka qarin jiray	That I used to hide from the people
Ooy dani i tidhi sheeg	I was forced to share

This stanza is repeated—or, as Karoone put it, allowed to "breathe," so its force can sink in. Then, in a more declaratory mood, Aamina states twice, "Let me take off its skin/peel." This declaration is emphasized rhythmically with an emphatic *diirka* (the skin/peel), echoed/reiterated by the instruments. But then Aamina hesitates again, ending in a phrase that trails off into silence:

Ma u tahay diyaar	Are you ready
Misa waaban daayaa?	Or should I let it be?
Ha i dilo jacaylkuye	And take it to my grave [lit. "May love kill me"]

In the second stanza, a smooth-voiced Kuluc responds, encouraging Aamina to talk plainly so that her lovesickness "can be treated." Then, echoing the musical phrasing of her initial secret, Aamina finally professes a love that refuses to go away:

Sida waqal daruureed	Like heavy rain clouds that
Da'ay waa dhawaadkii	Rained before the break of dawn
Caashaqan darrooree	This love begins
Intuu degay wadnaha	It has occupied my heart
Diga rogana waayaa	It keeps coming back
Inuu kaa durkana diid	It refuses to go away
Waana kula duljoogaa	I keep giving you my life

Finally, Kuluc shares that he has recently felt a similar ache in his heart ("Amba nabar damqaayiyo"; my own love wound hurts me). He concludes by saying that he is ready, as they "have been matched by God."

Buoyed by the memory of this song—and perhaps its outcome of voiced and *reciprocated* love—Gahayr phoned the girl back. Without saying anything else, he simply began to sing. Frustrated by a poor internet connection in the restaurant where we were meeting, he repeated this performance for me—first describing a painful secret, then outrightly declaring his love, via the words and melody first given voice by Aamina Cabdullaahi. Concluding his repeat performance, he told me that at this point the girl told him she needed time to think and hung up. After an agonizing night of waiting, she phoned to say that she would accept his invitation to begin a relationship.

After his successful serenading, Gahayr embarked on what he described as a happy and loving relationship. Over the coming years, the two young students learned together what it meant to be in a partnership, with all its ups and downs. And, Gahayr explained, love songs were to have a continuing role to play during the course of their relationship. Indeed, music served not only as a trigger for their relationship but also as a constant vehicle for raising difficult issues, or encouraging a certain kind of feeling in the other. This was a strategy that many of my interlocutors told me they deployed at one time or another. Women upset with their men might send a calaacal depicting women's suffering to get their partners to understand their disappointment or to orient the relationship in a certain direction. Men, similarly, would send songs containing otherwise-difficult-to-articulate messages in order to raise certain issues or to appease their partners in some way. In Gahayr's case, if the couple ever argued, he would find a song that contained the appropriate message and send it to his girlfriend. For instance, after one argument when his girlfriend did not want to speak to him, he sent her Axmed Gacayte's song "Inaan weli ku jecelahay" ([For proof] that I still love you). In this song, Gacayte acknowledges that his words might be received as "worse than poison" or "the wounds inflicted by a bow and arrow." But should his beloved ever doubt his feelings, she simply needs to ask "some of the people" who will confirm that she is the only woman for him. While Gahayr explained that mere words might be received as "worse than poison," as Gacayte put it, sending a song usually encouraged a more amenable response. After receiving a song from him, including this Gacayte song, his girlfriend would usually "immediately call, then you can solve your problems."

When I asked Gahayr to explain why his initial listening—and then his own (proxy) voicing of these songs—worked so effectively, he explained that songs are the ideal way to make sense of your own emotions and also the best way to convey these emotions to others. As another listener explained, when love first hits you, it is often hard to articulate or understand what you are feeling, but in songs "someone else is saying it for you." Songs work as a "container for feeling," a container that gives "shape and quality" to an otherwise hard-to-articulate sentiment (DeNora 2000, 74). Songs take you out of yourself and your inarticulateness for a moment, allowing you to sonically inhabit another's love experience—through another's words and voice. Listening thus helps you to "learn what love is"—as it has been felt and expressed by others. This, in turn, helps you to make sense of your own feelings and prepares you to share these feelings with others.

Yet songs do more than give sound to individual feeling. They also sound the possibility of dareen-wadaag (feeling-sharing)—a sharing that, importantly, requires a kind of social collaboration to make intimacy happen. As multivocal works whose authorship is distributed but that nevertheless sound from the heart, love songs model the possibility that one's difficult-to-articulate feelings might be made audible *through the voices of others*—yet still be heard as sincerely one's own. And as we saw in chapter 3, once released into the world the "voice" of these songs "belongs to everyone." This makes songs an ideal way to "pass love messages" between (potential) lovers and gives songs what one listener described to me as exceptional "say-it-for-me" abilities. And when one's own words fail, songs quite literally offer love aspirants the word, melody, and "voice" to break into intimacy. One female listener put it like this: "In Somali culture, [speaking about] love [is] prohibited . . . but the songs they say 'I love you' *inside* the music itself." Gahayr put it this way: "Songs are one of the best ways to convey to someone you love them." Or, as the second instance demonstrates, to show them that you *still* love them, despite a disagreement. What we have here, then, is a voicing-listening arrangement in which a listener first listens to make sense of their own feelings, and then a listening-turned-voicing in which a song first suggests sharing intimacy is possible, then comes to stand in for a listener's own hard-to-articulate sentiments, with another listener now occupying the position of a song's addressee.

There is, of course, always the possibility that the listener may not want to receive a song's message and may choose to interpret a song otherwise. As one proverb puts it, "Qofba meeshii bugtaa isagay belbeshaa" (each person takes it to where the wound burns). In the final instance, what a song does depends on the willingness of a listener to hear its message, to want to participate in the feeling-sharing intimacy that a song suggests. Luckily for Gahayr, like Maxamed Kuluc, the recipient of his revoicing also had her own aching love wound and was willing to listen in to the intimacy proposed in the song. Later she was also willing to accept Gahayr's proxy-voicing of Gacayte's words as an apology of sorts and to move past their disagreements. Songs' exceptional "say-it-for-me" abilities, combined with ears that listen with attention and intention, worked together to open the door for Gahayr to begin and then develop a new relationship.

Healing the Wounds of Love

"Music heals me," Huda said optimistically. "It helps me to keep going, day by day." Huda and I were sitting in our usual corner of a popular coffee shop in Jigjigayar one evening, discreetly listening to some of her favorite songs. Huda had begun by telling me about the role of music in her childhood. Born in Kuwait to Somali parents who had followed oil jobs in the

1970s, she was weaned on the "Somali greats" by her father, and this music had helped her to "feel Somali" while growing up abroad. She fondly recalled childhood evenings spent tuning her ear to her father's study when he would invite Somali musicians to gather and sing. In the early 2000s, she relocated to Hargeysa with her family. Now in her midtwenties and working as a nurse, Huda explained that "you need songs to give you a break from everything that goes on in your day. You just think about this song, why it was written, and you're curious to know everything about it." And when her work becomes emotionally taxing, Huda explained that she listens to songs to help her cope. Briefly putting her headphones in and listening to one of her favorite singers, she said, "makes me feel 'ah, I'm still alive.'"

While Huda had been speaking enthusiastically about music in her everyday life, as our conversation moved on from childhood memories to the healing powers of music, Huda's demeanor took on a comportment I had not seen in her before. At this point I had known Huda for over three years as a fiercely independent and unusually outspoken woman of incredible optimism. When we had met upon my return to Hargeysa, she had briefly mentioned that in the year I had been away she had married and divorced. At the time her tone suggested this was a topic out of bounds, and I had not broached the subject since. But to tell me about her favorite songs and to really explain what music meant to her, Huda would need to speak of pain. And it would be too much for one sitting. Over the coming weeks, in hushed tones punctuated by silence, laughter, and the melodic sound of the oud dancing along with the voices of her favorite singers playing from her smartphone, Huda recounted this story.

Huda first fell in love as a young university student. She explained, laughing at herself, that while in the cafeteria one day, walking with her gaze cast downward, she saw the feet of the acquaintance of a friend. She stopped in her tracks and slowly let her gaze creep upward, past his knees to his middle, and finally sneaking a glance at his face. She was immediately smitten. Over the coming months, she would make as many excuses as possible to spend time with him, and soon they became friends. After a few more months, they began dating (in secret, of course). While their relationship was only ever known to Huda's closest friends (and certainly not her parents), for years they were happy, learning together what it means to be in love. On occasion, Huda would send songs with a particular message to him, with instructions that he find a quiet place to listen. Songs shared in this manner, she explained, "are not for other people to hear," you must sit alone and really listen and absorb what the other person is trying to say to you, in both the lyrics of the song and the emotion in the voice. As for Gahayr, sharing songs helped Huda to articulate otherwise difficult sentiments, the task of raising sensitive topics somehow made easier by delegating words and sounds to the voice of another.

As Huda approached the end of her studies, her mother's incessant questioning about when she would marry began to take its toll. Wanting to orient her relationship toward marriage, at one point she sent her boyfriend a duet by Magool and Maxamed Kuluc, "Dadnimada aqoonso" (Recognize my humanity), in which Magool professes her undying love for a man she wishes to be with "until the grave," highlights the effort she has put into the relationship and pleads with him to "recognize [her] humanity," instead of rebuffing her. While her boyfriend did not want their relationship to end, unfortunately at the time he was responsible for feeding his family and lacked the financial stability to marry. Because of this situation, which is perhaps the number-one reason for first love relationships to fail in this setting, the couple went their separate ways.

But Huda's love challenges were only just beginning, and music was soon to take on a different role in her love journey. Shortly after Huda's break-up, her father came to her with a proposition. One of his cousins in London was returning to Hargeysa with the intention of taking a young bride. As the eldest and as-yet-unmarried daughter, Huda was an ideal candidate. While wary of this arrangement, Huda consented. The pair were married and spent a few weeks together before her new husband returned to London. While a spouse with a European passport is highly desirable to many locals, Huda explained that she immediately knew this union to be a mistake. Discovering shortly thereafter that her husband had failed to disclose a number of previous marriages further weakened the possibility of trust. She described this time as one in which she "could not find [her]self," and this feeling became so unbearable that she decided to seek a divorce before pregnancy could complicate matters.

While released from a difficult marriage, this ordeal threw Huda into a period of deep depression, defined by multiple layers of grief: heartache for a relationship of many years that had not ended in marriage, despair at being a divorcee before her twenty-fifth birthday, and anxiety about finding a partner who would accept this relationship history. In her despair, Huda turned to what she called her "crash" songs, or calaacal. For the next three months, she undertook a self-prescribed listening treatment regimen: she did nothing but go to work, bathe, eat, greet her parents, then lie on her bed alone in her room to listen to the love-pain of others.

How did this listening facilitate Huda's healing? In the first instance, Huda explained, listening to "crash" songs opened her up to a great deal of pain. When you listen to calaacal by the likes of Khadra Daahir or Magool, the sound of a song can "touch you deeply." Take, for instance, one of

Huda's favorites during this grieving period, Maandeeq's wistful "Ma jin baa ma jaan baa?" (Is he/it a jin or an angel?) Written by Cabdillaahi Direyee Sooraan, the song features just an oud, which periodically embellishes the vocal line but at other times leaves Maandeeq's voice bare. Alliterating somewhat unusually in "j"—a difficult letter to compose in—listeners also suggested the text of this song has a particularly memorable taste. And Maandeeq also does what Huda says all the best singers do—she "puts her voice on the words in a way that makes you feel like it happened to her." She begins, for instance, with a plaintive query low in her range, giving the effect of an uncertain whisper; the lyrics are intentionally ambiguous about whether the subject she is singing about is a man or love itself:

Ma jin baa ma jaan baa	Is he/it a jin or an angel
Mise jahawareer bay	Or is my life confused
Arrintaydu joogtaa?	Perhaps it is so?

After trading phrases with the oud player, in which she questions the direction her "love boat" has taken, the melody rises in pitch and Maandeeq's vocal delivery mimics the desperate, searching plea of the lyrics:

Allahayow janniyo naar	God, paradise or hell,
Adow kala jiheeyee	You direct people to each
Aniga jooge iga maqan	I don't know if my love is with me or not
Qalbigaygii lama jiro	My heart searches

The song continues on to question the loss of a love Maandeeq was willing to die for, laments that love has become "like heavy rain," expresses confusion over a man who has deceived her, and finds comfort in the promise that God will help her overcome this confusion—all sentiments that certainly resonated with Huda during this difficult period of her life. By the end, Maandeeq returns to a more contemplative delivery, leaving her fate to time:

Nabsiguna hadduu jiro	If fate exists
Hayska jalabuteeyee	Let it be
Loo joogi doonee	Time will tell

Taking listeners on a difficult love journey, Huda explained that this is a song that does not just "touch you deeply" but causes you to *feel* her. The sorrow audible in Maandeeq's voice, and the love-suffering tasted in the words and the melody, work together to take you to the highest place, a place outside yourself, yet also somehow deeply inside.

As we listened together, Huda seemed to restrain herself, not wanting to give herself over fully to Maandeeq's voice and the love-suffering entailed therein—at least not in my presence. These are not songs "just for listening for fun," she said. You must be ready to confront your pain—and, in a sense, to be intimate with yourself. Yet she explained that in the months following her divorce, this is precisely what she did. In the first instance, this listening worked to turn her own suffering inside-out—a process that is not unlike the way a song itself sonically indexes the very turning-inside-out of deeply felt internal sentiments, made possible by the voice as a medium that exists both inside and outside the voicing subject. Yet eventually opening herself up to her own pain by listening to songs about others' love-suffering became a source of comfort, reassuring her that she was "not alone in the emotional universe" (Levinson 1990, in Bicknell 2015, 18). These songs are, after all, distillations of the intimate experiences of multiple others. Listening in to others' love-pains provided Huda with an incredibly powerful source of comfort and a sense of suffering *with others*. As another friend put it, listening to calaacal reminds you that "sad days meet a lot of people [and] you are one of [those] people. . . . So, you just feel at home."

Beyond assuring Huda that she was not alone in the love-suffering universe, Huda credited these songs for giving her the strength to continue on. In between laments of love-suffering, she said, these songs also teach you that you can overcome pain. Love may be a matter of fate, as Maandeeq suggests. But rather than leading to resignation, these songs helped her to "accept that things happen for a reason," and, after accepting that, that she could *choose* how to respond. By risking bearing their love-pains to the world singers were singing a way past their pain, singing a way forward—singing the possibility of action, of moving on. My middle-aged friend, whose roommate in Sweden gave him an earful of Khadra Daahir, spoke similarly about what he called his "heartbreak and recovering songs." "Although the moment is painful and you are heartbroken," he said, "you look for people who are in a similar situation, and you look for answers. Some songs give you answers [in their words]. But others, *in their singing*, say 'I will pass this stage.'" We might say that in their very sounding—and the sharing of love-suffering this entails—love songs enable listeners to first listen in and then listen past their own love-suffering, providing a sonic roadmap of sorts for cultivating a qalbi-furan in the midst of heartbreak. And in actively orienting themselves to others' love-pains, listeners gain perspective on their own love problems, comfort in knowing that they do not suffer alone, and ultimately strength to continue on without closing off their hearts.

While in my early conversations with Huda speaking about this situation was obviously very difficult, by the end of my stay there was a new lightness in her voice. The lessons of the songs had begun to sink in, the work of attuning herself to others' love-pain paying off. With only a slight suggestion, she explained that she had finally decided it was time to date again. A specific suitor, alongside her favorite calaacal, had convinced her it was time to reopen her heart. So, for now, she has traded in her crash songs for a more optimistic playlist.

Remembering Love(-Pain), Cultivating Mercy

"Do you know this song," Cabdi asked, as the familiar voice of Xasan Aadan Samatar sang from his iPhone. "I think you've heard it before. Listen here. He is calling her 'Beerlula.' It means the one who catches him, who makes him feel. *Beer* means liver. She shook his liver." As strange as the liver-shaker or, literally, the "liver-quiverer" may sound, I was in fact well familiar with this song, and the famous encounter of the poet Hadraawi memorialized in its lyrics. While touring with a theater troupe in the 1970s, stationed overnight in a town in southern Somalia called Beledweyn, Hadraawi encountered a beautiful woman and was immediately smitten. He arranged to meet her the following day, but his troupe was called away early, dashing his romantic aspirations. He later transformed this encounter into a poem that alliterates in *b*, eliciting the nickname "Beerlula." The poem begins by invoking love itself—love that killed Boodhari (another *b*)—then explains that his skepticism about love has melted away, as love-pain overtakes his body (in language that certainly explains why love songs might be conceived of as anatomy lessons):[5]

Bi'i waa jacaylow!	O love, may you live forever!
Boodhari inuu dilay	That it killed Boodhari
Been baan u haystee	I took it for an untruth
Bi'i waa jacaylow	O love, may you live forever!
Boog aan la dhayinoo	An ulcerous wound that hasn't been salved and
Cidi baanan karinoo	That no one can nurse and
Beerkiyo wadnaha iyo	That is in the liver and the heart and
Bogga kaaga taalliyo	The side; [this wound] is present in you
Inuu yahay bir caashaqu	That love is [also] a weapon
Been baan u haystee	I took it for an untruth

The song goes on to describe the beauty of Beledweyn and Beerlula, before narrating Hadraawi's encounter and his reaction to being called away early (including praying for the gas tank to spring a leak) and, despite his love tragedy, finishes with a series of supplications and well-wishes to Beledweyn and Beerlula. In contrast to most songs, this one moves through a number of distinct sections: the melody (composed by Cabdikariin Faarax Qaareey "Jiir"), instrumentation, and vocal delivery notably shift to demarcate different parts of the story, each with its own feeling. The overall effect, like the encounter Hadraawi recounts, is one of taking an unpredictable journey: from the extensive use of the conjunction *oo* to set up anticipation in the listener (Orwin forthcoming); to the way the melody rises and falls to sonically convey the imagery in the lyrics (complete with overflowing rivers and anatomy lessons);[6] from the instrumental interlude and pauses and shifts of pace; to Samatar's varied vocalization, which includes everything from spoken passages to phrases belted at the top of his range.

Stories of Hadraawi's fateful encounter circulate widely with this song, often prompting animated debate—and, as I recounted in the introduction, sometimes speculation about possible veiled messages or interpretations. But Cabdi, a consultant in his early thirties, played this song for me for rather more personal reasons. As the final supplication to the "liver-quiverer" rang out, his demeanor took on a new seriousness, and he began to narrate how this song became entangled in his own love journey.

Born in southern Somalia, Cabdi had been displaced by war to Uganda. Just as for Huda, listening to music had been a way for him to "feel Somali" while away from home, and he recounted weekend trips from the rural town where he was going to high school to the nearest city, where he would scour local markets looking for tapes of his favorite singer, Maxamed Saleeban Tubeec. When he finished school, he moved to Hargeysa in search of work. There, he met a young woman, and they began dating. The first time this woman invited him for lunch, she put this song on before they ate. It was not a song that had been part of his schoolboy listening, and he was immediately captivated by its melody, and the encounter it describes. Like all of his "best songs," this is a song, he said, in which the words, the melody, and the voice "go well together, up and down," leaving you feeling "in a spiritual mood." The song thus first indexed a happy encounter. Yet its story of thwarted love soon came to take on new meaning. When the couple told her parents they wanted to wed, her parents refused. They did not want their daughter to marry someone from a different clan. She proposed eloping. This left Cabdi with what he described as a "dead decision"—choose the girl, and she is cut off from her family; leave the girl and abandon dreams of a life together. In the end the pull of family won, and they separated.

Cabdi eventually met another woman whose family accepted him, and they are now happily married with children. I was intrigued to find out, then, that "Beledweyn" is still a part of his regular listening repertoire. "Every time I'm out of the city for work, in the field, I have this song," he said, "and then I listen. When I listen I remember that time"—the woman who made his liver quiver and whom, like Hadraawi, he had to leave behind. He feels an especially strong sense of regret for the other woman, whose life has not been easy. She was married then quickly divorced and is now a single mother. Sometimes the painful feelings are so strong, he said, that he cannot listen for two or three months. "But then after awhile," he said, "I *have* to listen again."

When I pressed him as to why he would intentionally elicit these memories, he explained, firstly, that remembering love difficulties helps you to keep perspective on your present love situation. "We live in a hardship country," he said, where "it's hard for people to trust each other." Not everyone can succeed in love. In happy times remembering past love-pains can help you to more deeply appreciate where you are. In difficult times it can help you to remember that this too will pass. As DeNora (2000, 66) suggests, this kind of music-facilitated retrospection, which is aided by the fact that music is a temporal medium, an art form that moves through time, can be a critical "part of the work of producing one's self as a coherent being over time." Significantly, the self here is one modeled in "Beledweyn"—a self that, like Hadraawi (and Cilmi, and countless others) has known love, lived through love-pain, and made sense of that love-pain by giving it voice. And a self who, knowing this pain firsthand, ultimately wishes others well in their own love journeys.

Indeed, in addition to helping you to keep your own love journey in perspective, Cabdi explained, revisiting the feeling of love-*pain* also helps him to keep a sense of mercy in his heart. "Whenever you see a woman, you remember your girlfriend [and the difficulties she faced] . . . so you respect every woman. It gives you a kind of mercy. So, every week I *have* to listen, and remember her." While he is now happily married, this listening makes him think of the suffering that others might be going through. And remembering one's own love-pain by listening to the love-pain of others is a kind of "listening act" (Kapchan 2017) that many listeners I encountered explained has the unique ability to "soften the heart." Listening to a woman's calaacal, for instance, was cited by a number of men as a practice they used to foster patience toward their girlfriends or wives (and "listen to more qaraami" a prescription I heard men give each other when facing relationship problems). And as mentioned above, sending a calaacal to your husband or boyfriend after an argument was also a strategy deployed by women to encourage their partners to feel their frustration, forgive, or change their behavior. In his case, Cabdi explained that this type of listening is an excellent "inner feeling equipment method"—and the mercy this listening cultivates ultimately makes him a better husband to the woman who became his wife. What we have here is a form of listening in which songs work first as a "container for feeling" (DeNora 2000, 74) but also prompt the unfolding and replaying of feeling across time; songs also provide models of a feeling-self attentive to the love-pain of others, wherever they may be in their own love journeys.

The tenderness that this practice helps Cabdi to cultivate might also be why he obliged when his wife asked him to pick a song to mark *their* relationship, rather than just listening to one that reminded him of an old girlfriend. As "Beledweyn" stopped playing, he quickly changed gears and pulled up a newly published song on YouTube, one by Farxiya "Kaboyare" (little shoes), a young woman from his mother's clan in the south. Whereas "Beledweyn" is a song for remembering a past love and reflecting on hardship, this new song "Dhakac-dhakac" is a song for thinking about his current relationship, a song that he has intentionally set apart to mark his current relationship and to anchor feelings of intimacy with his wife. Well aware of the importance of "Beledweyn" in her husband's love history, for months Cabdi's wife pressed him as to why he did not have a song with which to remember *her* and their marriage. While traveling one day, his driver introduced him to a new song, and he was immediately taken by its catchy, lighthearted melody, its playful tone (Dhakac-dhakac is a children's game of hide and seek), and the gentle words of endearment it expresses. The song begins with a description of the necessity of love and the way it moves through the body (using strikingly similar anatomical references as those found in "Beledweyn").

Caashaqa waligii lagama dhergoo	You can never have enough love [i.e., be satiated]
Dhuuxiyo lafahuu u dhaadhacaa	It spreads in the bones and marrow
Dhuunta cunnadu ay martiyo	It moves in the food pipe
Dhiigiyo wadnahuu dhex socdaa	Blood and heart

In the bridge, Farxiya expresses her love's singularity before inviting her beloved to join her in the "play" in the song's upbeat refrain:

Dhegahaygu aday ku maqlaan	My ears listen only to you
Indhayguna aday ku dhugtaan	My eyes look only at you
Soo dhowow	Welcome
Dhabta aan ku saaree	I will put you on my lap
Dheesha dheesha	The play the play

| Dhakac-dhakac aan dheelne | Let us play dhakac-dhakac |
| Dhuumashow aan dheelnee | Let us play hide and seek |

In the second verse, the singer evokes the name of the man who "planted" this love in her and who is her "doctor of love" and can cure all her love wounds ("Dhaktarkii jacaylkana adiga ahow / Boogtani adigaa dhayi ka-ree"), before circling back through the bridge to the refrain.

Upon hearing these lyrics, Cabdi immediately texted them to his wife, describing the song as "so catching" and suggesting that this could be their song. Eventually, he brought her the music video on his phone's memory card, given to him by the driver from work. While at first his wife was not thrilled that he had chosen a song sung by a woman, he explained to her that she could listen to the song and imagine herself singing the words to him and know that he felt the same. This was a rare song, after all, about *requited* love. She agreed to this voicing-listening arrangement, and the song is now "theirs," something they can listen to individually to remember the other and sometimes together. After the kids have gone to sleep, he explained, he gets out his iPhone, and "we listen, and then we sleep on it." "Really, it's catchy," Cabdi continued, "we live here, but we imagine just like we are together in a good place, in a good life, not an unrecognized country like Somaliland, and just like we are living somewhere together, in a nice place." Listening together in this way to "their song" seems to foster a sense of imaginative intimacy and togetherness. As for "Beledweyn," this song also works as an anchor for the couple to reflect on where they are and where they might be going. As DeNora notes, musical memories "produce past trajectories that contain momentum" and may be "part of producing a retrospection that is, in turn, a resource for projection into the future" (2000, 66–67). In both cases, we see how the semiotic density of songs makes them especially ripe for "semantic snowballing" (Turino 1999, 235), for a layering of experiences, memories, moods, moments, and aspirations into a single song, that may be strategically tapped into by listeners to make sense of their own love life's unfolding.

Keeping the Romance Alive

While the cases presented thus far may suggest that experiences of love are only ever about love-suffering, Cabdi's listening of "Dhakac-dhakac" points to another kind of listening—listening as an activity undertaken to imagine what intimacy *could be* and to feel what successful love might be (and sound) like. The final case I explore is another case of listening to give form to romantic aspirations.

Aamina and Farxiya are sisters, in their late thirties and midfifties respectively. Born and raised in Hargeysa, they were displaced to Oslo in the late 1980s by the war between the SNM and Barre's regime. At the time, Aamina was a young teenager, and Farxiya was newly married. After more than twenty years abroad, both are part of a growing community of diaspora returnees who have recently relocated back to Hargeysa. Weaned on the "Somali greats" by their mother, they enjoy both old and new songs, but like many diaspora returnees who have lived in Europe or North America, they are also more open to songs produced by younger artists. They both prefer to listen to music alone, although Aamina's listening is often distracted by her six children who know where to find her phone and look up their favorite songs on YouTube. Her private listening thus comes while she is driving to work. While she told me that music is "probably xaaraan," and she has recently tried to start listening to *duco* (religious prayers), she admits that halfway through her commute she usually switches to music, as it helps her to relax and unwind—and, sometimes, to "get her into the mood."

Compared to most, Aamina and Farxiya have been luckier in love. Both were courted by well-to-do admirers in their late teens and happily married soon after, though Farxiya's early marriage was disrupted by the war. Both have been blessed with many children, as well as husbands who have not shown interest in taking second wives, even though their financial circumstances and aging first wives may allow them to do so. Neither sister listens to music with her husband: Aamina because her husband prefers gabay (classical poetry), and Farxiya because her husband prefers to listen to old songs by himself. Farxiya in fact explained that she teases her husband relentlessly when she finds him listening to qaraami, chiding him for being "too soft," for having a *qalbi-xabxab* (literally, a "watermelon heart"). When I asked Farxiya why she would not want her husband to be so romantically inclined, she explained that she fears he might start fantasizing about a romance with a younger woman. But, she mused, as long as this song-induced watermelon-heart softness is directed toward her, this listening might be okay, perhaps even beneficial to their marriage.

Like other lovers of new music, Farxiya and Aamina enjoy listening to whatever is popular and resonates with their moods and experiences at a particular time. They are especially fond of "romance" songs—songs composed or played at weddings, in which couples sing each other's praises (like Dhakac-dhakac) and that circulate like wildfire via WhatsApp (and often ended up crowding my own WhatsApp inbox). While Farxiya may find her husband's music-induced qalbi-xabxab potentially problematic, both sisters usually listen to foster this romantic softness in themselves. As we sipped sweet tea and nibbled cake one afternoon at my house, when

Aamina had managed to get away from her kids, smartphones armed and ready, they each quickly flipped through a series of songs, pausing briefly to explain what each was about. "I like this one," Farxiya said, playing snippets of a new BK song, "because I love BK's voice, it's nice. This song is called 'Laba baal,' which means 'two wings.'" Meditating on the theme of love-induced sleeplessness that we have seen elsewhere, the song describes a man awakening at night, so overcome by longing that he wonders if he should just let himself go (even in "romance" songs, love causes pain with potentially mortal consequences):

Badhtamaha habeenkii	In the middle of the night
Markaan soo baaraarugo	When I begin to wake from sleep
Beryimaysid caawee	[I feel] I might not make it through the night
Nafta bixi idhaahdaa	[I say to myself] Let my soul go

But instead of succumbing to this separation-induced love-pain, he is so pulled in by the beauty of his beloved that he wishes for two wings so he can fly to meet her the next day.

Bal haddaba bidhaan qurux	The shining beauty
Kama baaqan karayee	I can't stay away from her
Yaa i siiya laba baal?	Who will give me two wings?
Aan maanta boodoo	So I can fly
Berritaba la joogee	So I can be with her tomorrow

Like other fans of BK—who was then the most popular member of Xidigaha Geeska—the sisters explained that they like his songs because of his sweet and gentle voice, the way he "praises . . . and says nice words to women," and because of his reputation as a soft-hearted performer even known to invite his wife on stage so he can serenade her. BK, we might say, practices what he sings—or sings what he practices—and what he sings/practices is tender affection toward his wife. As we saw for Khadra Daahir, singers known to have "lived the song" (Butterworth 2014, 106) are especially revered. Moreover, the tender affection that BK professes is precisely what women often dream their lovers would bestow upon them, the kind of romantic words they wish they themselves might hear—yet that most men rarely express. And in the absence of husbands or lovers who might sing these sweet words themselves, BK's voice—known to sound from the heart and also available to and for others—provides his listeners with what Agawu (2001, 7) refers to as a kind of "hollow space," a space in which "active listeners and interpreters are invited to play, to invent, to dream, and, inevitably, to lie" (cf. Stasik 2016).

Indeed, as BK's gentle voice and the song's catchy upbeat melody sounded through Farxiya's well-loved Samsung smartphone, she explained what happens when she listens to these songs: "Sometimes, when the guy sings, I feel like he's saying it to me." Similarly, describing a duet she is especially fond of, Aamina explained that she "likes how the lady is speaking to the man, and the man to the woman, how they speak to each other." "You know," she continued, "sometimes when I listen to the songs that I like, I get into a mood, and I think about, you know, last time. . . . It's hard to explain, you get into a mood." When I pressed her about the nature of this "mood," she revealed that the mood she gets into is one of nostalgic reminiscing about her days of courtship and early marriage, days when her husband, like BK, "was still so romantic" and days before children when "we still had time for each other"—when they could walk the streets of Oslo holding hands and go out for a nice dinner; this is in contrast to their current married life in Hargeysa, where public displays of affection are taboo and dining with your wife may be seen as a sign of soft-heartedness most men prefer to avoid.

On hearing her sister speak this way, Farxiya pulled up a picture of herself before her wedding, exclaiming, "You see, I was very beautiful then!" While these songs do not intersect with specific moments as they did for Cabdi, the sentiments they express and the romance they sound allow Aamina and Farxiya to relive or reimagine their younger, more beautiful prechildren selves and their more romantic and attentive younger husbands. And they told me, somewhat conspiratorially, the romantically induced subjectivity these songs allow them to inhabit does indeed spill over into their personal lives. Aamina had just recently returned from a romantic child-free getaway weekend to the coastal town of Berbera—or what Farxiya teasingly described as her "second honeymoon"—after pressing her husband for months to rekindle the romance of their early marriage. Farxiya, for her part, recently bought a new set of bedroom furniture—much to the amusement of her age-mates, who told her this was the behavior of newlyweds—in part to keep her husband's song-induced watermelon heart focused squarely on her. Songs, in this case, afford listeners the "hollow space" (Agawu 2001, 7) they need to imagine romance, to "get into the mood"—and the courage to pursue romance with their husbands in their everyday lives.

Listening to Love

After one of my listening/love therapy sessions at a popular hotel, I ran into a group of male friends. I began chatting with them about my research and then casually asked them why it is that they like to listen to love songs. At first, my question was deflected, with two of the men suggesting I should instead talk to their friend who is known among his peers as the "expert" of love. (His love credentials? Falling so in love as a teenager that he branded the name of his beloved on his skin using a knife and hot charcoal.) But another of the men, Bilaal, sat quietly for a moment, considering his response. Then, in a comment that echoed Amran's statement that opened this chapter, he explained that he listens to love songs because love songs tell you everything you need to know about love; they can help you in any kind of love situation. When I asked him to be more specific, he effortlessly recited a version of the lyrics of a song by Saalax Qaasim,[7] which itself quotes a poem by Cilmi Boodhari:

Marna waa macaan	Sometimes it's sweet
Marna waa qadhaadh	Sometimes it's bitter
Hadba waa siduu	It depends on how
Kugu soo maree	It touches you

What love songs do, he continued, is "make love tangible" and "give it shape." Songs show you, he said, that "sometimes love has this shape"—it is like poison or the worst disease you've ever seen. Other times it "tastes delicious," like honey or camel's milk. Because a Somali poet has "traced love with his pen," others too can feel and understand love. Songs start in love, he said, and, in turn, songs guide love. There are, however, specific times that songs can make sense, and for him, this is when there's no one around, and the environment is very quiet, especially late at night. "Love without song," he concluded, "is like tea without sugar."

At first, I heard Bilaal's comments as a general confirmation of the indispensable role that love songs play in listeners' love lives. Tea without sugar is, for most Somalis, basically a non-option. As Amran put it at the outset of this chapter, "If you feel love, then you *must* listen to music!" In a setting where speaking about intimate matters is taboo, love songs are very often people's first port of call to learn about love. Love songs, as Bilaal suggested, teach you everything you need to know, they can help you through all manner of love challenges—whether this is making sense of the hurricane force of new love, learning to articulate love sentiments, coming to terms with heartbreak, evoking memories and imagining love futures, or fostering intimacy in existing relationships. And so deeply entangled in listeners' love lives are songs, that like tea without sugar, love without song is nearly unthinkable.

The more I have thought about Bilaal's comments, however, the more

I have come to understand that they help to explain not only the centrality of love song listening to listeners' own love journeys but also *how* it is that love songs "sweeten" love experiences, as it were. They highlight, in a sense, that the two themes that have run throughout this chapter—one about love songs' deep entanglement in listeners' love lives and one about the dialogic relationship between voices and ears—articulate at every turn. And, in fact, it is the nature of the voice in relation to attentive ears that imbricates songs so deeply in listeners' lives. Let me explain what I mean.

Love songs, as Bilaal noted, give "shape" to love. Songs start in love experiences that are "traced" by the pen of a poet and eventually given voice in a particular way—and Bilaal elsewhere told me that it is the words, melody, and unique voice of a singer that together make a song special. This voice *affords* listeners certain feeling opportunities. In the first instance, because a poet has already "traced love with his pen," songs give shape to listeners' own feelings of love, helping them to process and articulate their own experiences. It is a voice that takes listeners deep into themselves, yet ultimately one that assures otherwise lonely listeners that they are not alone. Songs, in a way, work to cut the sometimes lonely or "bitter" taste of love (as sugar does for tea). This is why, for instance, Weedhsame prescribed qaraami as a treatment to the patients in his love hospital. Yet the voice of love also opens outward to sweeten love experiences in other ways as well. As we saw in chapter 2, songs are the product of a collaborative feeling-sharing process that listeners can "taste" in the voice. And as we saw in chapter 3, this voice enters the world to be taken up by others, reinhabited, revoiced, belonging to, and made by everyone. This voice affords listeners the opportunity to feel *with others* and simultaneously suggests to listeners that this feeling-with-others is what makes love taste sweet. The voice of love, after all, becomes sweeter (and stickier!) when shared. Now love does not need songs to exist, but the intimacy my interlocutors desired does need dareen-wadaag (feeling-sharing) to be realized. For listeners like those we have met in this chapter, it is songs that encourage this feeling—and, indeed, that model the possibility of sharing one's feelings, via the voices of others. Just like sugar makes the taste of tea bloom, songs open into feeling opportunities that deepen how listeners experience the pain and promise of love. And for listeners who desire feeling-sharing in their own lives, love songs also open into a multitude of voicing-listening arrangements that in turn help listeners realize intimacy for themselves.

All of this, of course, depends on listeners, whose ears are an indispensable part of envocalizing love songs across time and space. Sugar does not add itself to tea; someone must intentionally scoop it in and stir it to dissolve just right. Similarly, we might say that the voice is not just *"for* the ear" (Cavarero 2005, 169), it *needs* the ear. As various listeners have noted, love songs only "make sense" under certain conditions, like the quiet solitude that gives listeners space to really pay attention—and, I would add, technological, political-religious conditions that temper how people listen and the "listening literacies" (Kapchan 2009) that they bring to the work of listening. The intimate possibilities afforded by the voice are ultimately realized by the attention and intention that listeners bring to the work of listening, listeners who approach listening as an "act," and who are deeply attuned to the affective possibilities of sound, poetry, and song. It is by aurally attending to the "pain and praise of others" (Kapchan 2017) that attentive and affectively attuned listeners are able to make sense of their own inexpressible love feelings, feel these feelings more deeply *with others*, and in turn cultivate the kind of qalbi-furan (open heart) that allows them to actualize intimacy in their own lives. We might say, in short, that listeners do not just listen to love songs, they listen *to love*. That is, they listen with attention and intention to voices that sing and model love, and they do so in order to love: to feel love, make sense of love, and actualize love in their own lives. This is a delicious act indeed, one that sweetens listeners' experiences of love, *and* the voices that carry love sentiments to future listening ears.

CHAPTER FIVE

Bodies of Music, Instruments of Love

"Like this," Cabdinaasir said, indicating that I should watch his right hand as it danced across the strings of his oud. He spoke gently but firmly, making sure I was really paying attention. I paused my own playing to watch as Cabdinaasir demonstrated how to play a tremolo. Vital to Somali oud (or kaban) playing—especially playing *with feeling*—the rapid and fluid movement required to produce this sound was foreign to my wrist, and the *riisha*, or plectrum, seemed to get stuck in the strings. But in Cabdinaasir's hands, the riisha vibrated across the strings so quickly that it almost disappeared. For my benefit, he slowed down the movement until I could copy him. Together we kept doubling the speed, until I could no longer keep up but had, at least, slightly improved. "Isbiidhka [speed] practice!" he implored. "Maalin kasta!" (Every day!)

Cabdinaasir and I were sitting cross-legged on the floor of his home in the Boqol Jirre neighborhood on the western edge of Hargeysa. It was a springtime afternoon, and you could feel the coming of the *gu'* rainy season. The air was heavy with humidity, making my kaban even harder to tune than usual. But after wrestling the temperamental pegs roughly into place, Cabdinaasir and I had played through some routine scales before he commanded me to play a song of my choosing, "bila buug!" (without the book). While Cabdinaasir could commit a melody to memory nearly immediately, I possessed no such skill and had taken to recording and notating the songs he was teaching me each week. But in this highly oral setting, this book of strange lines and circles was a crutch, and Cabdinaasir was slowly weaning me off it, encouraging me to listen more carefully, tune my ear to the pentatonic melodies of qaraami, and calibrate my inner metronome to the rhythms of hees. I settled on a simple Magool tune, "Ma tallabsan karo" (I can't take a step). Cabdinaasir seemed quietly pleased when I made it through one repetition by memory. But there was something missing in my tone and something hesitant in the vibration of the strings. He had stopped me, then, with a deliberate "like this," to demonstrate tremolo technique.

While I was far from mastering this skill, we played through the song together again, and he smiled mischievously as he effortlessly embellished the vocal line. Just as the quiver in the human voice communicates love-pain, Cabdinaasir's oud seemed to sing and cry at the same time. The motley crew of young artists and other passersby, who were assembling for an afternoon of qaad and conversation, began to clap and sing along, adding yet another texture to the sound we were producing together, bringing Magool's love-suffering lament to new life.

For a year of my stay in Hargeysa, this was our twice-weekly ritual. I had come to Cabdinaasir Macallin Caydiid—renowned as an *ustaad* (master) of the oud, veteran of the Somali National Movement (SNM), and *macallin* (teacher)—hoping to gain a better understanding of how Somali songs are put together. I did not set out to master the oud, nor to write about oud learning. I expected, rather, that these lessons might be a fun side project to my more "serious" research, a kind of "fieldplay" (Rice 1997, 107). Yet as the weeks passed and the songs in my repertoire grew, so too did my sense that the lessons I was learning seated cross-legged on Cabdinaasir's floor would go far beyond knowing how to pluck out a few melodies. I was, in an immediate sense, learning to listen, to watch, to move, to attend to my surroundings in sometimes subtly, sometimes radically different ways—even as my right wrist refused to cooperate. I was learning to respect and handle an instrument whose sounding evokes sentiments of love-suffering and its relief; war and its complicated aftermath; and frustration, pain, joy, and desire. And I was learning to negotiate space for my instrument's voice, as a good kabaniste (kaban or oud player) must, through and against the voices of others. I was learning, in short, to hone a set of sensibilities—musical, social, political, and affective—that are required to enable the voicing of love in contested urban terrain.

In retrospect, I should not have been surprised that my lessons were such a formative part of my research. As Qureshi highlights, instruments are "permeated with physicality and affect" (2000, 810). In short: "Instruments *mean*" (Qureshi 2000, 810; emphasis mine). For those acculturated into their specific sounds, instruments have the power to evoke a sense of place, a sense of home—to order collective memories and root experiences and feelings in sound (Stokes 1994).[1] And because instruments "mean" in such multifaceted ways, learning an instrument is always about more than acquiring technical skills. While I was naively unprepared for the sometimes frustrating, surprisingly intimate, and deeply transformative nature of my own oud lessons, I soon realized what apprentices of various stripes have long sensed—apprenticeship is always an intentional process of self-making through which subjectivities are shaped, and specific kinds of persons are made.[2] Whether through disciplining the body, learning to comport oneself in relation to other practitioners or nonpractitioners, coming to appreciate the sociopolitical and affective power of an instrument, or becoming increasingly competent in interpreting a set of signs (Rice 1994), apprenticeship is always about more than learning how to play an instrument. As Bryant (2005, 224) succinctly puts it, apprenticeship is about learning not simply to do "X" but "learning to become the *type of person* who can do X." It is about learning to "[emperson] a body of knowledge" that comprises a "set of values, both ethical and aesthetic" (Bryant 2005, 234).

This chapter is about learning to play the oud. Or, rather, it is about learning to become the *type of person* who can play the oud. This is a reflection on what it means to produce songs and sounds of love in a setting still marked by war, and what it means to be a musician in a place where musicians (and their instruments) have long been both revered and reviled. I begin this story with a consideration of the oud's history in Somaliland: an unraveling of the sonic and material meanings of the oud, and the various sociopolitical and aesthetic sensibilities that the instrument's sounding both indexes and creates. But anchored in my own oud apprenticeship, this chapter is primarily a reflection on the process by which one *becomes* the type of person who can play the oud, who can *sound* love, and who can enable others to voice love. It is a kind of "excavation" of "embodied data" (Hahn 2007, 13), a retrospective sorting through of the lessons I learned, some more consciously than others, sitting cross-legged on Cabdinaasir's floor and playing with him on stage. These lessons, more than any other part of my research, offered me an intimate and embodied perspective on the making of the voice of love. But perhaps above all else, this is the story of an encounter and the relationship between a novice and her elder mentor: a process that distills an additional layer of intimate possibilities into hees jacayl and one that is critical to the envocalization of love songs in live performance.

Sounding Love: A Brief History of Somali Oud Playing

When Weedhsame described a hospital where lovesick patients are treated with the oud—or, to be more precise, where the saline solution that drips from IV bags *is* the oud ("Sayloonku waa cuudka")—he drew on a widely held sentiment that there is something uniquely reparative about the instrument's sound. Indeed, across the Middle East, North Africa and Central Asia where it has long been played in secular and religious settings, the oud is especially revered for its healing powers. Among Arabs the oud is known as "the king, sultan or emir of musical instruments, 'the most perfect of those invented by the philosophers'" (Poché 2007, quoting Ikhwān al-Safā'). As a feature of Sufi musical-mystical quests, the instrument is said to express "the soul's longing to return to the divine" (Matar 2008). The oud has also been praised for the way its sound "places the temperament in equilibrium" and "calms and revives [the] heart" (Muhammad Shibab al-Din, in Goode 2008). Yet in Somaliland, the oud's soul-soothing powers cannot be separated from the instrument's checkered past. Consistently used to sound both love and freedom, the kaban's affective-aesthetic force is deeply entangled in a particular sociopolitical history and the lived experiences of the musicians in whose hands it sings. The instrument's complex and multivalent meanings were revealed to me in stories about legendary oud masters, in listeners' ideas about the instrument's sonic powers, and in coming to know my own oud teacher's history.

The kaban's complicated journey into Somali soundscapes begins with the story of Cabdullaahi Qarshe, the man affectionately known as "the father of Somali music." Born in Tanzania, Qarshe hailed from a family originally from the Sanaag region of eastern Somaliland, who held the title *muruud* (keepers) of the shrine of Sheikh Isaaq (the common ancestor of the Isaaq).[3] Upon his father's death, he moved with his mother to Aden, where he attended school. The British had recently established a radio station in Aden, and Qarshe recounts being especially drawn to the Hindi and Arab-language programs for the music that they played. Hearing this music led him to reflect on Somalis' lack of an instrumental musical tradition. "Want[ing] music to be for Somalis as it is for the other languages," when the opportunity presented itself to buy an oud, Qarshe took it (Qarshe, in Johnson 1996, 82). But this left him with a new challenge. To his well-regarded religious family, owning a musical instrument "was tantamount to blasphemy," so he did not know where to store his new purchase (Qarshe, in Hassan 2008, 67–68). Qarshe came up with a creative solution. He put the instrument in a box and convinced a friend to say it was his. Should anyone open the box and question its contents he could deny ownership. Then when he was due to set sail to Somaliland in the mid-1940s, his friend brought him the box and Qarshe and his prized-yet-clandestine instrument soon found themselves on Somali shores.

Once on Somali soil, Qarshe began his quest to develop a distinctly Somali musical form. He first pursued his musical interests alongside an Indian musician named Ina Beenaale and a Yemeni musician named Abdo Yusuf. They started experimenting with adding music to Somali poems, including that of Cilmi Boodhari, using the melodies of older genres of hees. Qarshe eventually moved to Berbera, where he found an Arab musician named Bakri who agreed to teach him the oud in exchange for a daily helping of qaad (an oud-learning arrangement not unlike my own). By this point, the belwo movement was in full swing and anticolonial sentiments were also on the rise. As his proficiency increased, Qarshe lent his new skill both to the causes of national freedom and to love: his first original composition was the political anthem "Ka kaacay! Ka kaacay!" (Wake up! Wake up!),[4] and his second was a love song for his first wife. While the songs that Qarshe and others in the belwo movement composed were derided by religious authorities as "evil"—and pejoratively dismissed by one sheikh as "songs of innovation" (Hassan 2008, 69)—Qarshe's expanding contributions were critical to the development of modern hees and the emergence of a distinctly Somali musical sound. Since its earliest introduction to Somali orature, the kaban and kabaniste have thus inevitably occupied a complex sociopolitical space: revered for sounding otherwise inarticulable desire (both individual and collective) yet reviled for inexorably challenging the status quo.

As music became increasingly accepted, and then central to the newly independent regime's project of Soomaalinimo, the oud cemented its position as an instrument iconic of "Somaliness." Even as an increasing number of new instruments were used in musical productions—from violins, flutes, and accordions to saxophones, organs, and electric guitars—the oud maintained a privileged position as "the center of gravity" of Somali music.[5] According to my oud-loving interlocutors, the instrument's humanlike "voice" (*cod*) lends the oud its uniquely affective powers: an ability to "repair you" and to "bring relief." Strung with five or six courses, the oud has the range of a male tenor or female alto; its vibrating strings, sounded by being struck with a riisha, produce sound in a manner similar to the vibrating vocal cords. Like a good singer, an oud may be described as having a *cod macaan* (sweet voice), and in skillful hands can *sing*, sounding with a depth of emotion unrivaled by other (nonhuman) instruments. A singer praised for having the voice of an oud—a compliment paid to Maxamed Mooge, for instance—is held in the highest regard. During the heyday of Somali music, musicians like Cumar Dhuule, Xudeydi, and "Jiim" Sheekh Muumin—so nicknamed for a virtuosity that drew comparisons to Jimi Hendrix—took oud playing to new heights, making their instruments sing and continuing to enable human voices to sing about love. Honing their craft in an increasingly cosmopolitan musical setting, these oud players embodied a continuity of sound and substance between new musical productions and the qaraami that came before.

Like all other aspects of life in then-Somalia, the oud and its sounding were to be indelibly affected by the implosion and eventual collapse of Barre's regime, and the spaces for music-making that the subsequent instability and violence restricted and precipitated. Barre's 1988 bombing campaign decimated Hargeysa's National Theater. Instruments were destroyed and artists fled to refugee camps. As Cabdinaasir was one of the only musicians active in Somaliland before, during, and after the war, his story is illustrative in this regard. And he once told me a story about two of his instruments that poignantly captures the place of the kaban—a relatively portable instrument—during this period of turmoil. When bombs rocked Hargeysa in 1988, Cabdinaasir and most other inhabitants of the city fled with few possessions. Like most other musicians, he had to leave his instruments behind. But one day when his company stopped to rest in a village, he noticed animals being watered with what he first thought was a large calabash. He explained to me, rather matter-of-factly, that when he was offered water from the same vessel, he realized it was one of his ouds, stripped of its strings and soundboard. Faced with this realization, Cabdinaasir said that he could not help but laugh. Responding to my confusion, he simply said: "There was nothing else to do." There was no other way to make sense of this destruction and this poignant loss of voice.

But before long Cabdinaasir was more happily reunited with another kaban. Soon after arriving at a refugee camp in Ethiopia (Camp Abokor), he heard someone playing an oud. He told me that he immediately recognized the voice (*cod*) of this oud as his own, so he asked for it to be returned to him. The other kabaniste did not want to relinquish the instrument, so Cabdinaasir made a proposition: to determine the instrument's ownership, a third party would inspect the instrument for seven distinct scratches that Cabdinaasir knew his kaban to have. When these markings were verified, the oud was given back to Cabdinaasir. Soon thereafter, Cabdinaasir and some artists in the camp organized themselves into an ad hoc band, later known as Kooxda Halgan (the Band of the Struggle). Like Qarshe before them, they used their art to sound both freedom and love. Kooxda Halgan became primarily known for their songs of resistance: they composed songs to support the SNM's struggle, including playing for soldiers on the frontlines.[6] The oud's contemporary sounding continues to recall this revolutionary use. Yet these musicians also played to provide entertainment to fellow refugees and "therapy" for lovesick listeners. Even in the midst of war, Cabdinaasir explained, "at least one in every five songs was a love song." People in refugee camps still fell in love, married, and experienced love(-suffering)—and yearned for the relief that only the oud could provide. As has always been the case, it remained the musicians' duty to soothe the wounds of their people, whatever their cause.

But fighting and its aftermath took its toll on musicians, including Cabdinaasir. When the SNM's stronghold at Beli-Gubadle was captured in 1990, he was so disheartened that he traded in his oud for a gun and joined the SNM's armed resistance. Cabdinaasir would not make music again until 1994, though by this time the political-artistic space had dramatically transformed. Many displaced artists did not return to Somaliland, and those who did had few instruments—and even less money and morale—with which to rebuild. For much of the 1990s, music-making was limited to private gatherings, the occasional performance at weddings, or NGO events, where songs were commissioned to promote various peace and development projects. But when the few instruments that had survived wore out, there was no money to replace them. The increasing presence of Salafism further squeezed to the margins the few musicians who were left and discouraged a younger generation from picking up the craft. And from sometime in the early 2000s, would-be musicians unperturbed by rising antimusic sentiments turned to the synthesizer: an instrument that could accomplish the work of multiple musicians and did not require the time, discipline, and resources available to an earlier generation to learn. By the time I was in the market for an oud and a teacher in 2015, one friend explained my challenges in these rather dire terms: "There used to be over a hundred professional-level oud players in Hargeysa. Today there are probably less than ten."

Yet rather than undermine its importance to Somali soundscapes—both as a physical instrument and "its embodied acoustic identity" (Qureshi 2000, 811)—the current musical environment seems to have deepened listeners' appreciation of the oud. Indeed, the postwar state of the music industry has only served to reimbue prewar sounds with greater significance, providing sonic continuity and comfort amid uncertainty. Qaraami still play over the radio and, as we will see in chapter 6, places like Hiddo Dhawr have further entrenched the sound of the oud as a quintessentially Somali sound. Younger artists are incorporating the oud into "live" television performances with greater frequency.[7] BK's success as a singer is sometimes credited to his own knowledge of the oud. And the last few years have seen increased interest from younger musicians and music lovers in learning to play the instrument. An oud-learning course at the Hargeysa Cultural Center, for instance, drew nearly twenty interested young people, whose enthusiasm was only dampened by the lack of instruments on which to learn (there were only three: mine, the teacher's, and one belonging to the center). Cabdinaasir, for his part, taught upward of thirty students, including aspiring musicians both from Somaliland and the diaspora. While the lack of instruments certainly presents a challenge to the transmission of oud-playing knowledge, the instrument remains an integral component of contemporary music-making and sonic notions of "Somaliness," perhaps somewhat stubbornly so. As Cabdinaasir once replied when I asked him about the instrument's future: "As long as I am Cabdinaasir, I will play this oud."

In contemporary Hargeysa, then, the oud is an instrument with multivalent meanings, whose body and sounding embodies and indexes a range of sociopolitical memories and values: from its clandestine original sea journey to an instrument lost and found in the midst of war, used to sound various projects of political freedom and revolution; from its early sounding of a new form of love poetry to the sonic therapy it continues to provide to conflicted hearts; and from an instrument that sounded "innovation" to one now associated with "heritage" and its preservation. Cabdinaasir summarized this complex position of the kaban and kabaniste to me with this well-known saying: *fanaanku waa ubax guddaafad ka dhex baxay* (artists are like flowers, growing in the rubbish). Given the current musical environment and the instrument's complex history, what does it mean to become the person who can play the oud? And what may this process teach us about the ongoing and intimate work of envocalizing love songs in contemporary Hargeysa? These are the questions that I now address.

Lesson One: On Perseverance and Finding Place

My first lesson on what it means to be the kind of person who can play the oud in Hargeysa had little to do with music-making. To learn the oud, I needed an instrument. And I needed a teacher. Despite my best efforts—or what I thought were appropriate efforts—for more than six months I succeeded in neither quest. But reflecting on my initial failures and what eventually gave way to acceptance provided a profound early lesson on the technical and social challenges that musicians face and the social obligations that come with belonging to a particular community of practice. This was a lesson in perseverance and a lesson in finding place.

My first challenge was caused by a faulty assumption: given the centrality of oud playing to Somali music, I assumed that I would be able to find an instrument and a teacher. But neither task turned out to be straightforward. A relatively recent addition to Somali oral arts, ouds have never been locally produced. Before the war, a steady stream of imports, mainly from the Arabian Peninsula, kept artists well supplied. A wealthy hotel owner, for instance, provided most of the instruments to Danan Hargeysa, with whom Cabdinaasir performed. But these arrangements dried up with state collapse. Musicians from the 1990s onward have relied on music-loving patrons and musicians in the diaspora to bring them instruments from Europe, Dubai, or another Arab country. This is the strategy I first adopted, though multiple promises by friends traveling through Dubai to bring me an instrument fell like dominos. "No one wants to be seen in the airport with an oud," a friend finally mercifully explained, after getting an earful of my frustration, "they're ashamed to be seen carrying an instrument." I had greatly underestimated the social burden and potential cost to one's reputation that an instrument might bring to someone not known to be a musician.

After much trial and error and a good dose of stubbornness, I eventually acquired an instrument. At the time it seemed serendipitous, though in retrospect it came about due to my increasing embeddedness in a local network of musicians who seemed to take care of their own. By this point I had befriended Khadra Daahir, whose home also served as an informal gathering place for artists young and old. A British-Somali singer I had met there called me one evening with a proposition: he knew from conversations at Khadra's that I was looking for an oud, and he had heard of a musician who would part with his instrument to raise funds to get to Muqdisho. Should I want it, we had to meet immediately. In a dark and dusty parking lot outside the university, after I had finished an evening lecture, I hesitantly climbed into the back seat of his car to inspect the instrument. It was, on my part, love at first sight. From the instrument's deep red ribbing and intricate wood purfling, to the finger oil stains that marked the ivory inlay of the fingerboard—evidence of the many songs it had already sounded—I was smitten. I paid half the requested likely-too-high sum on the spot and agreed to send the rest via Zaad the following day. I was assured in the following weeks that this was a fine instrument, an instrument with a *cod macaan* (sweet voice). Yet in nearly the same breath, I was warned to take care and made to promise not to be seen with it on the street, even though I lived within walking distance of Cabdinaasir's house. That the route from my house to his took me past a busy mosque with a conservative reputation raised particular fear that my instrument-bearing presence could be problematic. "You already attract enough attention," I was cautioned, "it's better for all of us [artists] not to provoke anyone. Promise, please, that you'll always carry your kaban in the car." While a symbol of soul-soothing "Somaliness," the kaban seems to serve as a constant reminder of the contradictory emotions—joy, relief, shame—that music and musicians bring.

Acquiring an instrument represented a significant step in my quest to learn the oud, but I was soon met with a new challenge: finding a teacher. Save for a few exceptions under Barre, music has never been formally taught. Aspiring musicians learn by being accepted into a musical collective, usually held together by a principal poet and/or musician, and then making music alongside others "who share a concern or a passion for something they do and learn how to do it better as they interact regularly," that is, a community of practice (Wenger and Wenger-Trayner 2015). Still naive to this process of musical transmission, my early quests to find a teacher were met with dead ends. One potential teacher, the kabaniste for Xidigaha Geeska, met with me, restrung my instrument, tentatively agreed to teach me, then disappeared into other musical obligations. Another lead was abandoned when I learned the potential teacher had demanded a year's worth of tuition upfront from another (European) student and failed to show up to many of their agreed meeting times; in the student's words, the teacher "never really taught anything specific." In retrospect, given Xidigaha Geeska's popularity, I could never have been seriously considered for membership. And, as I soon learned, meeting one-on-one for a structured lesson at a predetermined time and place is a peculiar notion indeed.

The silver lining to my possibly overpriced oud purchase turned out to be a fortuitous introduction. Two months after our parking lot dealings, I was again in the backseat of my oud-broker's car, instrument and bountiful offerings of qaad in tow, on the way to meet Cabdinaasir. The ustaad, my new musician-friend assured me, owed him a favor and would also surely be happy to meet a friend of the beloved mother of love, Khadra Daahir. Cabdinaasir greeted us warmly and to my pleasant surprise said he recognized me from my frequent attendance at Hiddo Dhawr. He tuned my instrument and indicated that I should copy his posture. My female anatomy led to some initial consternation, as I struggled to reach my arm around the body of the oud, which sat farther away from me than Cabdinaasir's was from his slim frame. He showed me how to hold the riisha—or the plastic stay from a men's shirt collar that most musicians here use, proper riishas (like ouds) being hard to come by. He seemed pleasantly surprised when I managed to repeat back a basic melody—though less pleased when, five minutes later, I had forgotten. Word that I was a "musician" in my home country somehow came out (a very generous assessment of some basic musical training), an electric guitar and a keyboard were summoned, and I was asked to play. "Do you sing?" Cabdinaasir queried, eager to know of my potential contributions. I fumbled my way through the few more popular songs in my repertoire that I knew by heart, much to the amusement and encouragement of the other musicians seated around the room's periphery. Cabdinaasir sat quietly in the corner, contemplatively watching and listening to my very amateurish ad hoc performance. Okay, he nodded at the end. She can learn.

That I had found more than a teacher, however, soon became abundantly clear. Cabdinaasir's living-room floor was nothing like the lesson space to which I was accustomed, and it was quickly apparent that the demarcation of our "lesson" time from the everyday flow of people, conversations, and collaborations that took place in his home was to be blurry at best. Cabdinaasir's wife and young stepsons cycled in and out, the young boys at first angling to have their picture taken with the "Hollywood" woman (I was the first white woman they had seen in person) and later coming simply to greet their *eedo* (paternal aunt). Friends and musicians from out of town came to pay their respects. The most cunning of the household's goats occasionally snuck inside. And, most significantly, other members of FanSan—a newly established musical collective under Cabdinaasir's mentorship—used his living room as a home base; it was a place to catch an afternoon nap, chew and converse, run through new compositions, and record new songs. These young musicians quickly took an interest in my presence and progress, offering me tips, singing along, asking for advice, and showing me what they were working on. Before long when we met in other social settings, they were (proudly) telling those around them "she is one of us" and asking me to affirm that I was part of them. Cabdinaasir, for his part, soon grew tired of my affinity for predictability. "Why do you keep calling me to ask this?" he chided one day when I phoned to ask if I could come for a lesson. "Just come over [unannounced] like everybody else!" I had not so much found a teacher, I realized, as I had joined a musical collective. And in so doing, I had gained membership in a "community of practice"—that is, a group of people who learn, live, and make music together in a space where "music is integrated into the rhythms of everyday life" (Weidman 2012, 22).

While my early oud-buying and teacher-finding quests were a source of frustration, once I had found my bearings, these early challenges cast into unique relief the social and musical significance of belonging to a community of practice. In the first instance, my own challenges gave me a heightened awareness of the obstacles that many others had also overcome to enter this space. Certain elements of my own background, to be sure, depart drastically from most local musicians: I am a woman, who was learning an instrument usually played by men; a foreign researcher with funds to buy an instrument, and not always held to the same moral standards as locals; and the child of parents who supported over a decade of formal musical training. Yet the more time I spent in Cabdinaasir's living room, the more I began to appreciate that perseverance and learning to carry oneself with a certain kind of integrity are critical skills for any aspiring musician. Except for the lucky few who came of age during the 1970s, Somali artists have long come into their careers against resistance on multiple fronts. Cabdinaasir's own history, for instance, bears a striking resemblance to Cabdullaahi Qarshe's. Like Qarshe, he was raised in Aden in a well-known religious family. He fell in love with music when he was nine, but as the son of a highly respected sheikh, he dared not pick up an instrument. Consequently, like Qarshe, he did not take up music until he moved away from home as a young adult—first to Qatar and eventually to Somaliland. The young members of FanSan told me similar stories of the challenges they had faced. The mother of one young poet, for example, had once flushed a flash drive of his poems down the toilet, fearful of the implications of pursuing an artistic path. A young male singer's relationship with his family was on tenuous terms, even though he had assured them he would not chew qaad and would be diligent in his prayers. Another young female singer had been allowed by her parents to sing only after intense negotiations during which she promised to stay in the family home and to always be fully covered while performing. Cabdinaasir even initially discouraged his own daughter, whose mother is also a singer, from pursuing music. He relented, eventually, as she had followed him around humming tunes "since she started crawling," and he realized he could not dampen her desire to sing. Lesson number one of what it means to become a musician, a lesson I was reminded of every time I put my kaban in the car instead of on my back: pursuing one's artistic passions comes at a price. Making art means accepting a life on the edges, a life of social trade-offs. Only those who "sing because they need to sing"—who, like Cilmi, are compelled by a kind of inescapable longing to outwardly express their inner sentiments—are likely to persevere.

Yet as aspiring musicians learn their place in the broader social context, they also enter a community of practice, where the novice not only learns how to make music but is socialized into the expectations and obligations of being an artist. As one singer explained to me, being a good artist depends not only "on the sweet voice" but also on one's "personality"—that is, how they treat their colleagues, how they treat their community, and how they treat the music itself. As Bryant (2005, 224) puts it, being the kind of person who can make music is often about not just being *good at* something, but also being *good*. For a community that is both revered and socially marginalized, maintaining an image of respectability and integrity through "good behavior" is particularly important and often a condition of membership. The chairperson of Xidigaha Geeska, for instance, explained to me that you can identify a good musician "by the ear," but before they are offered full membership they must go through a process of "assimilating the culture" of the group. This included, he explained, respecting other members and keeping their feelings private, refraining from sitting in public areas such as teashops, not shouting at others, and not asking others for money. Potential members must thus "stay with us for a long time, sit here and visit us again and again" until they understand the group's "culture"— until they "mix" like water with water rather than floating on top like oil. Only when he or she has "assimilated" these norms can aspiring artists be offered membership in the group.

While Xidigaha Geeska's reputation as Somaliland's preeminent music group means the bar for membership is particularly regimented, the fluid sociomusical space of Cabdinaasir's living room was one of acceptance but also expectation. Being one of them involved various obligations, some that I learned by overstepping invisible barriers and being corrected and some that I was more implicitly shown. These obligations included, for instance, being available to help with mundane everyday activities and a certain level of resource-sharing: shuttling children to Qur'anic school; driving young members to the power station to get their power turned back on; giving rides home after performances; and contributing to the costs of fuel and qaad. Significantly, while responding to requests for assistance was acceptable and seemed to signal that a level of intimacy had been attained (such requests are usually reserved for close friends and family, not strangers), giving perceived as charity was resisted. I was once reprimanded for sending money to a FanSan member after I had interviewed him; he was offended that I thought I needed to compensate him. Other obligations included active participation in the group's various musical endeavors: letting my Facebook wall become a space for the group's promotion; affirming in public that I was "part of them"; and being willing to perform on stage, even when I was not entirely comfortable or prepared to do so, as at a May 18 concert in Berbera where I was invited on stage to "play" an electric guitar (it was my presence not my musicianship that was important here—the guitar was not properly amplified).

Beyond these more tangible expectations, by watching how different artists interacted with each other, how they spoke of their work and musical trajectories, how they worked through challenges and responded to their objectors, and their expectations of me, I also came to understand the implicit code of conduct by which artists concerned with maintaining their integrity endeavor to work and live. Carry yourself with modesty and humility, on stage and in everyday interactions. Graciously accept praise from fans, while holding your resolve in the face of critics. Cultivate a sensitivity of how your actions affect the reputation of the entire artistic community and act, dress, and carry your instrument accordingly. Give credit where credit is due, and share your success with others. Use your God-given gifts not for fame and fortune but, as one young poet put it, "to give the people what they need"—whether it be relief from love-suffering or other social maladies. Aspire to improve not only your own musical voice but also your behavior. Perhaps we might amend lesson one as follows: following your artistic passions comes at a cost, but this cost can be mitigated by finding a place within a specific community of practice and learning to abide by the obligations of membership. Learning to (become the type of person who can) play the oud requires cultivating not only musical skill but integrity and respect for oneself and others—learning to live as a "flower," despite what your detractors might say.

Lesson Two: Watch, Listen, Move, Repeat

Having found my way to Cabdinaasir, and somewhat unwittingly into the ranks of FanSan, I was welcomed into a space where I could devote myself to learning the oud, however "unsystematic and communal" (Bryant 2005, 229) our lessons remained. Yet from my very first lesson, it was clear to me that I would need to adopt an approach to music learning that was completely foreign to my classical training. Given that Somali music is an entirely oral/aural tradition, I had to adopt what Rice (1995, 268) calls a "visual-aural-tactile" mode of learning that centers "observation, trial-and-error, and practice," rather than verbal explanation or note reading. As an "observing participant" rather than a "participant observer"—and one with markedly different engrained bodily habits of music-making—it also became apparent that, as for other novices, my own body would become a site of local action (Woodward 2008, Downey et al. 2015). This was a form of learning that would require fairly radical retraining of my body and my senses—a disciplining that, as Weidman (2012) points out, is deeply entangled in the production of a certain kind of subject.

The process went something like this: seated cross-legged on his living-room floor, Cabdinaasir would play for me, modeling proper posture and exaggerating the notes. I would watch and listen, then I would attempt to repeat back to him what I had seen and heard. We began by learning the pentatonic scales that form the basis of all songs, known to Somalis mainly in Italian (a legacy of colonialism): "do maggiore" (C major) and "si bemolle" (B♭ major), "re minore" and "mi minore" (D and E minor), "do dieses" and "fa dieses" (scales containing C# and F#).[8] I would watch Cabdinaasir's left hand and attempt to commit to memory the fingering patterns of each scale. We repeated this process for the different rhythmic patterns, whose names reflect Somali music's fusion of indigenous and cosmopolitan sounds—including "Fox" and "Samba," "Samba Sudani" and "dhaanto" (a traditional dance genre, which Cabdinaasir told me has a rhythm identical to reggae). When I struggled to hear the rhythm, Cabdinaasir would flip his instrument over, tapping out an exaggerated beat with the palm of his hand and fingers on the instrument's rounded back. Eventually we moved to lines of songs played in this manner until we had managed to put the whole song together. When I faltered, Cabdinaasir would wait to see if I could sort things out on my own. If I failed he would repeat a phrase until I too could play along—in a way encouraging me to recognize my own shortcomings and make sense of them myself, yet remaining attentively on-the-ready to assist if need be. In this manner we made our way through a selection of what I later learned were his own favorite songs to play: a series of classic *raaxeye* by Cabdullaahi Qarshe; a qaraami popularized by Cumar Dhuule, later sung by Khadra Daahir ("Xaafuun"); a set of more recent Magool songs, including "Miday laabtu doonto" (As the heart wants/takes me), a song we went on to play together often. On learning that I had been given the Somali name "Haweeya," he also taught me Rashiid Bullo's song by the same name, written for his wife—a song that Rashiid Bullo himself later recounted to me and that also gives quite a memorable anatomy lesson ("Haweeya, you have cut my artery with an axe! / If you were not in the heart valves . . . I would not have to sing for you"). And on my request, he patiently modeled one of his own compositions, "Waan ku aaminayaa" (I trust you)—a love song that "came to [him] on the breeze" one afternoon in 1994, the year he put down his AK-47 and decided it was finally time to take up his kaban again.

While my previous musical training served me well to a degree, I also soon realized that these lessons would require a reeducation of my senses and my body. My weak aural memory presented an early stumbling point. While adjusting to a visual-aural-tactile mode of learning was effective at Cabdinaasir's house, when I got home and tried to practice, I was completely at a loss. My ear was not the problem. I could hear a melody and repeat it back. And I had not previously thought I had issues with memory, having regularly memorized long and complex piano pieces. But it turns out that my *aural* memory is terrible. My initial response was to revert to what I knew: I took to recording our lessons on my phone and then went home and notated the songs from my audio recordings. Once I could *see* a song on paper, I had an easier time committing it to memory. At first, Cabdinaasir took this in stride, perhaps initially curious to see these songs represented so strangely on a page. On request, he added lyrics to my growing songbook and helped me mark down each song's scale and rhythmic pattern, as well as the original poet, composer, musician, and singer. And while he accommodated my book throughout the year, he soon grew tired

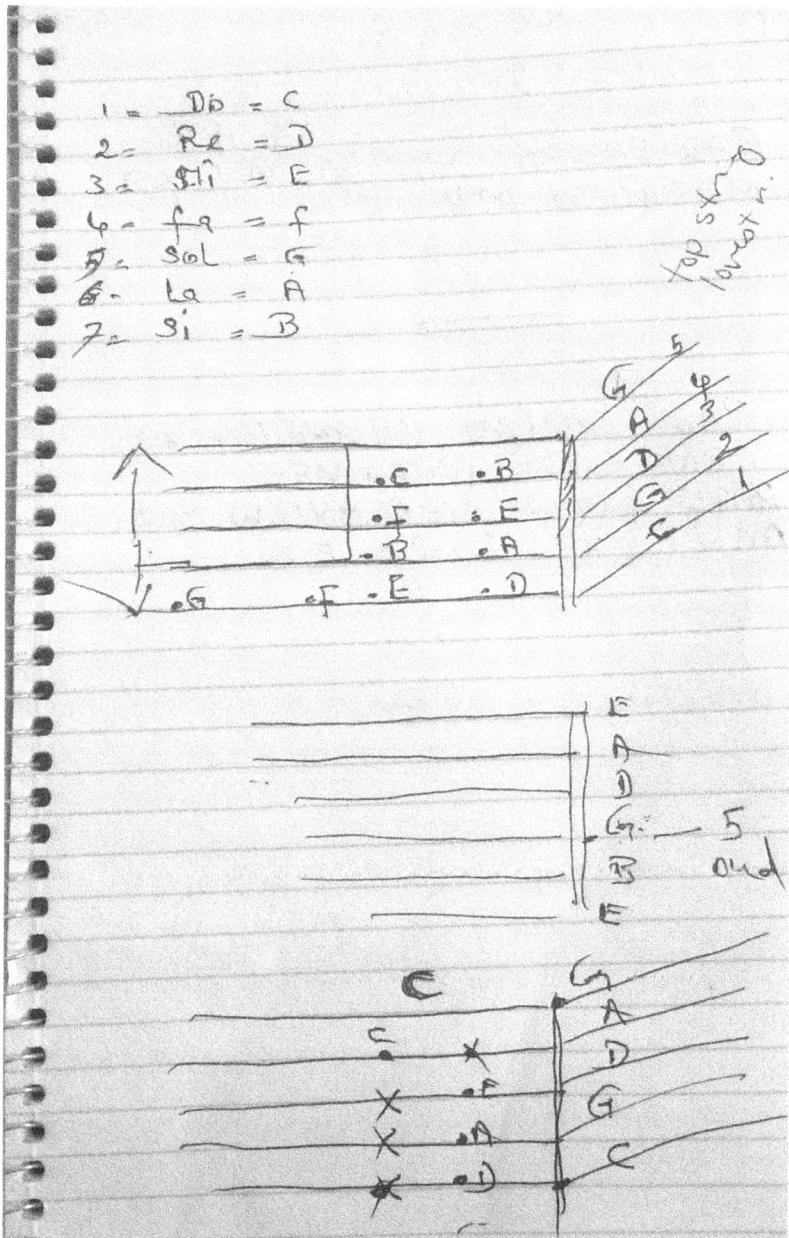

FIGURE 5.1. Notes from one of my earliest oud lessons, in Cabdinaasir's handwriting, showing the Somali names for different notes (from Italian) and how these map onto the oud (when the lowest string is tuned to a G; this string may also be tuned to an E). As a point of comparison, the middle diagram shows standard guitar tuning. The lower diagram shows the fingering for a C major ("do maggiore") scale.

FIGURE 5.2. Excerpt from my oud notebook of Cabdinaasir's song "Waan ku aaminayaa" with the lyrics added in his handwriting.

of my reliance on it, and at every turn encouraged me to put it away, listen, and feel the movement of the songs. Cabdinaasir would tell me that once he heard a melody, he would never forget it: he could immediately remember it and reproduce it, a skill forged through years of learning to listen. If I could not learn to listen, feel, and remember, my progress would remain slow and my repertoire limited.

While my book provided a temporary, if somewhat problematic, workaround to my weak aural memory, certain stubbornly ingrained bodily habits were harder to correct. While in performance the kabaniste often sits on a stool or chair, in more everyday music-making—as for most everyday activities like eating and chewing—sitting on the floor is the norm. And as Weidman (2012, 224) points out, sitting may be "a mode of bodily comportment tied into a whole complex of cultural, gender, and class proprieties." In Somaliland, while many houses have sofas, these are almost only ever used when welcoming unfamiliar guests. Sitting cross-legged on the floor is thus an expected position of familiarity, comfort, and convenience. It was also a position I found incredibly awkward, especially in a dress. Like Weidman's karnatic violin teacher who teased her for being "like a dog" who needed to be walked (2012, 224), my cross-legged awkwardness was often a source of amusement. And the fact that my feet frequently fell asleep and needed stretching elicited all manner of medical advice to improve my circulation ("Eat more meat!" "Drink more camel's milk!"). My feet-sleeping problem was never resolved, but I did learn to take cues from the way Cabdinaasir effortlessly folded his legs beneath him, modestly tucking his *macawis* (a saronglike men's garment) around his knees. And thanks in part to Khadra Daahir's insistence that I change into something "more comfortable" every time I arrived at her house, I quickly realized the practical and social value of wearing a loose-fitting *shiid* that allowed me to sit cross-legged without even my feet being seen. An ankle-length formless dress made of light cotton, a *shiid* is a garment usually worn by women at home; like sitting on the floor, donning a *shiid* indexes and necessitates a certain level of familiarity and intimacy. In time, I learned to dress and fold my legs in a way that allowed me to sit in a position of both modesty and familiarity, one that facilitated a level and intimate mode of interaction with others. Like the need to listen and feel the music in a certain way, this posture enabled an intimacy that was critical for learning how to play with and for others (more on this below).

Even more troublesome than my awkward sitting, however, was my delinquent right wrist. Years of piano and guitar playing had taught me to hold my hand in a restrained and steady way, and I struggled endlessly to reproduce the loose, rapid wrist movement required to play a tremolo. To my endless frustration, this was a technique I witnessed Somali novices perform with ease. And despite Cabdinaasir's careful demonstrations, and my attempts to practice *isbiidhka* (speed) at home, during my lessons my tremolo efforts usually resulted in my whole arm flailing around. This was one area of my playing that, at first, Cabdinaasir very explicitly tried to correct, as good oud playing critically relies on the sound produced by this movement. He not only interrupted my playing to demonstrate proper technique to me but often also physically placed his hand on my shoulder so the movement would need to come from my wrist. But a few months into our lessons, an incident led to a profound change of course. So deeply entrenched were my wrist movements, compounded by the fact that I had broken my right wrist a few years prior, that one day I simply announced I could not do it. Taking this news about my broken wrist in stride, however, Cabdinaasir would tell me—and more importantly, show me—that there are always ways to overcome and work through our own limitations. After mimicking his left hand for months, I had come to play the instrument with only my index and ring finger, assuming this was the "Somali" way of playing. I belatedly learned that Cabdinaasir could not properly bend his middle finger due to a rifle-cleaning accident. We carry our histories in our bodies. My own frustrated admission of vulnerability opened a new appreciation for the miraculously adaptable nature of our bodies and our ability to endure great hardship. Cabdinaasir's stories of losing and finding instruments in the midst of war—some irreparably damaged, others still able to make music—took on new import. His unused middle finger came to serve as a poignant visual counterpoint to the music he continued to defiantly make despite considerable hardship. While the kabaniste should ideally be able to listen, move, and feel in a particular way in order to create certain kinds of sounds, learning to play the oud also requires, in a sense, confronting the (hi)stories that our bodies hold, learning to work with, or work around, our own limitations. And from the gentle hand on my shoulder to the unspoken acknowledgment that we can play on despite our own imperfections, this was a lesson in perseverance of extraordinary intimacy.

As musicians the world over are aware, there is of course only one way to learn: practice, practice, and more practice. Time must be spent getting to know our own bodies, as well as the bodies of our instruments and their sonic potential and embodied limitations. The aim of this repetition is, as Bryant (2005, 229) puts it, "to make the song[s] such a natural part of one's bodily movements that thinking about [them] becomes like thinking about one's heartbeat: It can actually cause failure of the process." While Cabdinaasir played with such fluidity that he seemed to have been born with an oud in his hands, he reassured me by explaining that he had once

FIGURE 5.3. The author and Cabdinaasir during a typical oud lesson. Photograph courtesy of the author.

practiced for so long that the silver-plated strings made his fingers bleed. The tone he learned to achieve—that sometimes aching, sometimes joyful, nearly human sound—was the result of decades of practice, years of getting to know himself and his instrument, the potential in the grain of its wood. He once explained to me that wood needs breaking in like a horse; it takes years for an instrument to know the hands that play it. While there is a popular conception here that artistic skill is genetic, or is "in one's blood," Cabdinaasir was firmly of the view that instrumentalists (and poets and singers) need to hone their craft through practice and over time. Part of his work with the members of FanSan, he explained, was to get them to slow down, to resist the urge "to become stars overnight" without understanding the music first. Learning to become the type of person who can play the oud requires this slowing down, cultivating the ability to watch, listen, and feel; to know one's body and its capabilities and limitations; and to make peace, in a sense, with one's own embodied history and the processual nature of knowledge itself (Marchand 2010, 3). And it requires the commitment to repeat this until the movements become "second nature" (Weidman 2012, 219), until the song "keeps in your fingers" (*waa faro ku hayn*).

Lesson Three: Sounding Emotion, Feeling the Song

Learning to produce certain sounds and commit songs to memory, however, are only the first steps toward playing the oud well. As Bryant (2005, 229) notes, "Embodiment . . . does not necessarily mean mastery." I was reminded that I had a long way to go after my first onstage appearance at Hiddo Dhawr. After a few weeks of practice, I had Magool's "Miday laabtu doonto" sufficiently in my fingers that Cabdinaasir thought I was ready to perform. While the audience was reassuringly receptive to (or curious of) the "lady musician from Canada" (as I was later hailed on the street), when I showed a video of my performance to Khadra Daahir (never one to mince words) she watched intently, nodded some encouragement, then exclaimed: "You are playing the notes, but you aren't *feeling* the song. And why are you looking down at your instrument? Don't play like a machine. Move! Look up! See the people!" I was not, it seems, sufficiently "in" the music nor appropriately engaged with those around me. An accomplished kabaniste, I eventually learned, not only plays the notes but also learns to feel the song, the singer, and the mood of the space; the kabaniste must learn when to hold back, when to add *xawaash* (spice, i.e., ornamentation/embellishments),[9] when, as Cabdinaasir put it, to "let yourself go."

Developing one's own style and learning to engage in the affectively charged sonic dialogue that is the live performance of love songs, however, is no easy task. It requires bringing together technical skill, deep respect for the instrument's sociopolitical-affective power, awareness of one's sociomusical role as a performer, and an ability to "taste" (*dhadhami*) the love experience represented in the words and melody. One must learn, in short, to be *inside* the song. This requires cultivating a reflective awareness of one's own subjectivity and participation in an interaction alongside the ability to organize one's attention to the sonic and social forces at work in the performance space (cf. Berger and Del Negro 2002). I certainly came nowhere near mastering either the technical skills or sociomusical awareness required to perform well. Yet I did come to appreciate the explicit and implicit pedagogical modes by which this mastery may come about. Alerted to my own affective mistuning, I began to pay more attention to when and how Cabdinaasir added *xawaash* during performance (in contrast to his more simplified living-room demonstrations), especially when he "let himself go." While Somali oud playing does not involve the type of

FIGURE 5.4. Example of *xawaash*, added to the oud melody of Magool's "Miday laabtu doonto." The bottom system represents how I learned to play this song, with some simple embellishments: playing hammered-on notes, tremolo on accented notes, and using the low G as a drone. This is typical of how a kabaniste might play while accompanying a vocalist. The upper system represents more complex examples of *xawaash*, as demonstrated by Cabdinaasir during our lessons, and representative of how a kabaniste might play during the instrumental sections of a performance when freer to "let themselves go."

free-form improvisatory playing as jazz, a good kabaniste is highly adept at embellishing phrases and adding ornamentation to the vocal line, as well as riffing on the melody between vocal stanzas. Like Bryant (2005, 228) finds of saz players in Turkey, a good kabaniste "must find his or her own style, his or her own manner of ornamentation"—his or her own musical voice (cf. Duranti and Burrell 2004). This requires a deep knowledge of the musical rules (scale, rhythmic pattern) of a given song, as well as an acute understanding of the ways in which "emotion as a quality of sound" might be produced (Gray 2013, 42–43, referencing Cumming 2000, 3). Playing a note with vibrato, for instance, evokes a sense of longing, sometimes verging on crying. Upward or downward glissandi conjure a sense of emotions rising or falling. The elusive-to-me tremolo produces a sense of suspense, or anticipation—or when used as a drone, it provides a sense of grounding. Well-timed pull-offs or plucked notes serve as exclamation points at the end of a singer's phrase. And an instrumental riff making use of these techniques may express the kabaniste's own emotion on a given evening. As I began to recognize the musical-emotional effect of these sounds, I could then ask Cabdinaasir to show me the techniques that produced them. In this way, I began to develop a beginner's understanding of the intersection of technical skill and affective-aesthetic sensibilities, of the varieties of ornamentation I might draw on to make a song my own.

While technical elements may be explicitly taught, other social-aesthetic sensibilities are more implicitly transmitted. They are not, importantly, *unconsciously* acquired skills but rather sensibilities that are cultivated in informal spaces of music-making as well as through experience on stage. As Gray (2013, 69) finds among fado singers in Portugal, this is a process through which the aspiring artist "develops a vocabulary (gestural, sonic, performative) through which to express and to 'craft' (Kondo 1990) a particular kind of feeling self." Significantly, the informal and often intimate nature of my lessons proved to be an incredibly valuable space in which to familiarize myself with the voices of those with whom I later shared the stage. In Cabdinaasir's living room, I learned about singers' vocal ranges, repertoires, and idiosyncrasies as performers. Yet perhaps more importantly I also learned about their journeys into music and their love anxieties and aspirations—and how these experiences intersected with their performance styles. Knowing other musicians in this way is critical for effective performance. Indeed, when I asked Cabdinaasir how he chose songs on any given evening, he explained that it depends on the singer and what he knew of that person's situation—both in terms of their musical competence, vocal range, and repertoire but also in terms of their emotional state, if and how they could relate to the message of a given song, or indeed if perhaps they needed to sing a certain song to relieve their own love-suffering. The onstage rapport between musicians and singers begins off stage in these intimate social spaces. Learning to become the type of person who can play the oud requires cultivating a kind of heightened socioemotional awareness of those with whom one shares the stage.

Beyond being a space to cultivate this awareness, Cabdinaasir's home is where I first experienced playing, almost from the start, not for my own technical improvement but for others. As another young kabaniste explained, to be proficient is to be able to play for everybody, whether they are an experienced singer or a junior one. Both familiar faces and less frequent visitors would request performances, and when my playing reached a certain degree of competency, those present would sing along. While at first hesitant to play in the presence of others, remarking once that I could not remember the words and was not very good at singing, my assumption of what might be required of me was gently corrected: "Don't worry," I was reassured, "we just need you to play. We can't play, but we know the words, we will sing for you." Somali oud playing is not a solo art. It is, rather, a subtle dance between instrumentalist and vocalist, a sonic dialogue through which individual voices are showcased with, against, and through each other. Learning to do this requires becoming attentive to one's own bodily (and sonic) presence in relation to others' embodied presence (Csordas 1993, 138); it also requires the development of a "voice" that remains uniquely one's own. And it was in informal spaces of music-making like Cabdinaasir's home that I learned to adapt to the vocal styles and competencies of others. I also learned to listen to others' interpretations of songs, adjust my own playing to others' strengths and limitations, and (when feeling particularly brave) to practice embellishing phrases, experiment with my own style, and let myself "get lost" in the music. In lieu of formal rehearsal spaces, it is this space that provides musicians the chance to hone their own voice (human or instrumental) and to better understand the potential and limitations of each other's voices.

While competencies and sensibilities are forged in these informal spaces of music-making, it is on stage where these various elements of sociomusical training come together. While I certainly never achieved any level of mastery, I was fortunate to share the stage with others who had. On my final visit to Hiddo Dhawr during my main research stay, nearly a year after our first lesson, Cabdinaasir invited me to the stage. I settled myself in the back corner, adjusting my scarf and *dirac*. Aware of what I could play without my book, and what the singers could sing, we worked our way through a set of songs all of us could perform, with each performer bringing their own style, while also accommodating the voices of others. Cabdikariin Yare, one of FanSan's young members, took the stage first to perform "Wax dhintaad ka samirtaa" (You only let go when someone passes away) a song we had played together many times at Cabdinaasir's. Sahra Halgan— the venue's founder, and fellow SNM veteran—then took the mic, and we played through our familiar set of Magool songs. Abokor Buulo-Xuubay, the drummer, nodded with satisfaction as I adjusted to Sahra's early entry on one song, and Cabdinaasir smiled encouragingly as we replayed the final stanza of another, responding to the audience's applause. In the places he knew I was strongest, Cabdinaasir embellished the unadorned melodies I was playing, adding depth and emotion to the sound we were producing together—but in a way that drew attention back to me. Small adjustments were surely audible as I attempted to stay in time. Yet there was something satisfying in the give and take of his playing and mine, the communication between master and novice, the safety his instrument's voice provided for my fingers to experiment, and the way his fluid movements pulled me along. At the end of the set, I nodded, acknowledged the audience, and returned to my seat.

A year after meeting Cabdinaasir, and a year of learning to be the kind of person who can play the oud, it was from my seat in the audience that I could most fully appreciate the ustaad on stage and his seemingly effortless demonstration of what it means to be "in" the music. I watched with new appreciation as Sahra and Cabdinaasir spoke in simple glances, the chemistry between them palpable—forged through decades of performing together in times of war and peace. With the rest of the audience I sat mesmerized as Cabdinaasir's ring and index fingers danced across the strings. I smiled to myself with the intimate knowledge that these fingers had bled from his efforts to make these melodies second nature—fingers that had adapted to his own bodily limitations. I listened to the subtle sonic-emotional dialogue between singer and musician, musician and audience—a dialogue made possible only by a keen socioemotional reflexive attention to what was happening in the space. At moments, Cabdinaasir held himself back, playing in a way that showcased the singer or the audience singing along. In other moments, he let himself go, his instrument singing decades of unspoken longing, grief, and joy in a tone achievable only by those with an intimate understanding of their own bodies, their own voice, their relation to the bodies and voices of those around them, and an awareness of the affective power of their instrument. And at the end of the evening, he stood, taking an understated bow and nodding in modest acknowledgment to the audience and other musicians. He silently left the stage with his head held high and his evening's work complete.

Cultivating Sounds and Voices of Love

Since its original clandestine journey to Somali shores, the oud has come to occupy a complex sonic and social position in Somaliland. Learning to become the kind of person who can play the oud in Somaliland is thus inevitably a complicated and sometimes fraught undertaking. But with Cabdinaasir as my indefatigable guide, I learned that the kabaniste is a person of marked perseverance who undertakes their work with a keen sensitivity to the instrument's sociopolitical and affective powers. The kabaniste is also a person defined by certain sociomusical obligations and deeply embodied musical knowledge. And, as Cabdinaasir demonstrated so effortlessly when he was on stage, the kabaniste is also a person with an acute sonic-emotional-social awareness of their own voice and how it may be used to enable the voices of others.

But the lessons that I learned sitting cross-legged on Cabdinaasir's floor go beyond learning what it means to be the kind of person who can play the oud. These lessons also speak to the socially mediated nature of voices of love and, in so doing, add further depth to our understanding of songs' snowballing stickiness. Artistic ability in this context may be widely considered innate and in one's genes—indeed, were it not, the obstacles to overcome in pursuing an artistic path would likely be too great. But the apprenticeship process I have described in this chapter also suggests that the road from God-given gift to the stage is long and often difficult, requiring repetition, discipline, perseverance, and the crafting of a particular kind of "feeling self" (Gray 2013, 69). This is especially true for instrumentalists, but many of the same conclusions may be drawn for singers and poets; it is precisely for this reason that the various members of FanSan were similarly drawn to Cabdinaasir—to the quiet, exemplary mentorship he provided and to the musical wisdom he embodied. While someone might be born with an artistic gene, no one is born knowing how to play or sing or write verse in a way that will resonate with others. Musicians hone their craft with practice over time and within a community of practice defined by certain social, political, and musical obligations. Artists learn the emotive qualities of sound and how to produce them with their "voice"—whether in the alliteration and meter of a poem, through an instrument, or as singers. Poets, musicians, and singers find their voices in the presence of others. And yet, in the final instance, the voice with which the kabaniste or singer performs must be uniquely their own and must sound from the heart.

This last point is where my oud lessons join up with and more deeply illuminate one of the central claims of this book: that is, that love songs find their affective force in an aesthetics that privileges singing from the heart but through a voice that is nevertheless intimately multivocal. The affective power of both instrumentalists and vocalists undoubtedly lies in their ability to feel the song and to perform from the heart. But my oud lessons reveal that sounding from the heart depends on mediated, multivocal realities. Beyond their initial multivocal composition, each instantiation of a love song, each real-time envocalization—on stage, or in informal settings of music-making—is itself the result of a collaborative process that fosters an intimate self-awareness and socioemotional attentiveness to others. This is a process that we might say cultivates not only technical skill but also an ability to *feeling-share*. The intimate relations forged in the process of becoming someone who can sound love songs infuses these songs with another set of intimate possibilities that are integral to their snowballing stickiness. These intimate possibilities are perhaps most obviously realized in live performance. As we will see in the chapter to come, it is in these spaces that love songs' intimate world-building capacities—for performers, musicians, listeners, and broader publics—are put on full display, and an "aspiration for a narrative about something shared" (Berlant 1998, 281) is enacted in real time.

[CHAPTER SIX]

Staging Love

Dhallinyaro waa rajo-ku-nool, waayeelna waayo-waayo.
Youth live on hope, the elderly on nostalgia.

Somali proverb

On August 26, 2014, Hiddo Dhawr opened its doors in Hargeysa. Self-styled as a "cultural restaurant and tourism village," Hiddo Dhawr's opening marked the first time since 1988 that a live music venue had operated in Somaliland. And it opened to great success. Music lovers young and old quickly began to flock to Hiddo Dhawr—which roughly translates as "take care of heritage"—to take in the venue's one-of-a-kind entertainment. In a hall decorated with textiles and images of Somalis' pastoral heritage and displays of Somaliland patriotism, Hiddo Dhawr's musicians delight men and women with the live performance of love songs. Audience members hum along to popular melodies accompanied simply by an oud and drums, while enjoying traditional Somali dishes of *suqaar* (meat stew), *shuuro* (cornmeal porridge), *luxuux* (sorghum pancakes), and spiced tea (alongside more recent additions to Somali cuisine, like pasta, rice, french fries, and Fanta). And midway through the evening, audience members have the chance to take up the mic themselves: to lend their own voices to songs, or tell jokes and make others laugh. In Hargeysa's complex postwar urban landscape, Hiddo Dhawr has certainly not been without its detractors. But in the early years of its operation, the venue has established itself as an indispensable feature of the city's cultural (and political) landscape.[1]

Thus far in this book I have traced the collaborative and multivocal artistic process by which love songs come into being, explored how songs and singers' voices circulate across time and space, examined how listeners listen to love (songs), and traced the process by which musicians learn to sound love. Common to these chapters has been a focus on the types of intimate social relations distilled in and opened by love songs as they are animated by an ever-expanding number of voices across time and space. For the most part these voices have sounded behind closed doors—in artists' homes, bedrooms, cars, and quiet corners across Hargeysa. But at Hiddo Dhawr, voices that sing about love are put on full display to a live audience. Love-sufferers and singers, music aficionados and musicians, all of whom bring with them a lifetime of love song making and listening, are mutually and synchronously participants in a performance—or the live and collaborative envocalization of love songs in a specific time and place. As we have briefly glimpsed elsewhere, this is an incredibly powerful space for musicians and audience members alike. As the first music venue to operate in Somaliland in over a quarter century, Hiddo Dhawr's presence makes a clear political statement about the place of artists in the city. Yet the venue is revered not only as the city's first postwar theater but also as its primary frustration hospital—a place to set aside your troubles and find relief from whatever might be ailing you. The live staging of love songs, in short, seems to open space for the real-time enactment or embodiment of the intimacies that we have seen love songs enable throughout this book. And they do so in a space that is set up not as some radically novel performance venue but one deeply committed to "heritage preservation," a space that simultaneously celebrates Somaliland's past and lays claim to Somaliland's present—and its future.

This chapter tells the story of Hiddo Dhawr, Somaliland's first postwar music venue. This is a story about the politics of staging love (songs) in a conservative Muslim setting, a story that "like ink shows up the veins of a plant" (Barber 1987, 2) brings to the fore multiple lines of contestation. Yet I am not only interested in what Hiddo Dhawr reflects of the contemporary urban climate. I am equally concerned with the ways in which the venue, and particularly the live performance of old love songs, are implicated in contesting and (re)shaping Hargeysa's urban landscape—as a political statement but also as a space where audience members seem able to inhabit, for an evening at least, subjectivities and imaginaries otherwise not available to them. As Warner (2002, 444) points out, all performances are *poetic*, "say[ing] not only, 'Let a public exist,' but 'Let it have this character, speak this way, see the world in this way.'" This is, then, a story about the kind of public hailed into being by the live staging of love songs. By considering both the indexical *and* poetic nature of voices singing love in a particular historical moment, I am interested, in short, in what Hiddo Dhawr says about (and to) Hargeysa's postwar cityscape *and* what the venue does for those who cross its threshold "wearing the shirt of love."

A number of theoretical concerns and somewhat unresolved tensions run through this reflection. The first has to do with love songs' entanglement in Hiddo Dhawr's larger "heritage preservation" efforts and the force of the nostalgia that animates this mission. When Hiddo Dhawr opened just months before I began my research, I could not quite believe my luck. Going to Hiddo Dhawr on Thursday and Friday evenings quickly became part of my weekly routine. Like other audience members, I delighted in the ability to hear music performed live and often sat in awe, transfixed by Cabdinaasir's fingers dancing across his instrument, taken elsewhere by the longing in Sahra's voice. Yet from my very earliest visits, I was also perplexed by the entire mise-en-scène: artists performed decidedly urban music from Somalia's socialist era stripped back in instrumentation and recast as "classic" at a venue constructed to resemble a village of nomadic dwellings, all the while surrounded by somewhat incongruous pastoral images and symbols of Somaliland nationalism. But the more time I spent at the venue, the more I realized I needed to rethink my ideas about the kind of "force" (Dames 2010, 272) that this retrospective might represent. On the one hand, Hiddo Dhawr's mission of "heritage preservation" emerged from the kind of romanticizing nostalgia you might expect from diaspora returnees in a postwar city (not unlike the "colonial" nostalgia that has caused anthropologists discomfort elsewhere on the continent, cf. Bissell 2005). But at the same time, the venue's mission of "heritage preservation" played no small part in its establishment as a respectable (or at least acceptable) institution. And furthermore, there are undeniably "prospective" (Boym 2007, 8) and "subjunctivizing" (Brockmeier 2009, 228) elements to the way that audience members make sense of the selectively curated heritage that the venue has chosen to celebrate—including prewar love songs. The story I tell here is thus also a reflection on the multifaceted and unexpected ways that "nostalgia" animates ideas about the past *and* hopes for the future, while simultaneously shaping the work that love songs do in the present.

The second somewhat unresolved issue concerns love songs' somewhat paradoxical relationship to power.[2] On the one hand, the live staging of love songs in Hargeysa is clearly a political act. Yet Hiddo Dhawr is also a space that is in many ways *anti*political, one that encourages patrons to eschew the sociopolitical cleavages and gendered prohibitions that color everyday interactions in favor of a vulnerability that is ultimately a kind of "renunciation of power" (Gioia 2015, xi).[3] Indeed, Sahra quite explicitly described Hiddo Dhawr to me as an "antipolitical" project. This chapter is thus also a study in the ways that "popular culture creates power to resist power" (Fabian 1998, 69) and the (anti)political possibilities of voices that "stick" in a particular historical and cultural milieu. I tell this story in three parts: first, by tracing the more overt politics of the venue's founding and exploring how Hiddo Dhawr has managed to establish itself as a respectable (or at least acceptable) venue in the city; second, by outlining how the venue "speaks" in its setup and how and why love songs are entangled in a broader mission of "heritage preservation"; and finally by detailing what happens in a typical performance evening and the kinds of relations and imaginaries that these evenings provide to audience members. The "paradox" of love songs' relationship to power, however, means that this story pulls in some-times competing directions in ways that have never felt fully resolved to me. This is a story about politics and its disavowal, "heritage" and a desire for a different future, and the layered and complex power of voices that sing about love.

Making Space for Love Songs: From Vision to Venue

Like many restaurants, coffee shops, and cafes that have opened in Har-geysa in recent years, the story of Hiddo Dhawr begins in the imagination of two diaspora returnees: Ismaaciil Cawl, a Dutch-Somali businessman and development worker, and Sahra Halgan, a singer who had been living and working in France since the mid-1990s. Like many diaspora Somalis, they had both spent decades abroad longing for the home of their youth and dreaming of a return to Somaliland. Yet when they each managed to return, they came back to a very different city. As has also been the case for many other returnees, a certain "longing for what is lacking in a changed present" (Pickering and Keightly 2006, 920)—and especially "a different Somaliland," as one returnee put it to me—prompted a desire to contribute something to Somaliland's postwar recovery and development. But what is notable about Hiddo Dhawr is Ismaaciil's and Sahra's ability to materialize a *music* venue—the first to operate since 1988—in a political-religious environment where music-making is, as we have seen, not a neutral affair. Their success speaks to a range of telling factors: their personal biographies, Sahra's social and political capital, the way that music was incorporated into a project of "heritage preservation" that resonated with local as well as diaspora returnees, and the venue's eventual ability to "speak" to audiences in multifaceted ways. The story of Hiddo Dhawr's founding thus provides a fascinating glimpse into some of the complex sociopolitical-religious and local-diaspora dynamics that color Hargeysa's contemporary cityscape.

While Sahra Halgan is undoubtedly the public face of the venue, it was Ismaaciil who originally set things in motion. As we sipped spiced tea in the shade of one of the venue's distinctive outdoor seating areas one morn-ing, Ismaaciil, a soft-spoken man then in his thirties, began by telling me about a childhood and early adulthood lived in two places. Displaced by war in 1991 as a teenager, Ismaaciil explained that he found it "difficult to feel at home" in his adoptive Holland, yet found comfort in listening to Somali music and reading everything he could about his homeland. After finishing university, he took a job in the development sector that took him all over the world. Then in 2012 he returned to Somaliland for six months to work with some farmers. The Hargeysa to which he returned, however, was nothing like he remembered. "There were new buildings and new cars," he said, "and nothing I recognized from when I was young." Inspired in part by his travels abroad, where he had enjoyed visiting museums and cultural centers, he decided he wanted to return home and "build places that people would recognize" from prewar times, in the form of some kind of center devoted to preserving Somali heritage—especially the knowledge of the farmers and pastoralists with whom he had been working.

Ismaaciil's initial idea to build a village of *aqallo* (nomadic huts) and charge people to come and visit was met with laughter by the locals he told about his plan. But he eventually found a kindred spirit in Sahra Axmed Maxamed—better known as Sahra "Halgan"—whose involvement would become critical, providing what the manager described to me as the venue's "competitive edge." The granddaughter of Nimcaan Hillaac Dheere, a folklore dancer and singer, Sahra first rose to fame as a member of the SNM in the late 1980s. While still a teenager, Sahra worked as a nurse and sang to weary and injured soldiers to soothe their wounds. Mentored by Cabdinaasir Macallin Caydiid, she joined Kooxda Halgan and performed live for frontline troops and also recorded songs for Radio Halgan. It was her association with Radio Halgan that eventually earned her the "Halgan" ("struggle") in her name, a name that continues to recall her SNM activism in important ways. When the dust of war finally settled, Sahra continued to use her music to support postwar reconciliation work, and she proudly told me how she was the only woman to sing at the 1991 Burco Conference, when the SNM declared Somaliland's independence. Though intimately involved in the struggle, she became disillusioned with the interclan conflict that erupted in the mid-1990s. She fled this new violence, settling in France. As other immigrants and refugees, Sahra struggled to make a life for herself and her children in Lyon, eking out a living working in a cafeteria. Eventually she teamed up with two French (Algerian) musicians as the Sahra Halgan Trio. Together they have released two albums that combine what are described as "traditional" Somali songs with more recent compositions set to instrumentation that fuses north and east African sounds. The first album, *Faransiskiyo Somaliland* (France and Somaliland) (2016), includes a documentary about Sahra's homecoming; the second, *Waa Dardaaran* (Testament/last wishes) (2019) includes additional syncretic takes on a series of prewar "classics." Significantly, when Sahra tours with this group—including during a 2016 tour to Japan—she conceives of her artistic work as part of advancing Somaliland's demand for recognition. In her words: "When you flee to another country, you feel guilty. [But] when I had the chance to help my people I felt I had to show [the world] what's going on in Somaliland . . . I want the whole world to know there is a democratic, peaceful country called Somaliland with no Islamists" (in Grunebaum 2016). In both English- and Somali-language media coverage, Sahra is portrayed as a veteran, a patriot—often quite literally wrapped in the flag—and an artist who strives to use her craft to advance the cause of Somaliland's recognition.

Like Ismaaciil, during visits to Somaliland, Sahra was disillusioned with what she found. She was particularly saddened by the state of the artistic sphere. Artists, she said, "had no place to call home anymore," not least because the National Theater had never been rebuilt, and the government-built Waaberi apartments where artists had previously lived had been destroyed or reoccupied. Given the current state of the artistic sphere in Somaliland, she explained that people are nostalgic for a different Hargeysa and "want to relive the era where there was a national theater and people respected artists." Like Ismaaciil, in her tours abroad she had been impressed by venues dedicated to preserving and celebrating the culture and heritage of different locales. Driven by a shared commitment to "showcasing Somaliland's cultural productions," the pair met in Europe and began laying plans to establish some sort of cultural heritage center in Hargeysa. There were, it should be noted, certainly elements of a sentimental form of nostalgia in both Sahra and Ismaaciil's ideas for the venue, and in their imaginings of the Somaliland that they had left behind—a nostalgia marked by a desire to return to a time and place that no longer exists (if it ever did). This homeland- and history-fetishizing nostalgia has been observed in "diasporic imaginaries" across the globe (cf. Axel 2002, Kunreuther 2014). Yet their nostalgia also had a more tangible and future-oriented quality to it: rather than simply "articulating frustration with a changed present" (Omojolo 2009, 249), they planned to return to Hargeysa and create a space that would change the shape and feel of the city they once loved. The quality of the nostalgia that animated this project would come to shape the rather eclectic "heritage" on display, and the way that the venue has been received.

Once in Hargeysa, the pair set to work organizing the logistics of the future venue. They brought on board a local manager, Mustafe, and Sahra gathered her musical contacts, including fellow SNM veteran Cabdinaasir Macallin Caydiid. Other artists involved from early on included the kabaniste Karoone and the drummer Abokor Buulo-Xuubay (both musicians originally from southern Somalia), as well as local singers Caabi Mireh

Dacar, Cali Gacal, and Xasan Gacan. Younger singers, including Cabdi-kariin Yare and Deeqsan Cabdinaasir Macallin (Cabdinaasir's daughter) would eventually join the ranks of regular performers. In the early planning days, the group met at Gacan Libaax (a mountain northeast of Hargeysa popular for retreats) where they hashed out the venue's details, including its name. Intriguingly, one name the group considered was Dhaqan Dhawr (take care of culture). This name was ultimately rejected, however, for its similarity to the term *dhaqan-celis* (return to culture), a pejorative term used to describe diaspora youth who are sent to Hargeysa in the summers by parents afraid their children are losing their language and culture. While the alliteration in Dhaqan Dhawr would have resonated with Somali ears, sensitive to the possible associations the term might have elicited with a controversial group of diaspora returnees, they instead opted for the term *hiddo*, meaning "heritage." While they originally wanted to build in the more developed and densely populated Jigjigayar neighborhood, they were offered the use of land in the less-developed and more sparsely inhabited Bebsi area (named for a Barre-era soft drinks factory) by the bridge that joins Hargeysa's rather disparate sides.[4] The central yet somewhat out-of-the-way location also had the added security benefit of being quite close to the central military base and behind the heavily secured UNDP compound. With a grant from the Somaliland Development Fund and a loan, secured through connections not available to most locals, construction soon began.

While Hiddo Dhawr has generally been warmly received, it has certainly not been without its detractors. This is, after all, a setting where the very permissibility of music is contested and where many locals are wary of the potentially corrupting cultural influence diaspora returnees may bring. Perhaps predictably so, when Hiddo Dhawr opened they were visited by a group of religious leaders concerned about the nefarious activities mixed-gendered audiences may get up to and reports that the venue was serving alcohol. To allay these fears, they were invited to visit and see for themselves that alcohol was not being served. According to Ismaaciil, once they clarified that "heritage preservation" was their principal mission, these religious leaders agreed to leave them alone. And even though they remained opposed to the performance of music, they had weak grounds for further objection: Hiddo Dhawr does not serve alcohol (and even qaad is prohibited), female singers are always covered when on stage, and patrons are encouraged to dress modestly. Sahra, however, was more defiant in her response: "I struggled with this kaban," she told me, "I liberated the country with it and know its work. I have every right to practice my art." Patrons, similarly, have credited Sahra's SNM credentials and long history of using art to promote Somaliland's cause for Hiddo Dhawr's immunity to certain types of criticism. "It's Sahra Halgan!" one friend once remarked, "those religious guys can't touch her!"

The importance of the mission of "heritage preservation" and Sahra Halgan's sociopolitical capital is further revealed when the venue's success is compared to the fate of local artists who have breached certain religious and political protocols. Recall the cancelation of the concert of Nasteexo Indho, a singer from Puntland, over complaints from religious leaders that her online music videos, including recordings of concerts in Europe, suggested she "had a bad culture" and "didn't behave like a Muslim."[5] With no local (clan) relations to advocate on her behalf, Nasteexo Indho had little recourse but to accept the cancelation. On the political front, recall also the arrest of members of Xidigaha Geeska accused of flying a Somali flag at a concert in Muqdisho—an act tantamount to treason for Somalilanders. Both incidents serve to illustrate the complex political-religious environment in which artists operate. While Sahra herself has had her own rifts with the government and has been outspoken at times in her support for the opposition Waddani party, her SNM credentials mean she could never be accused of being anything but a patriot. Finally, the venue's mission of "heritage preservation" has guarded Hiddo Dhawr from (most) accusations of "bad culture," even though the "heritage" on display includes a curious mix of rural, pastoral material culture, and music from the more cosmopolitan-minded socialist era (more on this below).

In a setting where local-diaspora relations are sometimes fraught, Hiddo Dhawr's commitment to "heritage preservation" and Sahra's SNM credentials have also protected the venue from the type of criticism and harassment other similar diaspora-initiated projects have faced. Diaspora returnees occupy a complex place in Somaliland's postwar environment. On the one hand, as the (unrecognized) state lacks the ability to provide basic services, and foreign investment and development aid are severely limited by the country's lack of political recognition, Somaliland's postwar recovery has relied heavily on diaspora contributions. Everything from the city's two largest hotels (the Mansoor and Ambassador), largest university (the University of Hargeysa), and telecommunication and media giants (Telesom and Horn Cable TV) to hospitals (e.g., Edna Adan Hospital) and civil society organizations (e.g., the Nagaad Women's Network) were founded by diaspora members. Diaspora fundraising efforts have also supported critical infrastructure projects, such as the tarmac road to Ceerigabo, emergency health care, and drought relief. This, combined with the country's massive reliance on remittances, means that locals are often appreciative of, and dependent on, family members who live or have lived abroad. As one local politician put it, "Truly speaking, we [the locals] survived because of those of us abroad" (quoted in Ibrahim 2010, 46; addition his). Yet at the same time, this dependence often turns to resentment when returnees are perceived to come with a sense of entitlement to jobs for which they have few tangible qualifications. Holding a foreign passport often means returnees are eligible for ex-pat salary rates at NGOs that are often many times the rates paid to locals. And diaspora youth, many of whom were born abroad or have not lived in Hargeysa since they were very young, are frequently disparaged for having "lost their culture" (Mohamed 2015). So-called *dhaqan-celis* summer holidaymakers who push the boundaries of "acceptable" cultural mores—for such things as men wearing their hair longer, or women not dressing with sufficient modesty—often find themselves afoul of Guddida Wanaag Farista iyo Xumaan Reebista (Committee for Morality and the Eradication of Bad Behavior), who keep a watchful eye over summer diaspora crowds.

Hiddo Dhawr has managed, for the most part, to avoid the resentment some diaspora returnees face. But other diaspora-initiated entertainment venues have not fared so well. One restaurant known to pipe popular Western music into their dining area effectively had its speakers silenced after consistent complaints by local religious leaders. Another restaurant and arts venue, Cup of Art, was completely shut down. Opened in 2014, Cup of Art fashioned itself as a cosmopolitan, hipster-friendly artistic youth hangout that displayed the art of one of its founders (two sisters from the UK) and periodically hosted open mic nights. A July 2015 event, which featured a performance by Hargeysa's only English-language hip-hop artist, "Black East Hargeysa," ended in a police raid (after a tip-off that made dubious claims about the nature of the event), and comments to the owners to "go back where you came from."[6] When they opened a larger "Africa"-themed venue nearby—originally named "Black Mamba"—their sign, featuring a decorative mask, was destroyed by rock-throwing teenagers urged by the imam of a nearby mosque, who decried the figurative mask as un-Islamic. Accusations, entirely unfounded, of facilitating prostitution soon followed; they were also frequently harassed by security personnel who had the ear of the local Salafist imam, who sent them to check up on what was happening in the evenings. The situation was made worse for the owners because they were of mixed Somali-Turkish parentage (their father was a member of a seafaring Turkish community who had long lived in Berbera) and thus lacked paternal kinsmen/elders to negotiate on their behalf. By late 2016 the venue had completely closed its doors.

Hiddo Dhawr's commitment to "heritage preservation" is, of course, not a veiled maneuver to keep potential critics at bay, even if it has secondarily served this purpose. This focus is first and foremost born of a particular kind of postwar nostalgia that has resonated with local and diaspora audiences alike—if it did not, it would have failed as a business by now. Indeed, compared to the often-short lifespan of many businesses, restaurants and other institutions in the city, Hiddo Dhawr has shown remarkable staying power. But these incidents illustrate the tenuous sociopolitical environment into which Hiddo Dhawr was born and the delicate balancing act required to keep religious, political, and other social objectors at bay. As one cultural activist quipped to me, "You can't call Hadraawi un-Somali!" The poet and lyricist, after all, is celebrated and treasured as a national icon, so surely performing his poetry and song may be defended as legitimate pursuits of Somalilanders who, like Hadraawi, are also Muslim. In a setting where music's proponents and detractors both use "culture" as a rallying cry (Hadeed 2015), it is certainly no coincidence that Somaliland's first postwar music venue has come into being by presenting music as part-and-parcel of "traditional" culture, alongside displays of Somaliland patriotism, to be preserved and celebrated. In fact, I would argue that it could never have been otherwise. Not all acts of envocalization are equally welcome. But attending to the conditions that allow space for some voices to emerge over others is certainly revealing of Hargeysa's fraught sociopolitical-religious landscape and the complex and sometimes contradictory power dynamics that go into making a stage.

"Taking Care of Heritage" in Contested Urban Terrain

Considering the "backstage" work that went into opening Hiddo Dhawr gets us some way to understanding the significance of the venue in Hargeysa's contemporary cityscape. But to really get a sense of the kind of public that the venue summons into being, we also need to consider the entire mise-en-scène, and *how* it is that Hiddo Dhawr "speaks," as it were. This means accounting for the rather eclectic material and artistic heritage on display—and the particular way that love songs have been recast as part of the hiddo that needs care and celebration. Heritage projects like Hiddo Dhawr very often represent "a way of *talking* about the past" (Cassia 2000, 289). But they are also equally a discourse in and about the present. The hiddo of Hiddo Dhawr has a lot to say—sometimes speaking subtly, sometimes more overtly, often in multiple directions at once. Taken together, the venue represents a powerful statement about what it means, or *could* mean, to be a Somalilander, at least as imagined by two diaspora returnees who knew "a different Somaliland" and have dared to dream that some of that prewar Somaliland may yet return.

Put into practice, Sahra and Ismaaciil's commitment to "taking care of heritage" has resulted in a somewhat eclectic reconstruction of Somalis' rural pastoral heritage, some overt nods to Somaliland's struggle for independence, and the celebration of love songs from the prewar golden era of Somali music. Physically, the venue was designed to resemble a pastoral encampment, populated by *aqallo*, that is, thatched houses lined with woven grass mats (*caw*) that can be taken apart and reassembled quickly. This portability would have been critical for pastoralists who moved with their animals with the seasons. The thinking here was multifold. This design was, firstly, part of Ismaaciil's original vision, born of the dislocation he experienced upon returning to Somaliland. Echoing this, Mustafe explained that the idea here was "to set up a place where our people coming back from the diaspora can see how our traditional life looked like"—but also to expose those of the local urban postcollapse generation to "how things used to be." Mustafe further explained that their hope was for people "to feel the beauty of the Somali tradition, how life was different without our current modern [brick-and-mortar] houses." They wanted, in short, to make guests "feel that they were all born under an *aqal*." Sahra added a practical take on this choice. As they did not own the land where the venue was built, should they need to relocate, all of the venue's structures could be packed away and transported—much like a nomadic encampment.[7] It is also worth noting that *aqallo* have experienced a kind of resurgence as a result of war: when brick-and-mortar homes were destroyed or abandoned as people fled cities, people made use of their *aqal*-building skillset (see Mire 2007). Such dwellings are still the main constructions in displaced persons camps (like the "State House" IDP settlement, around the corner from the venue), though there the intricate textiles that were historically used have been replaced by whatever materials might be on hand, from old clothes and plastic sheeting to powdered milk tins hammered flat. The *aqallo* at Hiddo Dhawr, however, were not built in such haste: local women were commissioned to weave the *caw* and construct each *aqal*, a process that took months. The *aqallo* stand as a testament to a skillset somewhat refigured by war, and a celebration of a rich pastoral heritage.

In addition to the *aqallo*, the pastoral motif is carried throughout the venue's décor. Like an *aqal*, the walls of both music halls are lined with grass-woven textiles. In the smaller music hall, these textiles are complemented by the vibrant striped, red fabric used to make *garays* dresses, as well as paintings of a variety of pastoral implements like *gorof*, *haan*, and *xeedho* (wooden containers used for churning camel milk, and storing milk and dried meat). Several of these wooden containers also line the stage. In the larger Nimcaan Dheere Hall (named for Sahra's grandfather), tradi-

FIGURE 6.1. One of the *aqal* on the grounds of Hiddo Dhawr where patrons can dine and where artists gather backstage during performance evenings. Photograph by the author.

tional textiles are joined with photographs of pastoral scenes—the Goollis mountain range, a young girl with uncovered hair carrying a lamb, herds of camel crossing the semiarid landscape. Outside, images of "traditional" Somali food, as well as a large mural of the rock paintings found at Laas Geel, are painted on the exterior wall.[8] Two striking images of a man and a woman in "traditional" pastoral dress—the man sporting an Afro hairstyle, the women in a *garays* dress draped across one shoulder, her uncovered hair done up in braids—designate the men's and women's sides. Significantly, these displays might all be described as quintessentially "Somali." Yet for Sahra they were also subtle but intentional nods to certain underrepresented groups, or critiques of certain recent socioreligious trends. *Caw*, for instance, are always made by women, and Sahra was quick to point out that the entire venue was more or less built by women. As a woman whose own family objected to her singing career, in a setting where women's contributions are curtailed in public, showcasing and celebrating women's handiwork was especially important to her. In a Muslim setting that discourages figurative art, the murals on the walls also gave local painters with few opportunities to display their craft a large canvas to showcase their work. And for those who visit, these images serve to remind patrons that there were (are) different ways of looking Somali (ways that would not sit well with Guddida Wanaag Farista iyo Xumaan Reebista). Taking in the images on the bathroom doors, one friend memorably quipped: "We didn't always use to wear these cabaayas and jilbaabs," conservative Saudi-inspired fashions that now dominate everyday womenswear.

The venue's menu and seating arrangements also reflect this pastoral heritage, though here some accommodations have been made to meet the comfort and tastes of guests. As a daytime restaurant, Hiddo Dhawr is one of a few destinations in the city known for serving camel meat and milk and one of the few places you can get *shuuro* (cornmeal porridge). Other "traditional" staples, like *laxoox* and *suuqar* are served throughout the day and in the evenings, joined by more recent additions to Somali cuisine, and staples at most restaurants, like pasta, rice, french fries, chicken, and soft drinks. Somali *shaah* (tea with *xawaash*) remains a popular hot beverage option, though guests can also order *kapuchino*, a drink option that has taken the city by storm since 2014. Originally, the main seating option was stools fashioned from goat hyde (*kambadh*). But in response to complaints of sore backs and buttocks by city dwellers and diaspora returnees not used to such arrangements, some upright chairs and leather couches were later added. The venue's management may want visitors to "feel like they were all born under an *aqal*," but they also want them to be comfortable and come back again.

Significantly, much of the hiddo displayed at Hiddo Dhawr is common to most Somalis, including those in Somalia. And indeed, in the early in-dependence era and into Barre's regime, much of this pastoral hiddo was called upon to shore up ideas of pan-Somalist, clan-transcending national-ism or Soomaalinimo. The postcolonial state, for instance, was often re-ferred to as a she-camel named "Maandeeq," and references to Somalis' pastoral heritage abound in poetry and song from this era (sometimes to the consternation of Somalis whose heritage has little to do with camels, such as those from farming communities or various ancient coastal towns). Making Hiddo Dhawr a place to showcase Somaliland's cultural produc-tions thus also required some very overt nods to Somaliland's nationalist cause. Pastoral motifs are consequently joined by a number of overt na-tionalist symbols. In the center of the main courtyard is a flagpole, featuring both a flag and a 3D map of Somaliland. In Nimcaan Dheere Hall, one wall features a large printed banner of Somaliland's flag, flanked by the flags of over a hundred other nations (some others similarly unrecognized) and the byline "Dimuqraadiyad iyo Dadaal" (Democracy and effort). Even *girgire* pots—used for burning incense over charcoal (a staple in every home)—were reworked in nationalist terms. Lights shaped like *girgire* pots, with

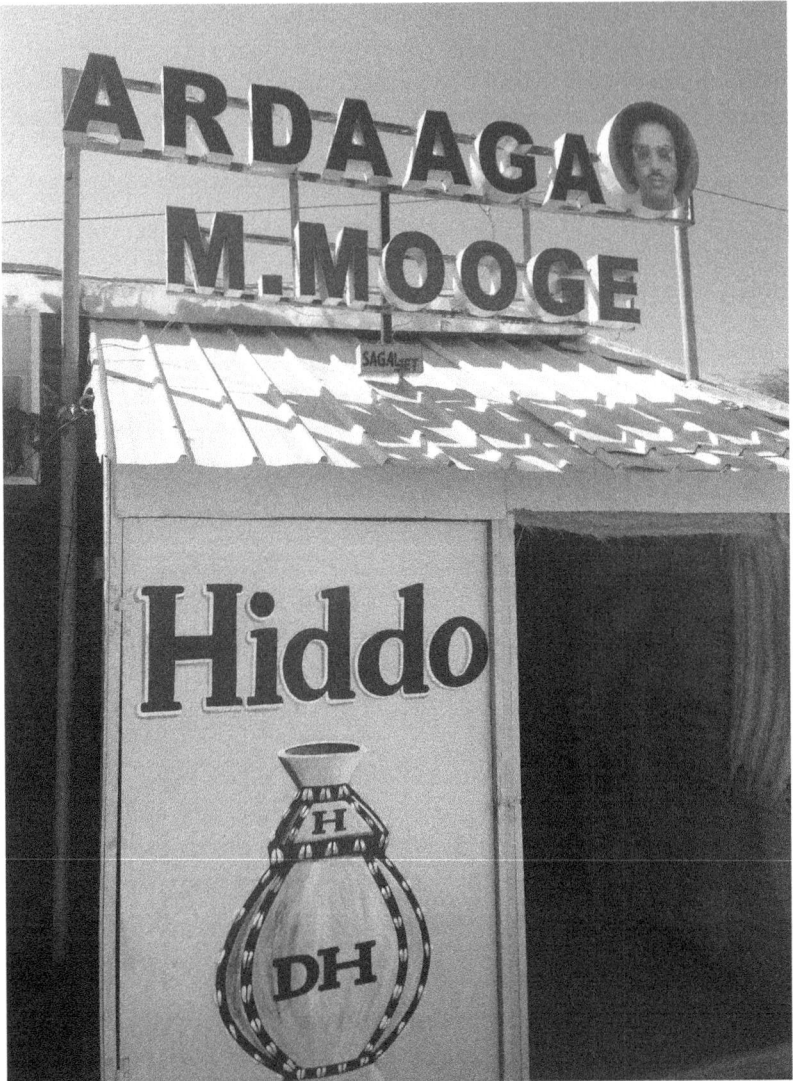

FIGURE 6.2. The entrance to Maxamed Mooge Hall, featuring a photograph of Mooge and the venue's logo: a painted *xeedho* (a wooden storage container). Photograph by the author.

charcoal painted a patriotic red, green, and white, line the main stage. In another nod to the SNM, the smaller hall was named after Maxamed Mooge, a singer-songwriter and SNM fighter who died during the struggle. A banner featuring Mooge's face and lyrics to one of his songs periodically sits near the stage of the smaller hall to remind patrons of the sacrifices made for Somaliland's independence. Joining pastoral images and textiles with nationalist symbols, Ismaaciil and Sahra's initial commitment to celebrating a "unique Somali*land* identity" has materialized in a way that works to instill a sense of nationalist pride, and mark out Somaliland as a distinct nation worthy of recognition.

While music was not part of Ismaaciil's original vision, as soon as Sahra was brought on board, celebrating Somalis' prewar musical heritage also became a central component of the venue's mission. In the context of the venue and the broader sociopolitical environment, there are three noteworthy features of the music that Hiddo Dhawr celebrates. Firstly, in contrast to the otherwise rural and pastoral heritage on display, the music performed at Hiddo Dhawr is of *urban* origins—and this is despite the fact that there are musical genres that would more closely align with the pastoral heritage on display, that is, *hees ciyaareed* (dance songs) and *hees hawleeddo* (work songs). The songs performed at Hiddo Dhawr comprise the songs we have encountered thus far in this book: so-called "old school" songs from the prewar golden era of Somali music, which were largely produced with the support of the socialist government. As we saw in chapter 1, these are songs that, in their time, made claims for greater freedom in matters both public and private and that were infused with the cosmopolitan sounds and sensibilities found in bustling urban centers across the continent in the 1970s. Even as many of these songs strategically used "'tradition' as an oratorical and moral weapon" (Kapteijns 1999, 140), these were songs that stretched social conventions and laid claim to new types of social relations. Described in their time as "modern" (Johnson 1996, Kapteijns 1999), these songs have now been recast as "classic." Sahra suggested that featuring this music was a natural choice, as these songs "transcend time and space," and are "in our genes." Choosing to celebrate this music cannot be delinked from the fact that the war decimated the artistic sphere, and people like Sahra are certainly nostalgic for the thriving music scene of prewar Somaliland, and a time when, as Sahra put it, "people respected artists." The impact of the war can be felt still, in a sense, in the fact that the songs' original instrumentation has been stripped back from the bands of the 1970s/1980s to include only simple drums and the oud.[9] But the effect of presenting this music as "transcending time and space" and "in our genes"—and accompanied by an instrument that has become iconic of Somaliness—has been to naturalize an urban genre of instrumental music as equally "Somali" as, say, camel-herding or gabay poetry. Like the images on the bathroom doors, refiguring these songs as "heritage" represents a claim to include more diverse experiences within the canon of what it means to be (a) Somali(lander). And given the current religious climate in the country, claiming an urban genre of *music* as equally part of Somali hiddo is no small statement.

The second striking feature of the music performed at Hiddo Dhawr is that all of the songs are *love* songs. This, to be sure, is partly a reflection of the overwhelming presence of love as a theme in Somali music. But the decision to only perform love songs was also a political one—or, in Sahra's reckoning an *anti*political one. Sahra herself certainly has a repertoire that includes everything from patriotic anthems to songs that address contemporary social problems, such as *tahriib* or tribalism, not to mention the music of Kooxda Halgan. Sahra was adamant, however, that Hiddo Dhawr is not the place for these songs. For its audiences, Sahra explained, the venue is to be an escape from precisely these things, a place to check divisive politics and other troubles at the door—a place where, as Idiriis told us, you should come "wearing the shirt of love." Sahra put it to me thus: "We live in one of the most restive, conflict-ridden regions. Killing and divisive political games dominate media coverage . . . [and] people become consumed with things like clan and tribalism. . . . People need a break from it. Here, we give them the chance to hear something different." These songs, to be sure, make a whole host of claims about gender relations, marriage, prevailing attitudes about love, and freedom of expression. But as we have seen throughout this book, love is also conceptualized as a kind of radical social leveler that may affect even the most unsuspecting victim, regardless of their clan, political leanings, or socioeconomic position. Even if it is the shared experience of love-*suffering*, "love," Sahra said, "is the only thing that binds people together, with no animosity."

The final pertinent feature of the music at Hiddo Dhawr is that it is always performed live. This is, firstly, a direct response to what Sahra sees as the weaknesses of young artists in Hargeysa and the diaspora. While they are few and far between, when groups like Xidigaha Geeska organize concerts in Hargeysa (or in London, for that matter), their performances are almost always lip-synched to prerecorded tracks. She recognizes, of course, that young artists work in extremely challenging conditions and that instruments are hard to come by (and even harder to learn in the current climate in Somaliland—not least because the city had no stage for twenty-six years). But her hope was that by exposing members of the post-collapse generation to a different musical environment, more young artists might be encouraged to make music in this way; music lovers, too, will have the chance to "feel" anew the music they have listened to for decades. Cabdinaasir's work with FanSan, and the young musicians who now regularly perform at Hiddo Dhawr, suggest she is succeeding in this regard, and the "liveness" of these performances fundamentally shapes the character of the music evenings. This emphasis on live performance, furthermore, also extends to the audience. During the participation section of the evening, early attempts to sing along to prerecorded tracks were quickly quashed. This is a time when you are meant to sing what you feel, to voice your own *run* (truth), even with voices that crack and wander out of tune. Musicians and audience members alike are encouraged to participate in the live voicing of love sentiments, and songs now recast as "heritage" are brought very much to life. Those who cross the venue's threshold are asked, in a sense, to live the songs in the moment, together, to quite powerful effect.

Taken together, the hiddo that is cared for and celebrated at Hiddo Dhawr presents a multifaceted argument about Somali(lander)ness, both past and present—one rooted, in part, in a nostalgia for "a different Somaliland," yet also one that makes a number of claims about who belongs in Somaliland today. The poetic force and effect of this argument, however, is most fully felt during the performance evenings. During these evenings, the heritage on display works alongside the live performance of love songs to open space for patrons to "try on" different ways of being, to dwell in a kind of mutual vulnerability. Let us now take a look (and listen) at how patrons—including me—typically experience these evenings unfold.

Performing Love, Enacting Intimacy

Thursday evenings in Hargeysa are a special time. The midday *duhur* prayers mark the unofficial beginning of the weekend. Streets become nearly impassable, as cars queue at qaad stalls to purchase supplies for chewing sessions that will undoubtedly stretch into the early hours of Friday. Majlisyo across the city swell beyond capacity. Buses fill with university students and commuters, relieved and ready for a day off. As the sun sets, restaurants and teashops fill up with groups of friends, eager to celebrate the week's end. And, since August 2014, a lucky group of men and women, young and old, make their way to Hiddo Dhawr for an evening of food, friends, and musical entertainment. Across the city, men and women pile into used white cars, taxis, and the occasional black SUV to make their way to the "Bebsi" area. From about 9 p.m. onward, lines of vehicles can be backed up to the bridge that joins the city's two halves, before snaking down an inconspicuous dark and dusty road. Security guards ask drivers to roll down windows and pop the trunk for security checks, before cars full of boisterous passengers maneuver into the haphazard parking lot that wraps around the venue's outer concrete wall. Through one more security queue, eager night-goers finally join the line inside to collect their prebooked tickets.

The manager flips effortlessly between his paper ledger and phone, matching reservation names with incoming Zaad (mobile-money) payments before directing patrons toward their seats.

On Fridays and summertime Mondays, when the venue hosts smaller music evenings, crowds are directed toward Maxamed Mooge Hall. But on Thursdays, the most popular night, patrons make their way to the larger Nimcaan Dheere Hall. The price of entry—which includes dinner and three or more hours of entertainment—means that audience members trend toward Hargeysa's more affluent. But even still, a fairly broad cross-section of Somalilanders, from students to retirees, pass through the venue's doors: groups of middle-aged women celebrating birthdays and weddings (sometimes with children and home-baked sweets in tow); politicians and businessmen entertaining potential partners; diaspora men and women on holiday for the summer, as well as more permanent diaspora returnees; groups of colleagues from local NGOs, with the occasional foreign guest; young couples out for a night of entertainment or an inconspicuous date; and groups of friends of more modest means, who have saved for a rare and special night out or are being treated by more affluent friends. As men are more likely to spend their evenings chewing, and this is one of the few places that women can come to enjoy a night out—suitable even for bringing teenage daughters and younger children—women often outnumber men, in sharp contrast to other hotels and restaurants.

While in daily interactions—in business, politics, education, and on the street—men and women are frequently segregated, at Hiddo Dhawr they mingle freely, laughing and joking with each other as they find their seats. Furtive eyes glance around to see who has arrived with whom and who is wearing what. The *cabaaya* and *jilbaab* that dominate women's streetwear are traded in for vibrantly patterned *dirac*—a dress worn at weddings and special events and here sometimes described as "traditional" attire. Groups of fashionably late women, sometimes in matching outfits, trickle in throughout the evening, delayed by the extra care taken to prepare themselves for a night out. Scarves are done up ornately to accent carefully chosen *dirac*—and even sometimes slip off onto women's shoulders to reveal carefully considered hairstyles. Indeed, young women friends explained to me that Hiddo Dhawr is the one place in town where you can, if you so choose, quite literally let your hair down (often to the consternation of the management, who are concerned with upholding Hiddo Dhawr's reputation). My friend Huda explained her choice of attire like this: "My *dirac* is simple. I love when I wear *dirac*, and I put my scarf like this," miming how she drapes her scarf over her shoulder, rather than using it to cover her hair. "I don't like to cover my hair when I'm here because I want to feel like a normal person. I don't care if people don't like it, it's my personality. I say 'this is my life.' It's better to have a good personality that people can see, and not be concerned about hiding something." While Huda's pious mother was at first opposed to letting her daughter go dressed like this to a music venue, she reminded her mother that "once upon a time they [women of her mother's generation] used to dress like this, so why are they hating it today? How many stages did you go to once upon a time?" She started to sing a song frequently performed at Hiddo Dhawr; her mother conceded that she had been at the concert where the song was first performed and that as a young woman herself she had enjoyed dressing up and going to such events. Assured that Hiddo Dhawr was a venue committed to preserving the "heritage" she herself had enjoyed, she consented to her daughter's nights out.

As the clock approaches 10 p.m., the anticipatory hum of the crowd swells as the artists take the stage, and the manager or one of the musicians swoops in to welcome guests, encouraging them to have a good time but informing them of the house rules: taking photos and videos of the musicians on stage is fine—and in fact Sahra herself often live streams performances on Facebook to hundreds of viewers—but photographing any guests who may make their way to the stage is strictly prohibited. This is meant to be a space where patrons should feel free to join in: to sing or dance, without the possible discomfort that documentation of such activities may bring (though taking selfies throughout the evening and posting them to Facebook is acceptable and even encouraged). And when the music begins, they move, clap, and sing along. While there is a hierarchy of sorts in the seating arrangement, with the coveted leather seats near the stage saved for politicians, business leaders, and special guests, when the music plays these distinctions fade. As one friend quipped, on finding himself seated near the president of the university where he was studying, "People can't help but move to the music together." The venue's house musicians take turns at the mic, oud and drums, performing classics by the giants of prewar Somali music we are well acquainted with by now—Cumar Dhuule, Khadra Daahir, Axmed Gacayte, Magool, Sahra Axmed, Maxamed Saleeban Tubeec, and others. The odd "lady musician from Canada" is also known to occasionally take the stage. Even though many in the audience were born decades after these songs were first sung, audience members energetically sing along or debate the real-world origins behind the songs. When taken by the music, guests join the artists on stage, dancing alongside them, patting them on the head, or showing solidarity with the sentiments in the songs by showering the artists with Somaliland shillings.

As patrons take in the music and sup on *shuuro*, *laxoox*, and *suqaar* or

FIGURE 6.3. Sahra Halgan (singing), Cabdinaasir Macallin Caydiid (oud), and Abokor Buulo-Xuubay (drums) perform in Maxamed Mooge Hall. Various pastoral implements (*haan, gorof, xeedho*) decorate the stage and are also represented on the walls. Photograph by the author.

french fries, seated on *kambadh* (or leather sofas) and surrounded by images of a rural past and contemporary patriotism, the energy in the room is palpable. Patrons both young and old credit the mood in this space to the unique "heritage" on display and the energy of the performers, singing love songs and playing live on stage. But how the venue is experienced depends on people's previous exposure to the hiddo on show. For those of Sahra's generation and older, Sahra suggested to me that the venue provides a kind of "nostalgia therapy." It does so by serving as a poignant reminder of "a different Somaliland"—a Somaliland with a flourishing arts scene, where men and women were freer to interact and dress as they please—and by providing patrons with the musical opportunities to relive joyous experiences from their youth. For instance, one friend in his fifties, Nuuradiin, explained that the music "takes you back" and "brings you the good things you know." Another middle-aged friend, Mukhtar, similarly explained that the "change of environment" that Hiddo Dhawr provides—a change that reminds him of a time when "singing together was normal"—helps "you to feel a bit of joy and refresh yourself."

For the venue's younger patrons who did not experience this music in real time, one patron suggested that going to Hiddo Dhawr is like attending a "university for the arts and culture": it exposes guests of the postcollapse generation to "a bit of a taste" of how Somali music used to be. And for the young patrons I met, this "taste" provides refreshment and relief, while also working to instill a sense of pride and a kind of direction to their ideas about Somaliland. One young patron, for example, said that coming to Hiddo Dhawr, "makes you feel that you are Somali." Huda, similarly, explained that Hiddo Dhawr is a place that "makes you feel alive, to feel your own culture, to know about a lot of things [which] teaches you day by day how you are different." Her friend Samira added that coming to Hiddo Dhawr is like being "in a different world," and the houses, the food, and the music on display "make you feel unique that you have your own Somali culture." Hanad put it this way: "Hiddo Dhawr . . . reminds the people of the old days, the materials, the food, and the oud. My generation, we forgot this system, but Hiddo Dhawr is teaching us how things used to be . . . you feel how things were, and you compare the situation to these new decades, and you think about where you are going in the future." His friend Cabdisalaan concurred: "If you know your culture, and how your people lived [before], [you] will know [who you] are now."

These comments make clear that Hiddo Dhawr's mission of heritage preservation is not lost on audiences. Yet rather than simply providing a somewhat romanticized and backward-looking retrospective, the comments above suggest that Hiddo Dhawr shapes not only people's ideas about Somaliland's past but also the direction the country is headed. This is the result of two related processes. One has to do with the sense of "Somaliness" that the venue works to instill in patrons of various generations. Writing about similar processes in Kenya, Nyairo (2005) has highlighted how such "romanticized returns" may "work as symbolic gestures whose purpose is providing the idioms and metaphors for confronting the past, thus becoming valuable tools in negotiating the political and even cultural impasse of the present" (in Ogude 2012, 162). Ogude, also writing about the Kenyan context, refers to this as a kind of "native cosmopolitanism" that is often deployed in the face of "an overwhelming global mass culture" (2012, 162)—and, in the Somaliland context I would also add, in the shadow of a war that radically disrupted Somalilanders' social, political, and artistic life. Patrons both young and old are energized by the physical and aural reminders Hiddo Dhawr provides of "Somali(lander)ness." This kind of retrospective, in turn, has what Brockmeier (2009, 228) refers to as a "subjunctivizing" force to it: in being reminded of this past, Hiddo Dhawr works to destabilize ideas of what Somaliland is and might yet be. Secondly and furthermore, this return-to-heritage-cum-native cosmopolitanism also seems to liberate audience members, in a way, to "try on" different ways of being in the present. Here again this is similar to what Ogude finds of the rise in popularity of "ethnic" theme nights in Nairobi's night clubs, where "the recourse to 'traditional' forms of music [works] to free the audience of those inhibitions of the open expression of pleasure" (2012, 157).

That Hiddo Dhawr provides more than just a retrospective on "Somali heritage" becomes especially clear during the audience participation section of the evenings. At around 11:30, the artists take a break, and the energy of the audience is channeled into a raucous joke-telling and sing-along session. For many attendees, the opportunity to sing and to listen to others sing in this setting is the most anticipated part of the evening—a time to really let loose, be yourself, and to feel with others. As Nuuradiin explained to me: "The aura of the place, the culture, the huts, the art side of it, the traditional artifacts displayed there and . . . when you play that music. . . . Actually, it's freedom. [You] can let it go. Let it loose. Nobody will judge you, you can sing your own song, you can be yourself." And this is precisely what happens when a large orange microphone is circulated through the audience. Those who wish (or are cajoled) take the opportunity to sing their favorite songs, or tell stories and jokes, in what Sahra described as a large group therapy session. While some shy away, others enthusiastically volunteer, eager to use this opportunity to get thoughts and feelings of love off their chests, nostalgically reminisce about earlier times, or simply to have fun and revel in the freedom to express themselves. Musical talent is not a prerequisite. Shaky voices that sing out of tune and forget the words are encouraged with clapping and laughter, and when others recognize the melody many more begin to sing along. What is important is that individuals sing *in their own voice* and use the time to express what they are feeling in the moment—remember that what makes a voice "good" in this context has long been linked to the perceived authenticity of emotion carried therein. As one young friend, Khaliil, explained, "This is the time when you can see the real emotions of the people who are there." As such, attempts in the venue's early days by audience members to sing along to prerecorded music were met with boos and are no longer welcome, suggesting that Sahra's mission of reintroducing an appreciation for live performance may be succeeding *and* that there is an expectation of authenticity and vulnerability in these performances. But I have seen all manner of other live participation encouraged, and special affordances even made to support those who are shy to sing. This was poignantly illustrated one night by Sahra's gentle encouragement of a women dressed in a pale pink jilbaab (common as streetwear, but almost never seen here) who loved to sing but was extremely shy; for modesty's sake, she performed with her back to the audience, to great applause.

What do people sing about? And what does this singing accomplish? As Sahra suggested, for those of her generation there is a clear element of "nostalgia therapy" in this singing: singing allows participants to return to earlier, happier, simpler times. Music, Sahra explained to me, is kind of like perfume—its sounds, like smell, work to trigger memories, to transport you to a different time and place (an observation well supported in literature on music and memory). Middle-aged men and women, both local and from the diaspora, revel in the opportunity to sing songs from their youth and to relive past love experiences. For others, including the venue's younger patrons with their own current love anxieties and aspirations, this is a particularly good time to get feelings and emotions of love off their chest. Most people, after all, are "victims of love" in one way or another, and I was told that singing in this setting is a good way to relieve the "psychological tension" you may feel. Hanad, for instance, explained that even though he does not like singing in public, and in fact abandoned dreams of being an artist because he thinks music might be xaaraan, at Hiddo Dhawr things are different. As we saw in chapter 4, listening to love songs almost inevitably makes you think about your own love history, your current challenges, and your future love journey. And watching performers sing about love *live*, Hanad explained, is "more touching" than listening to music at home because you can "read the lines on the face of the singer, and it touches [you]." This, in turn, opens space to let out bottled-up emotions and in so doing to find relief. Voicing your love feelings in song in front of others works as a kind of cure for whatever may be bothering you—echoing the suggestion, first made to me by Abokor Buulo-Xuubay (the drummer), that the venue is best described as Hargeysa's frustration hospital. Whereas listening to love songs privately may help you to feel like you are not alone in your love-suffering, singing and listening to others sing in this space allows you to hear and feel *and see* that you are not alone. Hiddo Dhawr, in short, provides a space where audience members become aural and visual witnesses to each other's love-pains and aspirations. It is a place to dwell defenseless in the "experiential richness of [one's] deepest emotional vulnerability" (Gioia 2015, xii). A place where the intimate social relations distilled in and opened by love songs are put on full display, and, if only fleetingly, shared. A place for dareen-wadaag (feeling-sharing)—for intimate belonging.

While many of the songs voiced in this space are about love-suffering, perhaps precisely because love in the real world is constrained by the very realities it has the possibility to transcend—particularly clan and socioeco-nomic status—"hearing something different," as Sahra put it, also provides audience members fodder not only to express their love woes but to imag-ine and fantasize about idealistic love futures. Love is, after all, a *future*-oriented emotion: it "project[s] into the future and infuse[s] . . . subjects with hope that their dreams of fulfilment will come to pass" (Fair 2009, 79). In pursuit of these love futures, the audience participation section is also one of the very rare physical spaces where I have witnessed the pub-lic expression of affection for another—a place where patrons might try to impress in serenade the person they are trying to woo. I was also told that Hiddo Dhawr is the best place in town to bring a date. While often discreet in their coupling, and likely to deny that what they are doing is "dating" (unless they are already married), couples might be seen exchang-ing flirtatious glances or stepping out for some private conversation in one of the *aqallo*. Young friends told me that there is nothing quite like sitting in an *aqal* with the person you love, with the love songs audible in the background serving as fodder to talk about your own love experiences and possible love futures. And for extra-special occasions or for those who want more privacy, at other times during the week a private performance by Sahra and some of the other musicians can be arranged (according to Huda, this makes for "the best date ever!") As Hanad explained, there are not many places in Hargeysa to take a girl, but Hiddo Dhawr is the best one "because you are just coming together, you are listening to music, you are sharing your stories, and everything is about your love." Another young patron similarly explained that at Hiddo Dhawr you cannot help but reflect on your own love journey—both painful experiences in the past, as well as your "love futures that might be coming up."

Back inside, when the audience has sufficiently vented their feelings for the evening, the musicians retake the stage for the second half. When the music begins again, the audience shows no signs of tiring, even as eve-ning fades into the early hours of the morning. Indeed, the energy seems to grow the longer the night wears on. During my main research period, more people would often even specifically arrive at this point to see Cab-dinaasir, who normally played the second set and in whose skillful hands the oud was dynamically brought to life. And while Cabdinaasir's absence is certainly deeply felt, there is still a fluidity and familiarity among the mu-sicians who continue to perform: in the subtle nods and smiles between artists, the seamless adjustments to the mood of the evening and to the en-ergy of the crowd. And like the best singers before her, Sahra adeptly car-ries in her voice and demeanor the experiences and emotions of the songs, whether they are about her or not. As she has told us elsewhere, "When you are singing, if you are not feeling it, you cannot transmit [the emotion] to the audience." Audience members concur that Sahra's ability to convey the emotion of the song—both in the painful quivering of her voice and in her bodily comportment and facial expressions—make her a particularly compelling performer to watch. In a nod to the musical lineage the venue endeavors to continue, Sahra frequently closes the evening by singing a short ditty composed by Rashiid Bullo for Radio Hargeysa to mark the end of an evening's program, which was also later sung on Radio Halgan. On some evenings Sahra replaces "Hargeysa" with Hiddo Dhawr: "Tani waa Hiddo Dhawr [originally "Hargeysa"] / Hirarka gabaan / Idin kala had-laysee / Habeen wanaagsan" (This is Hiddo Dhawr [originally Hargeysa], speaking to you from the short waves, good night).

When the music finally comes to an end in the early hours of the morning, guests are frequently reluctant to return to their cars, preferring to dwell in the energy and escape the evening has provided by continuing to chat and joke with each other in the venue's courtyard. By this point the mood is usually one not only of excitement but also of relaxation, as if those in attendance have let out a collective sigh of relief at the end of the work week. As I was told time and again, Hiddo Dhawr is the best place to relax and recharge: a place where you might find relief in the rhythm and sound of the oud and in listening to and singing love songs in the company of others; a place to come and clear your head of worries. Whether tired from housework, lonely and worried about a friend who has left on *tahriib*, anxious about one's own love life, or stressed about employment prospects, Hiddo Dhawr is a place that provides audience members with the opportunity to leave these worries behind. Huda explained it like this: "When everyone is singing, there is a positive energy everywhere, [there is] nowhere to be negative or sad. When you go to Hiddo Dhawr you will be happy, and this happiness carries you through the next week." Or, as Hanad told us at the outset of this book: "When you listen to the oud, by the time the evening comes to an end you feel repaired." Hiddo Dhawr is, after all, a place like no other in Hargeysa. A place where men and women can gather, freed for an evening not only from their personal worries but also from the gendered and socioeconomic strictures of daily life, and to listen and express emotions that are otherwise taboo. A place for dareen-wadaag, where it is all right—indeed, expected—to be happy, to have fun, to laugh, to dance, and to sing. As it indexes various socioeconomic contestations and performs alongside diverse heritage references, the voice of love live on stage calls into being an audience not only of ears but also of bodies—of social relations enacted in a particular time and place—where different ways of moving, dressing, singing, interacting, and expressing oneself are made possible.

Of Audiences and Alternative Publics

As the first live music venue to operate in Somaliland in over a quarter century, Hiddo Dhawr represents a particularly compelling entry into thinking about the politics—and the intimate world-building potential—of staging love (songs) in contemporary Hargeysa. The story of its founding by a pair of diaspora returnees indexes various sociopolitical-religious dynamics and contestations that define Hargeysa, a city where staging love songs was arguably only made possible as part of a larger project of heritage preservation spearheaded by an SNM singer-veteran. But I hope to have also shown that just as Hiddo Dhawr *reflects* something of Somaliland's sociopolitical climate, it also says something *about and to* the city it serves. In its commitment to heritage preservation and the live performance of prewar love songs, Hiddo Dhawr makes a "subjunctivizing" claim about what Somaliland could (or, in the founders' vision, *should*) be: a place where artists are respected, where war-induced ruptures with the past are repaired, and where certain sociopolitical cleavages and cultural and gendered prohibitions might be transformed. And in being mutually present to the performance of love songs in a space that also celebrates Somaliland's heritage, participants are freed to stretch social conventions, to "try on" different ways of being. Hiddo Dhawr is also a place, and crucially so, where the intimate potential of love songs is put on full display and where, for an evening at least, patrons may put on "the shirt of love": a shirt that allows the temporary suspension of daily troubles and divisions in favor of dwelling in shared vulnerability, a shared desire to belong.

In sharing some of my early findings about Hiddo Dhawr with others, I have been pushed on multiple occasions to consider how the venue may represent a "counterpublic" that is infused with elements of what Bakhtin referred to as the "carnival"—that is, a space characterized by the "free and familiar contact among people" (1984, 123), where certain hierarchies and prohibitions are suspended and the social order is inverted. I can see where such suggestions come from. Hiddo Dhawr does, on the one hand, provide a space where otherwise prohibited modes of interaction and expression are made possible. Hiddo Dhawr also seems to work as a kind of "dress rehearsal for better times," as Storey (1997, 130) conceives of the "carnival." And yet I remain convinced that the public hailed into

being by Hiddo Dhawr is *not* a "counterpublic," at least not in the way that
Warner defines the term: a public comprising a subaltern group, which
is "constituted through a conflictual relation to the dominant public . . .
[and] maintains an awareness of its subordinate status" (2002, 423–24).
While the venue certainly provides space to stretch accepted social norms,
it does so through recourse to heritage preservation and the *anti*politics
of love songs. As I have shown, the venue has only managed to establish
itself because of the mainstream sociopolitical capital of its founder—not
any subordinate status. The venue's patrons and musicians, furthermore,
would also not describe this space as "carnivalesque" or countercultural—
they are in fact committed to the opposite. Hiddo Dhawr may be a kind
of "dress rehearsal for better times," but it is also an encore performance
or reunion tour of sorts, made possible because of the multidirectional
retrospective-subjective-prospective fantasies about "Somali(lander)ness"
that it enables. As Barber highlights, the "tension between . . . continuity
and a deliberate, conscious creation of qualitatively new forms is one which
is never finally resolvable or determinable"; rather, "it is always changing
and taking different shapes in different historical, political, and economic
circumstances" (1987, 32). The same could be said, I would add, for the
work of intimacy, especially the kinds of intimacy that love songs enable.
What Hiddo Dhawr offers us is not an example of counterpublic making
but rather a glimpse into the complex ways that both forms of popular culture and intimacy "create power to resist power" (Fabian 1998, 69). And
this work is, I think, fundamentally rooted in love songs' own paradoxical
relationship to power: the challenge love songs inevitably present to the
status quo, yet their simultaneous ability to open space for vulnerability
and the "renunciation of power" (Gioia 2015, xi). What forms of popular
culture and intimacy say and do, and the line they walk between resistance
and conciliation, refusal and incorporation (cf. Dias 2012, 317), always depends on the historical moment in which they take form and the conditions
in which they are (re)animated (or envocalized).

I have, of course, only scratched the surface of the role Hiddo Dhawr and
the live staging of love songs are playing in the reshaping of postwar public
space in Somaliland. This is a story still in the making. As Barber (1987, 4)
reminds us, popular arts do not simply "reflect an already-constituted con-
sciousness" but may reveal a critique that is not yet fully formed. Perhaps it
would be apt to conclude that, as has always been the case for Somali audiences of the oral arts, *qofba meeshii bugtaa isagay belbeshaa*—each person
takes it to where the wound burns. The work of love songs, we might say,
depends very much on what their audiences need them to perform. It is
Hiddo Dhawr's audiences, the mingling of their voices with those of the

broader public(s) to which they belong, and the memories of all the other voices recalled in this mutual act of envocalization, that will ultimately be responsible for interpreting and reinterpreting, retrospectively redefining, and presently reimagining how love songs will continue to shape the contested everyday fabric of a nation unfolding.

Conclusion

Songs refer to aftermaths and returns, welcomes and farewells. Or to put it another way; songs are sung to an absence. Absence is what inspired them and it's what they address. At the same time (and the phrase "at the same time" takes on special meaning here) in the sharing of the song the absence is also shared and so becomes less acute, less solitary, less silent. And this "reduction" of the original absence during the sharing of the singing, or even during the memory of such singing, is collectively experienced as something triumphant. Sometimes a mild triumph, often a covert one. "I could wrap myself," said Johnny Cash, "in the warm cocoon of a song and go anywhere; I was invincible."

John Berger, *Confabulations*

Whatever you find me writing against, what I am surely writing for is the generativity of sound and complexity of intervocality. "It's stories 'all the way down.'"

Steven Feld, in an interview about *Jazz Cosmopolitanism in Accra*[1]

A week or so before my longest research trip to Hargeysa came to an end, I had a memorable if somewhat perplexing exchange with Khadra Daahir. As had become our Thursday routine, we had whiled away the afternoon chewing and chatting and, on this occasion, flipping through a book of song lyrics—an activity that had opened into stories and amusing corrections to the information that the amateur music enthusiast who had compiled the book had provided. While discussing one particularly painful calaacal, I turned to Khadra and simply asked: "What does calaacal feel like?" She looked at me, rather confused, and responded: "But Christina, haven't you ever been in love?" Then, "don't you love this man?" she demanded, referring to my partner, who was a frequent topic of conversation and there with us that afternoon. I responded, equally confused, in the affirmative. "Then how can you not know what calaacal feels like?" she rejoined. "Haven't you felt this pain before?" I hesitated momentarily, then explained that yes, perhaps there is sometimes pain involved in love.

I have had painful breakups. And when I am away from my partner, I miss him. Something pulls in the stomach. Something aches in the chest. "It's like that times a thousand," Khadra responded wistfully. Then, more somberly, and genuinely concerned for my well-being, she added: "Christina, I hope that one day you experience this love. I wish you could know this suffering too."

While I was by this point quite familiar with the near-synonymous equation of love with suffering in this setting, I was perplexed. I was not surprised that Khadra presumed my own experiences of love would mean I too would know the feeling of calaacal. Yet I was confused by her final pronouncement, and particularly by the genuine concern with which she wished (love) suffering upon me. Having herself experienced the depths of love's hurt, why did she hope this for me? In sounding the pains of unrequited love, does a calaacal not represent a kind of auditory demand that one's love prospects could be otherwise? Why would my friend, my surrogate mother (of love), not be happy for me and a relationship that brings contentment rather than suffering—the kind of relationship that love-sufferers from Cilmi onward seem to wish for themselves? Why wish pain on me? For the remainder of the afternoon, these questions percolated—and somewhat uncomfortably so. These questions continued to challenge me as I returned to the UK to wade through mountains of ethnographic material and then put pen to paper (or fingers to keyboard) in order to write this book. As I reach my conclusion, I am still unsure if I understand Khadra's suffering well-wishes. Yet reverberating through this exposition on the lives of love songs in motion, her statement takes on unexpected tones, both in relation to the work of love songs and the work of representing the voices that animate them in this book. I will return to these sometimes-discordant reverberations below. Let us first take stock, however, of the love song journey we have been on thus far.

In this book, I have tracked love songs as they move and are moved across and through Hargeysa's contemporary soundscapes, animated by an ever-expanding number of voices along the way. In a setting where "Afropessimist" narratives of war, piracy, famine, and refugees usually captivate media headlines and guide research agendas, exploring love songs in this way has served as a particularly compelling entry into thinking about what it means to live and love in an unrecognized postwar polity. Yet drawing on work in the anthropology of African popular culture, and in contrast to most other work on Somali oral poetry, I have argued for approaching love songs not simply as texts to be collected or as windows into other facets of sociopolitical life (though they offer us such insights in droves) but as "the terrain to be studied" (Barber 2007b, 5). This book is, then, an ode of sorts to the value and limitless potential of placing a form of popular expression at the center of ethnography inquiry.

Anchored in a dynamic understanding of genre, song-as-text, and the concept of envocalization, I have provided an ethnographic account of love songs *in motion*, highlighting the ways that love songs are continually made (intimate), affecting and being affected by the voices and ears they meet along the way. Importantly, we have seen envocalization to be about much more than weaving together words to outlast the here and now. Rather, it is a dynamic and ongoing process that requires the continual social and affective labor of myriad contributors. We have seen this to include the technical, emotional, and social work of poets, melody-writers, singers, and musicians who fix, sound, and perform love sentiments with words, melody, and voice; the work of music lovers who are intimately involved in making the voices of their favorite singers and who put songs to work in their own intimate lives; the surprisingly intimate work of musicians who learn to sound love, with and through the voices of others; and the creative behind-the-scenes work required to stage love songs in contested urban terrain. We have also seen this to include the labor of songs themselves, which work to articulate otherwise unsayable sentiments, as "container[s] of feeling" (DeNora 2000, 740) that help individuals make sense of their own love lives, as sites around which private and public memories, longings, and aspirations congeal, as articulations of belonging in contested postwar terrain—and to open space for intimacy wherever they travel. I have thus argued for an approach that holds together the human work by which texts are continually envocalized and made to "stick," as well as the affective and world-building labor that "sticky" genres themselves seem to perform. I hope to have shown the immense potential of approaching a genre *in motion*—that is, as a form of action best understood as constantly emerging from and in turn reshaping the lives of those who animate it.

Approaching love songs *in motion*, I have explored what love songs *are*, as well as what they *do* as they come into the world and are listened to, sounded, performed, and consumed. In an immediate sense, throughout this book we have seen love songs to be affectively charged textual-sonic objects that convey often otherwise inarticulable sentiments of love, which are conceived to come from "deep, deep within the soul" of those who give them voice. Yet one consequence of approaching love songs as dynamic, emergent, and always in motion is the realization that the being and doing of love songs cannot be easily disentangled. Songs are, after all, in Born's (2005, 7) formulation, "the paradigmatic multiply-mediated, immaterial and material, fluid quasi-object, in which subjects and objects collide and intermingle"—or "assemblages" that inflect existing social relations, produce new ones, and are always entangled in broader institutional and cultural forces (cf. Stokes 2010, 6). Love songs emerge from and represent intimate aspirations and experiences, very often of love-suffering. Yet as they articulate these experiences, they are also a distillation and enactment of the aspiration that love could be otherwise: in their original multivocal production and the stories they precipitate and that circulate with them, in the work they do in individuals' intimate lives, in the processes by which they are sounded, and in the spaces in which they are performed. Love songs, we might say, do what they are and are what they do.

As an ethnographic account of a *voiced* art form that is kept in motion by an ever-expanding number of voices, this book has also provided a reflection on "the voice"—as an embodied, sonic phenomenon, as a medium of communication, and as a marker of subjectivity. I have suggested that love songs' intimacy-opening power rests on what first appears to be a paradox. On the one hand, love songs work because the voice that gives them breath is conceived as providing unmediated access to the innermost sentiments of a love-suffering individual. The voice here works as an "iconic index" (Harkness 2015, 575), conveying emotion in sound and pointing toward a flesh-and-blood person who has personally suffered from love. Conceived as God-given, natural, and the possession of a unique love-suffering individual, it is the voice that is able to at once move listeners to "feel what [others] feel" and assure them that they are not alone in the emotional universe. The affective power of love songs rests squarely in a vocal ideology that figures the voice as providing "access to a 'pure interiority' linked with subjective self-presence" (Sterne 2003, 15) and that sets hees jacayl apart from other genres of orature and speech.

At the same time, however, we have seen that the voice is never produced in isolation and never simply the product or possession of a single individual: from the collaboration that gives birth to songs, to their (re)animation in circulation by myriad other voices, to the musicians who work together to bring live sound to songs, love songs are multivocal through and through. Multivocality is, after all, "a condition endemic to social existence" (Keane 2010, 77). Yet by attending to specific acts of envocalization, I have also shown this multivocality to take myriad forms. These forms, critically, extend our understanding of what multivocality may look—or sound—like. As has been documented elsewhere, multivocality might include the ordering of multiple perspectives or voices into a single narrative account (Englund 2015, 2018, Hill 1995), or it may be used to describe a democratic (possibly utopic) space in which multiple voices are audible.

But multivocality can also take other forms and encompass shifting voicing (and listening) arrangements, even as they articulate with a specific ideology of voice. In the first instance, songs are multivocal in the contribution of words, melody, sound and breath that work together to convey the "truth" of a love(-suffering) experience in a *singular* voice (in both a sonic and social sense). Songs are similarly multivocal in any given performance, where human and instrumental voices work together to enable the expression of love. Yet we have also seen the ears and voices of listeners to be critical to the snowballing "stickiness" of the genre as it moves across time and space. Songs are sounded, after all, in order to be heard and do what they do in part because they may be taken up by others, discussed, debated, constantly reimbued with new meaning, evoked, and refigured in others' intimate lives. We saw this to be the case in the way that fans *talk* about the voices of their favorite singers: talk that is animated by the perceived authenticity of a singer's voice yet in turn also works to make this voice ever more intimate and real. We also saw this to be the case in the way that fans listen to and revoice songs in their own intimate lives: where songs, in a sense, model the possibility of feeling-sharing to listeners and help listeners make sense of love in their own lives. Here we have a form of multivocality that is rooted in the "dialogic and embodied qualities of speaking and hearing" and that underscores "the link between felt audition of one's own voice, and the cumulatively embodied experience of aural resonance and meaning" (Feld 1998, 471).[2] This voicing arrangement adds a limitless time horizon to songs' multivocality, as well as an always intimately personal and multiply resonant dynamic to the way in which a song may be heard and (re)voiced in a given time and place. Taken together, I have highlighted that the multidimensional multivocal practices of voicing by which songs are envocalized does not work against an aesthetics that privileges singing from the heart, but are in fact critical to the way in which the voice is made intimate. In short, I have argued that the voice is made intimate by its very multivocal sociality.

This observation, importantly, does not undermine the notion that the voice may be the unique possession of an individual nor does it challenge the fundamentally multivocal nature of subjectivity and social life. Rather, I hope to have shown the value of simultaneously attending to an ideology of voice and practices of voicing that may at first appear to contradict each other. Exploring the processes by which something is made multivocal and how these processes intersect with specific ideologies of voice has the potential to further our understandings of the semiotic density of the voice. And here I have put forward the concept of envocalization as a theoretical and methodological tool that may assist analyses of musical genres and forms of speech. In the first instance, en*vocal*ization draws attention to the distinct possibilities and affordances of texts that are *sounded* or *vocalized*. And by centering the inseparability of talk and text as *voiced* phenomenon, envocalization reclaims the analyses of processes of entextualization and recontextualization from a trend toward the metaphoric. I have also specifically demonstrated that attending to processes of envocalization works to reveal how practices of voicing interact with different ideologies of voice. This approach surely has implications beyond how we think of love songs and could guide inquiry into how different kinds of voices gain different kinds of power, how ideologies of voice interact with different practices of voicing in specific contexts, and how these ideologies and practices are themselves both enabled and constrained by the broader "politics of voice" at work in a given setting. In Somaliland, such observations have clear implications for how we might think about voices in the male-dominated political realm. This is an arena where a multitude of voices have different kinds of power, where women do not always "speak" but are certainly not silent, and where voices gain power in ways that have sometimes confounded international observers—for example, through voting processes where the idea of a "secret" (and silent) ballot is paid little more than lip-service (see Pegg and Walls 2018). Indeed, voting is also often quite literally an act of "voicing," linguistically (to vote = *u codee*) and sonically: as an election observer in 2017 I regularly witnessed voters enter polling stations and vocally declare their choice. Beyond Somaliland, given the voice's status as a marker of subjectivity—and, as Kunreuther (2014, 22–23) puts it, "the medium that generates social meanings and social positions, or all that is classically thought of in anthropology as 'culture'"—such observations have implications for how we think of the variety of mediating practices by which persons and social worlds are made. By what semiotic ideologies (of voice or otherwise) and everyday practices of interaction is intimacy or authority—or any other number of social or political phenomena—achieved elsewhere? How might ideas of personhood be revised to account for the interplay of ideas/ideologies of individuality and relationality and processes of becoming that do not always sit easily together?

Finally, as an exposition on the work of love songs, and the ideologies of voice and practices of voicing by which songs gain their affective power, this book has also provided a reflection on the work and nature of intimacy. Indeed, while what songs are and do is always in flux, I have argued that in contemporary Hargeysa, the primary work of love songs is the distillation, creation, mediation, and facilitation of uniquely *intimate* social relations. In a setting where music-making is contested, where expressions of love are taboo, and where various socioeconomic and clan cleavages define every-day interactions, these are intimate relations that transcend what otherwise might divide and that are predicated on a form of dareen-wadaag (feeling-sharing) that is made manifest through the voice. Yet there remains an un-resolved tension, I think, regarding what this intimacy is and does. This intimacy is something distinct from, for example, the somewhat abstract "sentimentalism" that pervades "intimate publics" elsewhere, publics com-prised of strangers who usually do not meet face-to-face (cf. Berlant 2008, Stokes 2010). The intimacy of love songs in Somaliland is something far more tangible and the public it stitches together something more famil-iar. As would perhaps be expected, this intimacy is wrapped up in broader ideas about gender, the expression of emotion, romance, and marriage. But the pull and promise of this feeling-sharing is also inseparable from the challenges faced by youth with uncertain future prospects and the force of nostalgia in the lives of an older generation coming to terms with the course of Somaliland's sociopolitical and religious trajectory. Often, this intimacy is a form of therapeutic relief—from love-suffering but also from other types of anxieties and frustrations. Yet even here, we should not underestimate the profound impact this can have on the course of indi-viduals' (love) lives and love songs' power in the political realm. Indeed, we have also seen that this intimacy may have subtle political undertones or even overt (anti)political overtones. In its very embrace of vulnerabil-ity, this intimacy may represent a demand for a different kind of politics. If we can conclude anything, it might be that this intimacy, like the songs it opens into or out of, is always in motion and always a *potential*. The type of public it summons into being is thus necessarily underdetermined and dependent on the work invested into it and on what its members need it to perform. Perhaps we might conclude, following the late poet Gaarriye, that what a love song is and does always depends "on how it's tended and by whom," "the spot in which it's planted," and "who needs it and for what its husk is hulled or boiled."[3] *Qofba meeshii bugtaa isagay belbeshaa*: each person takes it to where the wound burns.

Given all of this, what might we make of Khadra's wish for me that I too may feel calaacal and may know what it means to suffer from love? What might this investigation of the intimacy-opening powers of love songs and of the voice reveal about this pronouncement? In retrospect, the answer is in one sense so glaringly obvious that my confusion is somewhat em-barrassing. In wishing me suffering, Khadra was wishing me love. More specifically, she wished for me to experience a particular kind of love—an all-consuming "love [that] loves the difficult things" (Farid al-Din al-Attar, in Gabobe 2014, 29), a transformative and transcendent heartbreaking and heart-opening kind of love that she believed would enrich my understanding and experience of love and of being human. Khadra wished for me a kind of love that she herself had known, a love that, despite its spine-breaking, rib-snapping, sleep-depriving, and potentially fatal effects, was somehow a part of her—but not yet a part of me. This realization, however, brought about a new conundrum. Her comment threw into relief the possible incommensurability of our love worlds in a way that profoundly unsettled me. If I had not "tasted" this love, what could I really understand about Khadra and about the love songs that give voice to these experiences? As an anthropologist, how could I write about "love" if I did not yet fully understand what my interlocutors took for granted when speaking about the phenomenon they called jacayl? What was I to do—as a friend, as an ethnographer—about this rupture, this distance between our respective (love) experiences?

Reverberating through this reflection on the work of love songs, however, I have come to understand this distance as a space of possibility, imagination, and vulnerability. What first appeared as a knowledge chasm began to look and sound like an invitation—a call to learn something of another, to imagine another's pain, and to open the door to feeling and the possibility of feeling-sharing. And, indeed, it is this very space that necessitates love songs, and it is in this space where songs most forcefully resound. Do hees jacayl not also call out into a void of unknown listeners, present and future, "hear my pain," and in so sounding, "share this suffering with me"? In this space, the reverberations of hees jacayl echo: "Dwell with me for a moment, regardless of who you are or where you come from, imagine that we could be otherwise. Know that you are not alone." Love songs, importantly, do not make this space disappear. But full of sound this space somehow feels smaller, "less acute, less solitary, less silent" (Berger 2016, 99)—pregnant with intimate possibility. Singers and their fans, love doctors and their patients, music teachers and their students, performers and the audiences who lend them their ears, friends, acquaintances, strangers, lovers, maybe even ethnographers: all are welcome. As Weedhsame put it to me, in one way or another "when we let our emotions show, we are *all* calaacal." "I want you to know this suffering too" is not only a statement about Khadra's wishes for my love life but also an index of a desire for "something shared" (Berlant 1998, 281); it is a desire for a void to be filled with sound, with her voice and mine too—an invitation to feeling-share with others. Perhaps we can never fully comprehend the varieties of emotions, experiences, and relations covered by the category of "love," separate from our own embodied knowledge and expectations. But in the space between, there is room for something else.

Opening this space and resounding through it: that is the work of love songs—and perhaps the work of ethnography too.

Acknowledgments

One of the central arguments of this book is that the voice may be at once deeply personal and uniquely one's own yet also intimately multivocal—both in the way a single voice may condense a multiplicity of voices and in the way the voice in circulation may be continually taken up by others. This is, I think, equally the case for love songs and the kind of ethnography I aspire to write. This book is thus written in my own voice, but it is also the distillation of a chorus of many voices. Some of these voices are audible in the preceding pages; others speak more subtly. This work belongs to all of them.

I am profoundly thankful to and humbled by the women and men who let me into their lives in Hargeysa. To the friends who introduced me to the city, housed and fed me, and offered their companionship: *waad mahad-santihiin saaxibayaal.* To the artists, young and old, who shared their music and stories with me: *mahadsanid, suugaantaada oo waarta ku rajeynayaa.* I am especially grateful to the members of FanSan and Hiddo Dhawr who welcomed me in their midst and opened their homes and hearts to me. For teaching me innumerable lessons of love, life, and music—and for trusting me with their voices—I will be eternally indebted to Khadra Daahir Ciige and Cabdinaasir Macallin Caydiid. I am profoundly grateful for the time I got to spend with each of them when they still walked among us. For deepening my knowledge of Somali language and verse, I am thankful to Xasan Daahir Ismaaciil "Weedhsame," Dr. Martin Orwin, Abdihakim Abdilahi Omer, and the late Cabdiraxmaan Faarax "Guri Barwaaqo." Abdihakim has been a patient and trustworthy teacher and research assistant for many years, and I am grateful for his curiosity, diligence, and friendship. Martin and Weedhsame have also been critical sounding boards for various ideas and projects in the years since I began my research, and for this I am eternally thankful.

This book would not be what it is without the intellectual and moral support of colleagues and friends in the UK and beyond. I am deeply grateful to Harri Englund, who trusted my anthropological instincts before I fully understood what they were and who has gently yet profoundly helped to shape my ethnographic voice. Corinna Howland, Rosie Jones-McVey, Julia Modern, Amy Binning, Alice Pearson, and Andrea Grant were there from the beginning; they have suffered through more drafts of various bits of this book than I dare to recall, providing helpful guidance and encouragement at each turn. Karin Barber and Rupert Stasch provided invaluable feedback on this work at an earlier stage, helping me to sharpen my argument and encouraging this work's prospects as a book. Generous comments from Amanda Weidman and an anonymous reviewer further helped me to hone my argument. I am also grateful to Rashel Pakbaz and Leonard Enns for assistance with the notations that appear in this book (though all errors are my own), Stefania Merlo for making the map, and John Clark for designing and helping to build the companion website. Thanks also to the editorial team at the University of Chicago Press who have patiently shepherded this book into fruition: Mary Al-Sayed, Fabiola Enríquez Flores, Mollie McFee, and Elizabeth Ellingboe.

My research and writing were made possible through the generous support of a number of funders and institutions. My research was funded by the Social Sciences and Humanities Research Council of Canada and the Cambridge International Trust (Smuts Memorial Fund). An early-career fellowship funded by the Leverhulme Trust and Isaac Newton Trust supported transforming this research into a book. King's College has been my home in Cambridge since I began my PhD; a travel grant when I was a student facilitated my initial research, and research funding provided during my years as a college research associate helped me with some of the costs of transforming my work into a book.

None of this would have been achievable without the unwavering support, presence, and encouragement of my family: Peter and Cath Woolner; Jodie, Josh, Elliott, and Regan Pulsifer; Steven Woolner and Julie Young; and Kenedid and Maia. I am especially grateful to my parents, Peter and Cath, who have never once questioned the value of a decade spent at university; they have eagerly asked after draft chapters to read, and their home in Addis Ababa was a welcome respite during research trips. I am particularly grateful for the sharp eye of my mother, who has copyedited nearly everything I have written since I started my undergrad degree many moons ago. And finally, Kenedid, who has been a sounding board for this project since its infancy and who has provided invaluable research assistance and moral support at every turn. His limitless patience, enduring encouragement, and love echo through these pages. Maia and I are lucky to have you.

A version of chapter 5 was previously published as "'Out of Time' and 'Out of Tune': Reflections of an Oud Apprentice in Somaliland," in *Ethnomusicology* 65, no. 2 (2021). A version of chapter 4 was published as "Listening to Love: Aural Attention, Vocal Iconicity, and Intimacy in Somaliland" in *American Ethnologist* 49, no. 2 (2022). I am grateful to the Society for Ethnomusicology and the American Anthropological Association for permission to incorporate my previously published work into this book.

Glossary

abwaan/abwaanid (m/f). A poet; historically, a title given to poets held in high regard, today used more generally.

bad. "Sea"; also refers to the genre of a poem (whether this be the scansion pattern, general theme, or emotion that a song depicts).

belwo. A short, lyrical poem popular in the 1940s, reportedly first composed by Cabdi Sinimo; from the Arabic *balwā* or *balā'*, meaning "trial," "tribulation," or "calamity"; sung to a standardized tune, with the introductory formula "*belwooy, belwooy, hoy belwooy!*"

calaacal. "Complaint," "lament," or "wailing"; a genre of love song that reflects on painful love experiences of longing, loss, or unrequited love.

cod. "Voice" or "sound"; may refer either to the voice of a person or that of an instrument; with a definite article (i.e., *codka*), refers to the singer of a specific song; in its verbal form, it may refer to the sounding of a specific melody (*codee*), or voting (*u codee*).

dhaanto. A dance genre (*hees ciyaareed*); also refers to a specific poetic meter with midlength lines and two alliterative words per line (used in belwo and qaraami) and a specific rhythmic pattern popular in love songs.

foorjo. A genre of love song in which the singer derides a lover for treating her/him badly, usually involving insults.

gabay. A genre of classical poetry, historically composed by and for men, on topics related to politics and philosophy; considered the most prestigious of classical genres. Each line comprises two hemi-stiches, each containing the alliterating sound.

hees. "Song"; one of two broad categories of Somali orature (alongside maanso) and includes poems that are sung to melodies with musical meter; prior to 1960, generally used to describe work and dance songs, now includes popular music about love and politics.

hees ciyaareed. Dance songs, historically used in courtship rituals and still performed today.

hees hawleeddo. Work songs, sung to accompany various work-related activities (like camel watering, animal herding, millet pounding, etc.).

hees jacayl. Love songs.

hees siyaasadeed. Political songs.

jiifto. A short-lined poetic meter used in both maanso and hees, especially popular since the 1960s; each line requires a single alliterative word.

kaban/kaman. A Somali term for the "oud" (*cuud* in Somali, *'ūd* in Arabic); a short-necked, pear-shaped instrument fashioned from wood, and strung with either five or six courses.

kabaniste. A person who plays the kaban (oud).

laxamiste. The person who composes the melody of a song; often a musician but may also be a poet or another inspired party.

laxan. The melody of a song.

luuq. The melodic motif to which oral poems were performed, comprising three or more pitches of an anhemitonic scale; guided by the scansion of the poetry, and lacks a consistent musical meter.

maanso. "Poetry"; one of two broad categories of Somali orature (alongside hees), including classical genres (like gabay and *buraanbur*) sung to a luuq, and more recent genres that are recited.

qaraami. An early genre of love song, usually credited to Cabdullaahi Qarshe, characterized by simple oud accompaniment and long melismatic phrasing; from the Arabic *gharāmī*, meaning "amorous" or "passionate."

riyaaq. A genre of love song that focuses on the beauty of requited love, or praise for one's partner.

waddo. "Road"; also refers to the (anhemitonic pentatonic) scale of a song.

xawaash. "Spice" or "aromatics"; refers to the spice mix added to both savory dishes and tea (usually including some combination of cardamom, cinnamon, and cloves); also used to refer to the vocal or instrumental embellishments musicians add to a song.

Notes

1. This includes French Somaliland (now Djibouti), Italian Somaliland, British Somaliland, the Ogaaden or Somali region of eastern Ethiopia, and northeast Kenya (previously the Northern Frontier District).

2. Most commentators (and Somalis themselves) describe Somalis as belonging to one of five main clan families: the historically pastoralist Dir, Darood, Hawiye, and Isaaq—all of whom share a common ancestor "Samaale"—and the Digil-Rahaweyn, agro-pastoralists who live in the interriverine area of southern Somalia (some of whom speak May-May). The Isaaq are concentrated in Somaliland, although they also live in Djibouti and Ethiopia; the Dir live primarily in Djibouti, western Somaliland, and parts of Ethiopia; the Darood live in southern Somalia, eastern Somaliland, and parts of Ethiopia and Kenya; and the Hawiye are dispersed across the Somali region of Ethiopia and parts of southern Somalia. I should note that "clan" is not as fixed as many commentators often make it out to be (especially those influenced by I. M. Lewis's structural-functionalist accounts of the region), and clan intersects with a number of other kinds of cleavages political, economic, generational—in how it shapes group relations.

3. For a vernacular perspective and critique of the horrors of *tahriib*, see Weedhsame's poem "Galiilyo," available at https://www.poetrytranslation.org/poems/catastrophe.

4. The Isaaq can be subdivided into Habar Madaago and Habar Jeclo. The Habar Madaago comprises the following subclans: Habar Garhajis (Habar Yunis and Ciidaggale), Arab, Habar Awal (Ciise Muuse and Sacaad Muuse), and Ayuub. Habar Jeclo includes Muuse Sheikh Isaaq, Imran, Toljecle, and Sanbuur.

5. For more theoretical discussion of the ontology of music, as well as the rejection of the idea-text-performance of earlier musicological accounts, see Cook and Everist 1999, Bohlman 1999, DeNora 2000, Agawu 2003, and Born 2005. For examples of studies that employ this approach ethnographically, see Stokes 2010, Impey 2018, Gray 2013, and Gill 2017.

6. Some exemplary works include Abu-Lughod 1986, Coplan 1994/2008, Askew 2002, Impey 2018.

7. There is a large body of literature on Somali orature, most of it by linguists and historians. Linguistic studies tend to focus on the technical features of Somali verse,

and some of the social correlates of the form of specific genres. Among historians, poetry is frequently used as an oral source on historical events or as commentary on a range of social issues. On the linguistics side this includes the extensive body of work by B. W. Andrzejewski (see Hayward and Lewis 1996 and Finnegan and Orwin 2011 for compilations and commentary) and more recent work by Martin Orwin. For work on poetry and politics, see Laitin 1977; Samatar 1982, 1989, 2010; Rirash 1992; Ahmed 1996; Johnson 1996; Afrax 1994, 2010; and Cabdillaahi 2009. For uses of poetry as "history from below," or commentary on issues ranging from migration to gender relations, see Abokor 1987/1993, Jama 1991, Hassan, Aden, and Warsame 1995, Adan 1996, Kapteijns 1999/2009, and Kapteijns and Ali 2001.

8. The notable exception to this is the work of Lidwien Kapteijns (with Maryan Omar Ali), though as an historian Kapteijns is generally interested in love songs as a window into understanding gender relations and other related themes.

9. One early critique of Barre's regime took place in the Siinley debate, which began as a series of tape-recorded poems exchanged between Hadraawi and Qays. Both poets were arrested, imprisoned, and forced into exile at various times. Hadraawi also later became a staunch supporter of the SNM.

10. I draw in particular on dynamic anthropological approaches to text/entextualization influenced by Bakhtinian dialogism, including Bauman and Briggs 1990, Silverstein and Urban 1996, and especially Karin Barber 2007a/2007b.

11. Agawu's call to treat African music *as text* is part of an effort to revalue African music as a performed art, one that necessarily means focusing less on "origins," classificatory schemes, and the kinds of contextual (and often "functional") explanations historically put forward by ethnomusicologists.

12. For example, Bakhtin 1981, Bauman and Briggs 1990, Barber 2007a/2007b, Berlant 2008.

13. For other work on the affective dimensions of genre, or "structures of feeling," see Williams 2015 [1977], Berlant 2008, Sharma and Tygstrup 2015, Gill 2017.

14. See, for example, Cole and Thomas 2009, Stasik 2016, Archambault 2017, and Johnson 2018.

15. Here I have in mind a large body of work on challenges faced by Africa's incredibly young population, including Ferguson 2002, Durham 2004, Cole and Durham 2007/2008, Weiss 2009, Masqualier 2005/2013, Honwana 2012/2013, and Schielke 2015. The material on "waithood" also intersects with research on gendered relationships and marriage (especially work by Masqualier and Honwana).

16. For instance, Bissel's (2005) work on engaging colonial nostalgia or Piot's (2010) work on nostalgia for the future.

17. Performance studies have similarly challenged the idea of context as some objective field in which texts are created, prompting a shift in focus to processes of contextualization. For an overview of this shift, see Bauman and Briggs 1990.

18. Here I build on a significant body of anthropological literature, much of it influenced by Peircean semiotics, that has looked to the "voice" as a site where music and language meet (Feld and Fox 1994, Feld et al. 2004, Gray 2013), and where different types of meaning collide (Besnier 1990, Turino 1999, Eisenlohr 2018a/2018b).

19. In Peircean terms, Turino (1999, 237–40) suggests that the affective power of musical genres defined by an aesthetics of sincerity rests in large part on the singing voice's (and related gestural cues) perceptions as a decent sign, that is, a sign that is interpreted to be real, direct, or natural.

20. See, for example, Hill 1995, Irvine 1999, Keane 2000, Englund 2018, Fisher 2019, Weidman 2021.

21. This includes the intersection of citizenship, sex and familial relations (Berlant 1997, Mody 2008, Povinelli 2006); the "embarrassing" or unofficial aspects of national culture that nevertheless create a sense of national belonging (Herzfeld 2005, Stokes 2010); the mass mediation of publics that depart from the Habermasian model (Berlant 2008, Kunreuther 2014); technology and ecological deterioration (Weston 2017); witchcraft (Geschière 2013); and ethnography itself (Shryock 2004, Chrysagis and Karampampas 2017). See also Sehlikoglu and Zengin 2015.

22. I am grateful to Amanda Weidman for this articulation of what I have in mind by the term "politics of voice."

23. The name Miimley comes from the fact that all of the poems alliterate in *miin* ("m"). Somali orature has a long history of poetic debate. The best-known debate chains include Guba, from the early twentieth century, in which poets debated issues related to interclan politics, as well as Siinley and Deelley, both from the 1970s, in which poets criticized and defended Barre's regime.

24. https://www.theguardian.com/world/2018/apr/18/somaliland-poet-naima -abwaan-qorane-jailed-for-three-years-in-crackdown-on-writers.

25. Warsame (2002) links this trend to changing notions of property rights that accompanied urbanization from the late colonial period onward.

26. Islam permits men to marry up to four wives, should their financial circumstances allow them to treat each wife equally. The practice of polygamy, however, is one that Warsame (2002, 58) contends most women find "degrading" and psychologically traumatizing. Women might accept that men are allowed to take additional wives, but they are rarely happy with it and often contend that it is impossible to treat multiple wives equally.

27. In total, I interviewed sixty artists and arts sector employees, including representatives of Walaalaha Hargeysa, Waaberi, Iftiin, General Daa'uud, Danan Hargeysa, Kooxda Halgan, Xidigaha Geeska, FanSan, Radio Hargeysa, Radio Halgan, Horn Cable TV, the Hargeysa Cultural Center, and Hiddo Dhawr.

CHAPTER ONE

1. For more on this archive, see Woolner 2021b or the liner notes of *Sweet as Broken Dates: Lost Somali Tapes from the Horn of Africa* (Ostinato Records, 2017). The archive was the source of most of the tracks found on that album.

2. This overview is based on observations made by others (Abokor 1993, Johnson 1996, Orwin 2003, O'Dubhda 2009, Andrzejewski 2011) and my own observations of how these terms were used in Somaliland during my research.

3. For a further discussion of this distinction, see Orwin (2003) or Afrax (2013).

4. Two famous poetry debates of the 1970s, Deelley and Siinley, as well as Miimley, use jiifto. According to Weedhsame, upward of 80 percent of all songs produced since the 1970s use jiifto. For a discussion of the rise of jiifto, see Afrax (2013).

5. Cumar Dhuule sings lines from Cilmi's poem "Caashaqa haween" (The love of women). For a discussion and translation of the original poem, see Abdillahi and Andrezejewski (1967).

6. The Ka'bah is the black monument located at the center of the Great Mosque in Mecca. All Muslims pray facing the Ka'bah, and its circumambulation is a key part of the pilgrimage.

7. Gabobe (2014) and Laurence (1993, 59) report the former; Martin Orwin and Khadra Daahir suggested the latter to me.

8. For examples of some of this poetry, see Abdillahi and Andrezejewski 1967, Gabobe 2014, or the companion website.

9. As reported in Abdullahi (2008, 79), with spelling amendments.

10. Dark, glossy gums are a mark of beauty.

11. Excerpts from the poem "Qaraami" (Passion), in Laurence (1993, 57–58).

12. One notable exception to this is the late nineteenth-century poem "A Broken Betrothal," by Raage Ugaas. This poem movingly describes the bodily pain caused by the marriage of his betrothed to another man and love-lamentations so loud they were mistaken for a roaring lion. See Andrzejewski and Andrzejewski (1993, 9) for an English translation.

13. These include an early book by Hodan's son, Rashiid Maxamed Shebeele, *Ma Dhabaa Jacayl waa loo Dhintaa?* (Is it true one died for love? [1975]), and more recent titles like Cabdirashiid Maxamed Ismaaciil and Idiris Yuusuf Cilmi's *Cilmi Boodheri iyo Jacaylkii Taamka Ahaa* (Cilmi Boodheri and love that causes sorrow/pain [2016]) and *Cilmi-boodhari Caashaqiisii* (Cilmi Boodhari's love [2014]) by Maxamed Xirsi Guuleed "Abdibashir." In English, Cilmi is the focus of Jamal Gabobe's 2014 PhD dissertation in comparative literature and an article by Abdullahi and Andrezejewski (1967). There are also discussions of Cilmi and/or translations of his poetry in the work of Laurence (1993), Kapteijns (1999), Johnson (1996) and Andrezejewski and Andrezejewski (1993).

14. This story is well documented in a variety of Arabic, Persian, and Turkish sources, which vary slightly on the details of the nature of the relationship between Qays and Leyla and the cause of his death (Cook 2007, 99–101). This story is dramatized in the 1970s Somali play *Leyla iyo Qays*, and references to the similarities between Qays and Cilmi also abound—for example, the song "Qays iyo Cilmuu Dilay" ([It] killed Qays and Cilmi), sung by Axmed Mooge and Sahra Axmed.

15. While love sickness did not receive nearly as much attention as melancholy in such texts (cf. Gill 2017, Stokes 2010), it is periodically described as a disease related to the balance of the humors (blood, phlegm, yellow bile, and black bile) or an affliction that so preoccupies the mind, heart, and liver that its sufferers are left unable to eat, drink, or sleep (Biesterfeld and Gutas 1984, 23).

16. Gabobe (2014) reports this interpretation being given to him by Muuse Goth. One of the authors of the recent book *Cilmi Boodheri iyo Jacaylkii Taamka Ahaa* (Ismaaciil and Cilmi 2016) was originally of this view, basing his conclusion in part on the references in Cilmi's poetry to "Canab," which literally translates as "grapes" and that

he took as a reference to wine and a kind of divine intoxication. His coauthor eventually convinced him this was an erroneous interpretation and that "Canab," which is also a woman's name, was used as a stand-in for "Hodan" (substituting women's names for each other was a common poetic practice). Together they rewrote the book, a process they recounted to me after the book's launch at the 2015 Hargeysa International Book Fair.

17. This story is recounted in a number of written sources, including Johnson (1996), Laurence (1993), and Mukhtar (2003). My own account here relies mainly on accounts given to me personally, including by Rashiid Bullo.

18. The first three lines were widely recited to me, the fourth line is as reported by Mukhtar (2003), and the fifth by Cabdullaahi Qarshe (in Hassan 2008).

19. There is some discrepancy about what the terms *heello* and *qaraami* refer to. The strictest definition of qaraami was given to me by Weedhsame, who limited qaraami to songs that use dhaanto meter and deploy one of a series of approximately seventy named laxan (melodies), mostly attributed to Qarshe. In my own oud lessons, my teacher used qaraami slightly more generally to refer to songs from the 1940s and 1950s, many of which were composed by Qarshe. Today, most lay listeners use the term to refer generally to prewar love songs and specifically to those with simpler instrumentation (mainly the oud, drums, violin, and flute).

20. The following five belwo are taken from Johnson (1996, 60–66), with some minor alterations to the Somali spelling and the translation of *curuqyada*.

21. A slightly different version of this belwo is available in Johnson (1996, 61); I have included the lines that were later sung by Dhuule.

22. From an English translation of the poem "The Evils of the Balwo" by Sheikh Muhammed Hasan (in Andrzejewski and Lewis 1964, 151–52).

23. The recording of the gabay notated in figure 1.1 is available on the companion website and on YouTube (https://www.youtube.com/watch?v=BrjT5A9FkGA&t=8s). Composed by the poet-warrior Sayyid Maxamed Cabdille Xasan in 1904, this poem has been described as a kind of "state-of-the-union" address, as it sets out the Sayyid's political vision. The poem is alternatively known as "Gudban" (Moving across) and "Gaala-leged" (Defeating the infidels). See Afdub and Kapteijns 1999.

24. The transcription on which figure 1.2 is based comes from a recording of Ibraahin Garabyare accompanied by the musician known as Xuseen Cabdi "Caydaruus" on the oud and some women chorus singers (available at https://www.youtube.com/watch?v=YE7oVy6mICQ). Only the first three stanzas are notated. The belwo melody, with slight variation, is still used up to the present, though the invocation is more commonly sung as "laylay." A number of examples are included on the companion website.

25. The recording that this transcription is based on is on the companion website and also available on YouTube (https://www.youtube.com/watch?v=YE7oVy6mICQ).

26. See Jama (2015) for a brief discussion of why this might be the case. While he challenges this interpretation, the first explanation he mentions, that is, that marginalized clans are over-represented because singing was still a stigmatized profession, is by far the most common explanation I have heard.

27. Translations taken from Kapteijns (1999, 203).

28. This interpretation was suggested to me in a personal correspondence with Dr. Jama Musse Jama.

29. The Somali text of this excerpt was provided to me directly by Weedhsame.

30. From the song "Oo shiikh baa wuxuu yidhi," sung by Aamina Cabdullaahi, quoted and translated in Kapteijns (1999, 6).

CHAPTER TWO

1. As discussed in chapter 1, one of the biggest changes in postwar music is the reliance on electronic recording/editing software/playback. But authors who have explored similar changes elsewhere have highlighted that recording technologies need not always undermine notions of authenticity or "liveness" in music (cf. Meintjes 2003, Auslander 2008, Bicknell 2015, Weidman 2014b/2021). The reverse, of course, may also be true (cf. Grant 2017).

2. The love experiences of men and women are almost always sung by male and female vocalists respectively, though a singer may sing a song inspired by a member of the opposite sex when it describes a situation that transcends gendered experiences of love.

3. For examples of songs he wrote about these experiences see "Nabaadiino," or "Laxaw" (quoted in chap. 1).

4. While not common, it is permissible to marry one's cross-cousin (the children of one's mother's brother, or father's sister).

5. This idea of "trading places" is developed in phenomenological terms by Duranti (2010) in his reading of Husserl.

6. This is not unlike what Wikan finds when her Balinese interlocutors suggest that to create a text that will resonate with one's audience you need both "feeling" and "thought," but the "feeling" must come first—"for without feelings we'll remain entangled in illusions" (1992, 462–63, quoting a Balinese poet-philosopher interlocutor).

7. As an aside, I do not think it is a coincidence that the types of experiences that compel responses are so frequently based in love-*pain*. As Levinas (1998) highlights, "to see a person in pain is to be presented with an opportunity to feel suffering for the suffering for another" (in Throop 2012b, 409)—one that in turn places a kind of ethical demand on us to respond (Throop 2012a, 160).

8. This is a process which closely parallels Jodi Halpern's (2001) work on "clinical empathy," which advocates viewing empathy not as "detached inference" or "projection" of one's own emotions onto another but as an "experiential way of knowing about another's emotional states"—a form of knowing that requires both "affective attunement" *and* a more intentional form of perspective-taking.

9. I am grateful to Mohammed Ahmed (who also happens to be a Canadian Olympic medalist) and Kenedid Ali Hassan for assistance translating this poem.

CHAPTER THREE

1. Without venturing into psychoanalytical literature, I will note that work on the voice as fetish is rooted in the notion that the voice represents the classic Lacanian "objet a" (Stokes 2010, Durham Peters 2004, Dolar 2006).

2. Here I build on the work of Cody, who highlights that "certain semiotic forms lend themselves to particular regimes of entextualization," and that the resulting publicness of a text is an "effect of particular acts of entextualization" (2009, 288). In this case, the textual-sonic-vocal nature of songs, combined with a specific ideology of voice means that love songs are envocalized in a specific way, resulting in a particularly intimate public.

3. For the full text, translation and analysis of this poem, see Orwin (2006).

4. This is not unlike what Kunreuther (2014) and Englund (2018) find of radio publics in Nepal and Zambia respectively, especially in the face-to-face interactions of Gogo Greeze with his public. I do not think it is a coincidence that these two cases also involve oral/aural media, as opposed to print.

5. The recording is available on the companion website and on YouTube (https://www.youtube.com/watch?v=x_p5FQHW5X0).

6. The original poem for this song is available in Faarax (2015, 106), which also includes an analysis of the linguistic features of the poem. My transcription here includes some sung additions that are not part of the original poem and fall outside the poetic meter.

7. Available at https://realworldrecords.com/releases/new-dawn/.

8. The comments are taken from the comments section of various of Khadra's songs on YouTube. Some have been translated from Somali.

9. See https://www.bbc.com/somali/articles/cw0d8ew8px2o.

CHAPTER FOUR

1. Here I have in mind Peirce's notion of diagrams—that is, icons "which represent the relations . . . of the parts of one thing by analogous relations in their own parts" (1932, 157). I develop this idea, alongside the notion of "vocal iconicity," more fully in the article version of this chapter that appeared in *American Ethnologist* (Woolner 2022). For a similar perspective, see Eisenlohr's (2018) work on "suggestions" of movement in Muslim devotional poetry in Mauritius.

2. See, for instance, Hirschkind 2001/2006, Larkin 2014, Kapchan 2009/2017, Eisenlohr 2018a/b, Gill 2017.

3. From the English translation of the poem "Uurkubbaale" (Seer), available at https://www.poetrytranslation.org/poems/seer.

4. The concept of "tarab," which is central to religious and secular musical traditions across the Arab world, also highlights these parallels (cf. Racy 1998, Hirschkind 2006, 36).

5. Translation adapted from Orwin (forthcoming).

6. Cabdikariin Jiir has explained how he intentionally composed the melody to "match" the referential content of the lyrics. For example, in one passage the lyrics describe an overflowing river that waters farmland out of which crops grow; the melody begins low in the vocalist's range, matching the water flowing at ground level, but then rises as the lyrics describe bountiful crops springing up from the ground. In another section that references various organs the rise of the melody also mimics their relative

location in the abdomen (i.e., the melody is lower when describing the liver, but rises when mentioning the heart). See https://www.youtube.com/watch?v=354GtILGNGs.

7. The song is called "Moogiye jacayl waa maxay?" (Unknown to me, what is love?). Most recorded versions I have listened to use slightly different lyrics than those Bilaal quoted to me.

CHAPTER FIVE

1. See also Feld 1996, Qureshi 2000, Impey 2018, Gill 2017.

2. See, for example, Rice 1994, Wacquant 2004, Downey 2005, Bryant 2005, Weidman 2012.

3. This account is based on Qarshe's own description of his upbringing and interest in music, as recounted in Hassan 2008 and Johnson 1996 (in the preface written by Qarshe, and in Johnson's narrative).

4. For the lyrics and translation of this song, see Johnson 1996, 84–90, or Hassan 2008, 69–70.

5. This phrasing comes from Ahmed Samatar, interviewed on "Reconstructing Somalia: Love Songs at the Birth of a Nation" (https://afropop.org/audio-programs/reconstructing-somalia-love-songs-at-the-birth-of-a-nation).

6. For examples of these performances featuring Cabdinaasir, see "Faqash way tegaysaa" (The regime is being chased away), available on the companion website.

7. See, for example, *Xidigaha Geeska*'s 2017 Eid Concert, featuring Maxamed Miyir on the oud (who we met in chap. 2): https://www.youtube.com/watch?v=vBx5bR8h78Q.

8. Amongst Somali musicians, these names correspond to a set of five notes, learned as oud fingerings, that may be played as either major or minor scales (that is, the same name is used regardless of which note is the tonic). The scale known as "mi minore" (E minor) for instance, is the scale I learned to play "Xaafuun" (as notated in figure 1.3), as well as the scale I learned to play "Miday laabtu doonto," in G major (as in figure 5.2). What is important for novices to learn are the different sets of notes/fingerings, practiced in ascending/descending arpeggios; the tonic shifts as necessary.

9. *Xawaash* usually refers to some combination of cinnamon, cardamom, cloves (when added to tea), and the addition of cumin when added to savory dishes.

CHAPTER SIX

1. This chapter builds on a podcast (Woolner 2016), and preliminary research findings presented in a book chapter (Woolner 2018).

2. By extension, I also address here a perennial question in the study of African popular culture: that is, when, where and how forms of popular culture may constitute a practice of resistance. Fabian (1998, 69) points out, however, that "the issue of power and resistance . . . cannot be reduced to determining whether or not, or when and where, expressions of popular culture qualify as acts of resistance" (1998, 69)—popular arts are, after all, both constrained and enabled by particular configurations of power,

and emerge from the same "cultural habitus" as less "liberated" forms and traditions (Okome and Newell 2012, 41).

3. In his ambitious account of the global history of love songs, Gioia similarly points out this paradoxical nature of love songs. He suggests that love songs have always represented a challenge, "demand[ing] not only freedom of expression, but other freedoms in matters both intimate and public" (2015, xi). Yet inasmuch as they are also "the quintessential music for those moments when we let down our guard, leave ourselves defenceless, and accept the experiential richness of our deepest emotional vulnerability," love songs "also resemble the renunciation of power" (2015, xi).

4. Hargeysa's postwar urban development has been rather uneven, with most business concentrated on the southwest side of the riverbed, especially around the Mansoor Hotel. The construction of Ambassador Hotel (and associated UN and NGO villas) and redevelopment of the airport have begun to even out development, though the city still remains fairly divided. See Ibrahim 2010 or Gandrup 2016.

5. See freemuse.org/news/somalia-concert-cancelled-for-objectionable-shows-in -europe/.

6. As recounted by Yusuf Serunkuma in an unpublished PhD dissertation chapter draft shared with me, and in conversations with the owners.

7. Indeed, during the late stages of this book's production I learned that Hiddo Dhawr had moved to a new site on the western edge of the city where Sahra now owns the land.

8. While decried by some religious leaders as a "house of the devil" for the pre-Islamic, figurative images they feature (Mire 2011, 81), Laas Geel is a protected site, and also arguably the country's biggest draw for non-Somali tourists.

9. For a sample of the instrumentation of this era—including the use of synthesizer, saxophone, drums, guitar and bass—see *Sweet as Broken Dates: Lost Somali Tapes from the Horn of Africa* (Ostinato Records, 2017). Track 11, a famous song written by oud-legend Xudeydi ("Uur Hooyo" [Mother's womb]), features Cabdinaasir Macallin Caydiid on the guitar, playing as part of Danan Hargeysa.

CONCLUSION

1. Interview with Justin Burton. Available at http://iaspm-us.net/iaspm-us -interview-series-steven-feld-jazz-cosmopolitanism-in-accra-and-sound-sentiment/.

2. Feld (1998, 471) names this phenomenon "intervocality," a term he intentionally uses for its relationship to both "intertextuality" and "intersubjectivity."

3. Excerpts from the translation of "Uurkubbaale" (Seer) (http:/www.poetry translation.org/poems/seer).

References

Abdillahi, Mohamed Farah, and B. W. Andrzejewski. 1967. "The Life of 'Ilmi Bowndheri, a Somali Oral Poet Who Is Said to Have Died of Love." *Journal of the Folklore Institute* 4 (2/3): 191–206.

Abdullahi, Mohamed Diriye. 2008. *Culture and Customs of Somalia*. Westport, CT: Greenwood Press.

Abokor, Axmed Cali. 1987. *The Camel in Somali Oral Literature*. Translated by A. A. Xange. Uppsala: Scandinavian Institute of African Studies.

———. 1993. *Somali Pastoral Work Songs: The Poetic Voice of the Politically Powerless*. Uppsala: EPOS, Research Programme on Environmental Policy and Society, Department of Social and Economic Geography, Uppsala University.

Abu-Lughod, Lila. 1986. *Veiled Sentiments: Honor and Poetry in a Bedouin Society*. Berkeley: University of California Press.

———. 1990. "Shifting Politics in Bedouin Love Poetry." In *Language and the Politics of Emotion*, edited by Catherine Lutz and Lila Abu-Lughod, 24–45. Cambridge: Cambridge University Press.

Adan, Amina H. 1996. "Women and Words: The Role of Women in Somali Oral Literature." *Comparative Studies of South Asia, Africa and the Middle East* 16 (2): 81–92.

Afdub, Mursal Farah, and Lidwien Kapteijns. 1999. "'The Defeat of the Infidels': A Poem by Sayyid Muhammad 'Abd Allah Hasan of Somalia." *Sudanic Africa* 10:27–47.

Afrax, Maxamed Daahir. 1994. "The Mirror of Culture: Somali Dissolution Seen through Oral Expression." In *The Somali Challenge: From Catastrophe to Renewal*, edited by Ahmed I. Samatar, 233–51. Boulder, CO: Lynne Rienner.

———. 2010. "Toward a Culture for Peace: Poetry, Drama and Music in Somali Society." In *Whose Peace Is It Anyway? Connecting Somali and International Peacemaking (Accord, Issue 21)*, edited by Mark Bradbury and Sally Healy, 72–74. London: Conciliation Resources.

———. 2013. *Between Continuity and Innovation: Transitional Nature of Post-Independence Somali Poetry and Drama, 1960s–the Present*. PhD diss., SOAS, University of London.

Agawu, Kofi. 2001. "Introduction to Special Issue: The Landscape of African Music." *Research in African Literatures* 32 (2): 3–7.

———. 2003. *Representing African Music: Postcolonial Notes, Queries, Positions*. New York: Routledge.

Ahmed, Ali Jimale. 1996. *Daybreak Is Near . . . Literature, Clans and the Nation-State in Somalia*. Asmara, Eritrea: Red Sea Press.

Ahmed, Sara. 2014. *The Cultural Politics of Emotion*. 2nd ed. Edinburgh: Edinburgh University Press.

Andrzejewski, B. W. 2011 [1963]. "Poetry in Somali Society." *Journal of African Cultural Studies* 23 (1): 5–11.

Andrzejewski, B. W., with Sheila Andrzejewski, trans. 1993. *An Anthology of Somali Poetry*. Bloomington: University of Indiana Press.

Andrzejewski, B. W., and I. M. Lewis. 1964. *Somali Poetry: An Introduction*. Oxford: Oxford University Press.

Appadurai, Arjun. 1986. "Introduction: Commodities and the Politics of Value." In *The Social Life of Things: Commodities in Cultural Perspective*, edited by Arjun Appadurai, 3–63. Cambridge: Cambridge University Press.

Archambault, Julie Soleil. 2017. *Mobile Secrets: Youth, Intimacy, and the Politics of Pretense in Mozambique*. Chicago: University of Chicago Press.

Askew, Kelly. 2002. *Performing the Nation: Swahili Music and Cultural Politics in Tanzania*. Chicago: University of Chicago Press.

Auslander, Philip. 2008. *Liveness: Performance in a Mediatized Culture*. London: Routledge.

Axel, Brian Keith. 2002. "The Diasporic Imaginary." *Public Culture* 14 (2): 422–28.

Bakhtin, Mikhail. 1981. *The Dialogic Imagination: Four Essays*. Translated by Michael Holquist and Caryl Emerson. Edited by Michael Holquist. Austin: University of Texas Press.

———. 1984. *Problems of Dostoevsky's Poetics*. Manchester: Manchester University Press.

Banti, Giorgio, and Francesco Giannattasio. 1996. "Music and Meter in Somali Poetry." In *Voice and Power: The Culture of Language in North-East Africa: Essays in Honour of B. W. Andrzejewski*, edited by R. J. Hayward and I. M. Lewis, 83–127. *African Languages and Cultures*, Supplement 3.

Barber, Karin. 1987. "Popular Arts in Africa." *African Studies Review* 30 (3): 1–78.

———. 2007a. "Improvisation and the Art of Making Things Stick." In *Creativity and Cultural Improvisation*, edited Elizabeth Hallam and Tim Ingold, 25–41. Oxford: Berg.

———. 2007b. *The Anthropology of Texts, Persons and Publics: Oral and Written Culture in Africa and Beyond*. Cambridge: Cambridge University Press.

———. 2018. *A History of African Popular Culture*. Cambridge: Cambridge University Press.

Barthes, Roland. 1977. *Image, Music, Text*. London: Fontana Press (Harper Collins).

Bauman, Richard, and Charles L. Briggs. 1990. "Poetics and Performance as Critical Perspectives on Language and Social Life." *Annual Review of Anthropology* 19:59–88.

Berger, Harris M., and Giovanna P. Del Negro. 2002. "Bauman's Verbal Art and the Social Organization of Attention: The Role of Reflexivity in the Aesthetics of Performance." *Journal of American Folklore* 115 (455): 62–91.

Berger, John. 2016. *Confabulations*. London: Penguin.

Berlant, Lauren. 1997. *The Queen of America Goes to Washington City*. Durham, NC: Duke University Press.

———. 1998. "Intimacy: A Special Issue." *Critical Inquiry* 24:281–88.

———. 2008. *The Female Complaint: The Unfinished Business of Sentimentality in American Culture*. Durham, NC: Duke University Press.

Besnier, Niko. 1990. "Language and Affect." *Annual Review of Anthropology* 19:419–51.

Bicknell, Jeanette. 2015. *A Philosophy of Song and Singing: An Introduction*. New York: Routledge.

Biesterfeld, Hans Hinrich, and Dimitri Gutas. 1984. "The Malady of Love." *Journal of the American Oriental Society* 104 (1): 21–55.

Bissell, William Cunningham. 2005. "Engaging Colonial Nostalgia." *Cultural Anthropology* 20 (20): 215–48.

Blacking, John. 1973. *How Musical Is Man?* Seattle: University of Washington Press.

Bohlman, Philip. 1999. "Ontologies of Music." In *Rethinking Music*, edited by Nicholas Cook and Mark Everist, 17–34. Oxford: Oxford University Press.

Born, Georgina. 2005. "On Musical Mediation: Ontology, Technology, Creativity." *Twentieth-Century Music* 2 (1): 7–36.

Boym, Svetlana. 2007. "Nostalgia and Its Discontents." *Hedgehog Review* 9 (2): 7–18.

Brockmeier, Jens. 2009. "Reaching for Meaning." *Theory and Psychology* 19:213–33.

Bryant, Rebecca. 2005. "The Soul Danced into the Body: Nation and Improvisation in Istanbul." *American Ethnologist* 32 (2): 222–38.

Butterworth, James R. 2014. *Andean Divas: Emotion, Ethics and Intimate Spectacle in Peruvian Huayno Music*. PhD diss., Royal Holloway, University of London.

Cabdillaahi, Rashiid Sheekh "Gadhweyne," ed. 2009. *War and Peace: An Anthology of Somali Literature*. Translated by Martin Orwin with Maxamed Xasan "Alto." London: Progressio and Pointe Invisible.

Cavarero, Adriana. 2005. *For More than One Voice: Towards a Philosophy of Vocal Expression*. Translated Paul Kottman. Stanford, CA: Stanford University Press.

Chrysagis, Evangelos, and Panas Karampampas, eds. 2017. *Collaborative Intimacies in Music and Dance: Anthropologies of Sound and Music*. New York: Berghahn.

Cody, Francis. 2009. "Daily Wires and Daily Blossoms: Cultivating Regimes of Circulation in India's Tamil Newspaper Revolution." *Journal of Linguistic Anthropology* 19 (2): 286–309.

Cole, Jennifer, and Deborah Durham, eds. 2007. *Generations and Globalization: Youth, Age, and Family in the New World Economy*. Bloomington: Indiana University Press.

———. 2008. *Figuring the Future: Globalization and the Temporalities of Children and Youth*. Santa Fe: School for Advanced Research Press.

Cole, Jennifer, and Lynn M. Thomas, eds. 2009. *Love in Africa*. Chicago: University of Chicago Press.

Cook, David. 2007. *Martyrdom in Islam*. Cambridge: Cambridge University Press.

Cook, Nicholas, and Mark Everist, eds. 1999. *Rethinking Music*. Oxford: Oxford University Press.

Coplan, David B. 1994. *In the Time of Cannibals: The Word Music of South Africa's Basotho Migrants*. Chicago: University of Chicago Press.

———. 1997. "Eloquent Knowledge: Lesotho Migrants' Songs and the Anthropology of Experience." In *Readings in African Popular Culture*, edited by Karin Barber, 29–40. Bloomington: Indiana University Press.

———. 2008. *In Township Tonight! South African Black City Music and Theatre*. 2nd ed. Chicago: University of Chicago Press.

Csordas, Thomas J. 1993. "Somatic Modes of Attention." *Cultural Anthropology* 8 (2): 135–56.

Cumming, Naomi. 2000. *The Sonic Self: Musical Subjectivity and Signification*. Bloomington: Indiana University Press.

Dames, Nicholas. 2010. "Nostalgia and Its Disciplines." *Memory Studies* 3 (3): 269–75.

Das, Veena. 2006. *Life and Words: Violence and the Descent into the Ordinary*. Berkeley: University of California Press.

DeNora, Tia. 2000. *Music in Everyday Life*. Cambridge: Cambridge University Press.

Dias, Juliana Braz. 2012. "Popular Music in Cape Verde: Resistance or Conciliation?" In *Music, Performance and African Identities*, edited by Toyin Falola and Taylor Fleming, 316–28. New York: Routledge.

Dolar, Mladen. 2006. *A Voice and Nothing More*. Cambridge, MA: MIT Press.

Downey, Greg. 2005. *Learning Capoeira: Lessons in Cunning from an Afro-Brazilian Art*. New York: Oxford University Press.

Downey, Greg, Monica Dalidowicz, and Paul H. Mason. 2015. "Apprenticeship as Method: Embodied Learning in Ethnographic Practice." *Qualitative Research* 15 (2): 183–200.

Ducaale, Boobe Yusuf. 2002. *The Role of the Media in Political Reconstruction*. Hargeysa: Academy for Peace and Development.

Duranti, Alessandro. 2010. "Husserl, Intersubjectivity and Anthropology." *Anthropological Theory* 10 (1–2): 16–35.

Duranti, Alessandro, and Kenny Burrell. 2004. "Jazz Improvisation: A Search for Hidden Harmonies and a Unique Self." *Ricerche di Psicalogia* 3 (27): 71–100.

Durham, Deborah. 2004. "Disappearing Youth: Youth as a Social Shifter in Botswana." *American Ethnologist* 31 (4): 589–605.

Durham Peters, John. 2004. "The Voice and Modern Media." In *Kunst-Stimmen*, edited by Doris Kolesch and Jenny Schrödl, 85–100. Berlin: Theater der Zeit Recherchen 21.

Eisenlohr, Patrick. 2018a. *Sounding Islam: Voice, Media and Sonic Atmosphere in an Indian Ocean World*. Oakland: University of California Press.

———. 2018b. "Suggestions of Movement: Voice and Sonic Atmospheres in Mauritian Muslim Devotional Practices." *Cultural Anthropology* 33 (1): 32–57.

Englund, Harri. 2015. "Multivocal Morality: Narrative, Sentiment, and Zambia's Radio Grandfathers." *HAU: Journal of Ethnographic Theory* 5 (2): 251–73.

———. 2018. *Gogo Breeze: Zambia's Radio Elder and the Voices of Free Speech*. Chicago: University of Chicago Press.

Faarax, Cabdiraxmaan C. ("Guri Barwaaqo"), with Maxamed Axmed Xasan "Qodax." 2015. *Bad Macaan: Murtidii iyo Middii Xasan Xaaji Cabdillaahi "Xasan Ganey."* Hargeysa: Hal-aqoon Publishers.

Fabian, Johannes. 1998. *Moments of Freedom: Anthropology and Popular Culture*. Charlottesville: University Press Virginia.

Fair, Laura. 2009. "Making Love in the Indian Ocean: Hindi Films, Zanzibari Audiences, and the Construction of Romance in the 1950s and 1960s." In *Love in Africa*, edited by Jennifer Cole and Lynn M. Thomas, 58–82. Chicago: University of Chicago Press.

Faudree, Paja. 2012. "Music, Language, and Texts: Sound and Semiotic Ethnography." *Annual Review of Anthropology* 41:519–36.

Feld, Steven. 1998. "They Repeatedly Lick Their Own Things." *Public Inquiry* 24:445–72.

———. 1996. "Waterfalls of Song: An Acoustemology of Place Resounding in Bosavia,

Papua New Guinea." In *Senses of Place*, edited by Steven Feld and Keith H. Basso, 91–135. Sante Fe: School of American Research Press.

Feld, Steven, and Aaron Fox. 1994. "Music and Language." *Annual Review of Anthropology* 23:25–53.

Feld, Steven, Aaron A. Fox, Thomas Porcello, and Danial Samuels. 2004. "Vocal Anthropology: from the Music of Language to the Language of Song." In *A Companion to Linguistic Anthropology*, edited by Alessandro Duranti, 321–45. Malden, MA: Blackwell Publishing.

Ferguson, James G. 2002. "Of Mimicry and Membership: Africans in the 'New World Society.'" *Cultural Anthropology* 17 (4): 551–69.

Finnegan, Ruth, and Martin Orwin. 2011. "Introduction: Carried by a Mystic Wind: B. W. Andrzejewski on the Somali Passion for Poetry and Language." *Journal of African Cultural Studies* 23 (1): 1–3.

Fisher, Daniel. 2016. *The Voice and Its Double: Media and Music in Northern Australia*. Durham, NC: Duke University Press.

———. 2019. "To Sing with Another's Voice: Animation, Circumspection, and the Negotiation of Indigeneity in Northern Australian New Media." *American Ethnologist* 46 (1): 34–46.

Fox, Aaron A. 2004. *Real Country: Music and Language in Working-Class Culture*. Durham, NC: Duke University Press.

Frankema, Ewout, and Marlous van Waijenburg. 2018. "Africa Rising? A Historical Perspective." *African Affairs* 117 (469): 543–68.

Frow, John. 2005. *Genre*. London: Routledge.

Gabobe, Jamal Abdi. 2014. *Elmi Bodari and the Construction of the Modern Somali Subject in a Colonial and Sufi Context*. PhD diss., University of Washington.

Gandrup, Tobias. 2016. "Enter and Exit: Everyday State Practices at Somaliland's Hargeisa Egal International Airport." *DIIS Working Paper 2016: 3*. Copenhagen: Danish Institute for International Studies.

Geschière, Peter. 2013. *Witchcraft, Intimacy and Trust: Africa in Comparison*. Chicago: University of Chicago Press.

Giannattasio, Francesco. 1988. "The Study of Somali Music: Present State." In *Proceedings of the Third International Congress of Somali Studies*, edited by Annarita Puglielli, 158–67. El Pensiero Scientifico Editore.

Giffen, Lois A. 1971. *Theory of Profane Love among the Arabs: The Development of the Genre*. New York: New York University Press.

Gill, Denise. 2017. *Melancholic Modalities: Affect, Islam and Turkish Classical Musicians*. Oxford: Oxford University Press.

Gioia, Ted. 2015. *Love Songs: The Hidden History*. New York: Oxford University Press.

Goffman, Erving. 1981. *Forms of Talk*. Philadelphia: University of Pennsylvania Press.

Goode, Erica. 2008. "A Fabled Iraqi Instrument Thrives in Exile." *New York Times*, May 1. http://www.nytimes.com/2008/05/01/world/middleeast/01oud.html?_r=1&hp=&oref=slogin&pagewanted=all.

Gracyk, Theodore. 2001. *I Wanna Be Me: Rock Music and the Politics of Identity*. Philadelphia: Temple University Press.

Grant, Andrea M. 2017. "The Making of a 'Superstar': The Politics of Playback and Live Performance in Post-genocide Rwanda." *Africa* 87 (1): 155–79.

Gray, Lila Ellen. 2013. *Fado Resounding: Affective Politics and Urban Life*. Durham, NC: Duke University Press.

Grunebaum, Dan. 2016. "Sahra Halgan Sings Recognition for Somaliland." *Japan Times*, August 21. https://www.japantimes.co.jp/culture/2016/08/21/music/sahra-halgan -sings-recognition-somaliland/.

Guuleed, Maxamed Xirsi "Abdibashir." 2014. *Cilmi-boodhari Caashaqiisii*. Stockholm: Eurosom Bokförlag.

Habermas, Jurgen. 1989 [1962]. *The Structural Transformation of the Public Sphere: An Inquiry into a Category of Bourgeois Society*. Translated by T. Burger with F. Lawrence. Cambridge, MA: MIT Press.

Hadeed, A. 2015. "Who Decides What's Good for Somali Music: Goth or Good?" *Sahan Journal*, February 27. http://sahanjournal.com/abdi-good-bashir-goth# .WWShasYZM0o.

Haeri, Niloofar. 2017. "Unbundling Sincerity: Language, Mediation and Interiority in Comparative Perspective." *HAU: Journal of Ethnographic Theory* 7 (1): 123–38.

Hahn, Tomie. 2007. *Sensational Knowledge: Embodying Culture through Japanese Dance*. Middleton, CT: Wesleyan University Press.

Halpern, Jodi. 2001. *From Detached Concern to Empathy: Humanizing Medical Practice*. New York: Oxford University Press.

Hardt, Michael. 1999. "Affective Labor." *Boundary 2* 26 (2): 89–100.

Harkness, Nicholas. 2014. *Songs of Seoul: An Ethnography of Voice and Voicing in Christian South Korea*. Berkeley: University of California Press.

———. 2015. "The Pragmatics of Qualia in Practice." *Annual Review of Anthropology* 44:573–89.

Hassan, Dahabo F., Amina H. Adan, and Amina M. Warsame. 1995. "Somalia: Poetry as Resistance Against Colonialism and Patriarchy." In *Subversive Women: Historical Experiences of Gender and Resistance*, edited by Saskia Wieringa. London: Zed Books.

Hassan, Kenedid A. 2018. "Pan-Somalist Discourse and New Modes of Nationalist Expression in the Somali Horn: From Somali Poetic Resistance to Djibouti's *Gacan Macan*." In *Music and Dance Research in Eastern Africa: Current Research in Humanities and Social Sciences*, edited by Kahithe Kiiru and Maina wa Mūtonya, 48–62. Nairobi: French Institute for Research in Africa (IFRA) and Twaweza Communications.

———. 2019. *Guux*. In *Bloomsbury Encyclopedia of Popular Music of the World*, volume 12, *Genres: Sub-Saharan Africa*, edited by Heidi Carolyn Feldman, David Horn, John Shepherd, and Gabrielle Kielich, 164–67. New York and London: Bloomsbury Academic.

Hassan, Mohamed-Rashid Sheikh. 2008. "Interview with the Late Abdullahi Qarshe (1994) at the Residence of Obliqe Carton in Djibouti." *Bildhaan: An International Journal of Somali Studies* 2:65–83.

Hayward, R. J., and I.M. Lewis, eds. 1996. "Voice and Power: The Culture of Language in North-east Africa: Essays in Honour of B. W. Andrzejewski." *African Languages and Cultures*, Supplement 3.

Herzfeld, M. 2005 *Cultural Intimacy: Social Poetics and the Real Life of States, Societies and Institutions*. 2nd ed. London: Routledge.

Hill, Jane H. 1995. "The Voices of Don Gabriel: Responsibility and Self in a Modern Mexicano Narrative." In *The Dialogic Emergence of Culture*, edited by Dennis Tedlock and Bruce Mannheim, 97–147. Urbana: University of Illinois Press.

Hirschkind, Charles. 2001. "The Ethics of Listening: Cassette-Sermon Audition in Contemporary Egypt." *American Ethnologist* 28 (3): 623–49.

———. 2006. *The Ethical Soundscape: Cassette Sermons and Islamic Counterpublics.* New York: Columbia University Press.

Hollan, Douglas, and C. Jason Throop. 2008. "Whatever Happened to Empathy?" *Ethos* 36 (4): 385–401.

———. 2011. Introduction to *The Anthropology of Empathy: Experiencing the Lives of Others in Pacific Societies,* edited by Douglas Hollan and C. Jason Throop, 1–23. Oxford: Berghahn.

Honwana, Alcinda. 2012. "'Waithood': Youth Transitions and Social Change." In *Development and Equity, An Interdisciplinary Exploration by Ten Scholars from Africa, Asia and Latin America,* edited by Dick Foeken, Ton Dietz, Leo de Haan, and Linda Johnson, 28–40. Leiden: Brill.

———. 2013. *Youth and Revolution in Tanzania.* London: Zed Books.

Ibrahim, Mohamed Hassan. 2010. "Somaliland's Investment in Peace: Analysing the Diaspora's Economic Engagement in Peacebuilding." *DIASPEACE, Working Paper #4.* https://www.unaoc.org/ibis/wp-content/uploads/2011/11/DIASPEACE_WP4.Pdf.

Impey, Angela. 2018. *Song Walking: Women, Music and Environmental Justice is an African Borderland.* Chicago: University of Chicago Press.

Irvine, Judith. 1999. "Registering Affect: Heteroglossia in the Linguistic Expression of Emotion." In *Language and the Politics of Emotion,* edited by Catherine A. Lutz and Lila Abu-Lughod, 126–61. Cambridge: Cambridge University Press.

Ismaaciil, Cabdirashiid Maxamed, and Idiris Yuusuf Cilmi. 2016. *Cilmi Boodheri iyo Jacaylkii Taamka Ahaa.* Hargeysa: Ponte Invisibile (Red-Sea Online).

Jama, Jama Musse. 2015. "Against the Odds." *Review: Culture in Defiance.* Prince Claus Fund. Reprint available online at http://www.jamamusse.com/2018/11/02/against-the-odds/.

Jama, Zainab Mohamed. 1991. "Fighting to Be Heard: Somali Women's Poetry." *African Languages and Cultures* 4 (1): 43–53.

Johnson, Jessica. 2018. *In Search of Gender Justice: Rights and Relationships in Matrilineal Malawi.* Cambridge: Cambridge University Press.

Johnson, John William. 1996 [1974]. *"Heelloy": Modern Poetry and Songs of the Somali.* London: Haan Publishing.

———. 2010. "The Politics of Poetry in the Horn of Africa: A Case Study in Macro-level and Micro-level Tradition." In *Milk and Peace, Drought and War: Somali Culture, Society and Politics,* edited by Markus Hoehne and Virginia Luling, 221–44. London: Hurst Publishing.

Kapchan, Deborah. 2009. "Learning to Listen: The Sound of Sufism in France." *World of Music* 51 (2): 65–92.

———. 2017. "Listening Acts: Witnessing the Pain (and Praise) of Others." In *Theorizing Sound Writing,* edited by Deborah Kapchan, 277–93. Middleton, CT: Wesleyan University Press.

Kapteijns, Lidwien, with Maryan Omar Ali. 1999. *Women's Voices in a Man's World: Women and the Pastoral Tradition in Northern Somali Orature, c. 1899–1980.* Portsmouth, NH: Heinemann.

———. 2009. "Discourse on Moral Womanhood in Somali Popular Songs, 1960–1990." *Journal of African History* 50:101–22.

Kapteijns, L., and Maryan Omar Ali. 2001. "'Come Back Safely': Laments about Labor Migration in Somali Love Songs." *Northeast African Studies* 8 (3): 33–46.

Kassabian, Anahid. 2013. *Ubiquitous Listening: Affect, Attention and Distributed Subjectivity.* Berkeley: University of California Press.

Keane, Webb. 2000. "Voice." *Journal of Linguistic Anthropology* 9 (1–2): 271–73.

———. 2002. "Sincerity, 'Modernity,' and the Protestants." *Cultural Anthropology* 17 (1): 65–92.

———. 2010. "Minds, Surfaces, and Reasons in the Anthropology of Ethics." In *Ordinary Ethics: Anthropology, Language and Action,* edited by Michael Lambek, 64–83. New York: Fordham University Press.

Kondo, Dorinne K. 1990. *Crafting Selves: Power, Gender and Discourses of Identity in a Japanese Workplace.* Chicago: University of Chicago Press.

Kunreuther, Laura. 2014. *Voicing Subjects: Public Intimacy and Mediation in Kathmandu.* Berkeley: University of California Press.

Laitin, David. 1977. *Politics, Language, and Thought: The Somali Experience.* Chicago: University of Chicago Press.

Larkin, Brian. 1997. "Indian Films and Nigerian Lovers: Media and the Creation of Parallel Modernities." *Africa* 67 (3): 406–40.

———. 2014. "Techniques of Inattention: The Mediality of Loudspeakers in Nigeria." *Anthropological Quarterly* 87 (4): 989–1015.

Laurence, Margaret. 1993 [1954]. *A Tree for Poverty: Somali Poetry and Prose.* Hamilton, Ontario: McMaster University Library Press.

Levinas, Emmanuel. 1998. *Entre Nous: On Thinking-of-the-Others.* Translated by Michael B. Smith and Barbara Harshav. New York: Columbia University Press.

Levinson, Jerrold. 1990. *Music, Art and Metaphysics: Essays in Philosophical Aesthetics.* Oxford: Oxford University Press.

Lewis, I. M. 1989. *Ecstatic Religion: A Study of Shamanism and Spirit Possession.* 2nd ed. London: Routledge.

Lipps, Theodor. 1979. "Empathy, Inner Imitation, and Sense-feelings." In *A Modern Book of Esthetics,* 5th ed., edited by Melvin Rader, 370–82. New York: Holt, Rinehart, and Winston.

Marchand, Trevor H. J. 2010. "Making Knowledge: Explorations of the Indissoluble Relation Between Minds, Bodies, and Environment." *Journal of the Royal Anthropological Institute,* Special Issue (Making Knowledge): S1–S21.

Marcus, George E. 1985. "Ethnography in/of the World System: The Emergence of Multi-sited Ethnography." *Annual Review of Anthropology* 24:95–117.

Masqualier, Adeline. 2005. "The Scorpion's Sting: Youth, Marriage and the Struggle for Social Maturity in Niger." *Journal of the Royal Anthropological Institute* 11 (1): 59–83.

———. 2013. "Teatime: Boredom and the Temporalities of Young Men in Niger." *Africa* 83 (3): 470–91.

Matar, H. 2008. "The Sound of Love." *New Statesman,* November 10. http://www.newstatesman.com/music/2008/11/dhafer-youssef-arabic-oud-jazz.

Maybin, Janet. 2017. "Textual Trajectories: Theoretical Roots and Institutional Consequences." *Talk and Text* 37 (4): 415–35.

Mazzarella, William. 2004. "Culture, Globalization, Mediation." *Annual Review of Anthropology* 33:345–67.

Meintjes, Louise. 2003. *Sound of Africa: Making Music Zulu in a South African Studio.* Durham, NC: Duke University Press.

Meyer, Birgit. 2011. "Mediation and Immediacy: Sensational Forms, Semiotic Ideologies and the Question of the Medium." *Social Anthropology* 19 (1): 23–39.

Middleton, Richard. 2000. "Rock Singing." In *The Cambridge Companion to Singing*, edited by John Potter, 28–41. Cambridge: Cambridge University Press.

Mire, Sada. 2007. "Preserving Knowledge *not* Objects: A Somali Perspective for Heritage Management and Archeological Research." *African Archeological Review* 24:47–71.

———. 2011. "The Knowledge-Centered Approach to the Somali Cultural Emergence and Heritage Development Assistance in Somaliland." *African Archeological Review* 28:71–91.

Mohamed, Nadifa. 2015. "Somalis Returning to the Motherland Are Finding Their Foreign Ways Out of Favour." *The Guardian*, September 11. https://www.theguardian.com/commentisfree/2015/sep/11/diaspora-somaliland-hargeysa.

Mody, Perveez. 2008. *The Intimate State: Love-Marriage and the Law in Delhi*. London: Routledge.

Mukhtar, Mohamed Haji. 2003. *Historical Dictionary of Somalia (African Historical Dictionary Series, No. 87)*. Lanham, MD: Scarecrow Press.

Navaro-Yashin, Yael. 2012. *The Make-Believe Space: Affective Geography in a Postwar Polity*. Durham, NC: Duke University Press.

Nelson, Kristina. 1985. *The Art of Reciting the Qur'an*. Austin: University of Texas Press.

Newell, Stephanie, and Onookome Okome. 2014. "Introduction: Popular Culture in Africa: The Episteme of the Everyday." In *Popular Culture in Africa: The Episteme of the Everyday*, edited by Stephanie Newell and Onookome Okome, 1–24. New York: Routledge.

Nyairo, W. Joyce. 2005. *"Reading the References": (Inter)textuality in Contemporary Kenyan Popular Music*. PhD diss., University of the Witwatersrand.

O'Dubhda, Fiacha. 2009. "On the Musical Patterning of Sculpted Words: Exploring the Relationship between Melody and Meter in a Somali Poetic Form." *Journal of the International Library of African Music* 8 (3): 97–116.

Ogude, James. 2012. "The Invention of Traditional Music in the City: Exploring History and Meaning in Urban Music in Contemporary Kenya." *Research in African Literatures* 43 (4): 147–65.

Okome, Onookome, and Stephanie Newell. 2012. "Measuring Time: Karin Barber and the Study of Everyday Africa." *Research in African Literatures* 43 (4): vii–xviii.

Omojolo, Bode. 2009. "Identity and Nostalgia in Nigerian Music: A Study of Victor Olaiya's Highlife." *Ethnomusicology* 53 (2): 249–76.

Orwin, Martin. 1995. *Colloquial Somali: The Complete Course for Beginners*. London: Routledge.

———. 2003. "On the Concept of 'Definitive Text' in Somali Poetry." *Bulletin of SOAS* 66 (3): 334–47.

———. 2006. "The Worldly and the Unworldly in 'Jacayl Dhiig ma lagu Qoray' by Maxamed Ibraahim Warsame 'Hadraawi.'" *Research in African Literatures* 37 (3): 15–27.

———. 2021. "Lyric Voice in *Hees* and *Maanso* Poetry: Some Initial Thoughts Concentrating on *Hees-Hawleed*." *Bildhaan: Journal of Somali Studies* 21:64–78.

———. Forthcoming. "Conjunctions and Language Flow in Beledweyn by Hadraawi." In *Fetschrift for Hussein "Tanzania,"* edited by Jama Musse Jama. Pisa: Red Sea Online (Ponte Invisible).

Pegg, Scott, and Michael Walls. 2018. "Briefing: Back on Track? Somaliland after Its 2017 Presidential Election." *African Affairs* 117 (467): 326–37.

Pickering, Michael, and Emily Keightly. 2006. "The Modalities of Nostalgia." *Current Sociology* 54 (6): 919–41.

Pierce, Charles Sanders. 1932. *Collected Papers of Charles Sanders Pierce.* Volume 2, *Elements of Logic.* Cambridge, MA: Harvard University Press.

Piot, Charles. 2010. *Nostalgia for the Future: West Africa after the Cold War.* Chicago: University of Chicago Press.

Poché, Christian. 2007. "'Ûd." *The New Grove Dictionary of Jazz*, 2nd ed. Accessed via Oxford Music Online: http://www.oxfordmusiconline.com/subscriber/article/grove/music/28694?q=ud&search=quick&pos=1&_start=1#firsthit.

Povinelli, Elizabeth. 2006. *The Empire of Love: Towards a Theory of Intimacy, Genealogy and Carnality.* Durham, NC: Duke University Press.

Qureshi, Regula. 2000. "How Does Music Mean? Embodied Memories and the Politics of Affect in Indian 'Sarangi.'" *American Ethnologist* 27 (4): 805–38.

Racy, Ali Jihad. 2003. *Making Music in the Arab World: The Culture and Artistry of Tarab.* Cambridge: Cambridge University Press.

Rice, Timothy. 1994. *May It Fill Your Soul: Experiencing Bulgarian Music.* Chicago: University of Chicago Press.

———. 1995. "Understanding and Producing the Variability of Oral Tradition: Learning from a Bulgarian Bagpiper." *Journal of American Folklore* 108 (429): 266–76.

———. 1997. "Towards a Mediation of Field Experience and Field Methods in Ethnomusicology." In *Shadows in the Field: New Perspectives for Fieldwork in Ethnomusicology*, edited by Gregory Barz and Timothy Cooley, 101–20. New York: Oxford University Press.

Rirash, Mohamed Abdillahi. 1992. "Somali Oral Poetry as a Vehicle for Understanding Disequilibrium and Conflicts in a Pastoral Society." *Nomadic Peoples* 30:114–21.

Rojek, Chris. 2001. *Celebrity.* London: Reaktion Books.

Salois, Kendra. 2014. "Make Some Noise, *Drari*: Embodied Listening and Counterpublic Formations in Moroccan Hip Hop." *Anthropological Quarterly* 87 (4): 1017–48.

Samatar, Said S. 1982. *Oral Poetry and Somali Nationalism: The Case of Sayyid Mahammad 'Abdille Hasan.* Cambridge: Cambridge University Press.

———. 1989. "Oral Poetry and Political Dissent: The Hurgumo Series." *Ufahamu: Journal of the African Activist Association* 17 (2): 31–52.

———. 2010. "Somalia: A Nation's Literary Death Tops its Political Demise." In *Milk and Peace, Drought and War: Somali Culture, Society and Politics*, edited by Markus Hoehne and Virginia Luling, 205–20. London: Hurst Publishing.

Schafer, William J. 2008. "Ragtime." In *The New Encyclopedia of Southern Culture*, volume 12, *Music*, edited by Bill C. Malone, 113–17. Chapel Hill: University of North Carolina Press.

Schafers, Marlene. 2015. *Desiring Voice: Female Subjectivities and Affective Publics in Turkish Kurdistan.* PhD diss., University of Cambridge.

Schielke, Samuli. 2015. *Egypt in the Future Tense: Hope, Frustration, and Ambivalence before and after 2011.* Bloomington: Indiana University Press.

Sehlikoglu, Sertaç, and Aslı Zengin. 2015. "Introduction: Why Revisit Intimacy?" *Cambridge Anthropology* 33 (2): 20–25.

Seremetakis, C. Nadia. 1991. *The Last Word: Women, Death, and Divination in Inner Mani.* Chicago: University of Chicago Press.

Shabeele, Rashiid Maxamed. 1975. *Ma Dhabba Jacayl Waa Loo Dhintaa?* Muqdisho.

Sharma, Devika, and Frederik Tygstrup, eds. 2015. *Structures of Feeling: Affectivity and Public Culture*. Berlin: De Gruyter.

Shelemay, Kay Kaufman. 2006. "Music, Memory and History." *Ethnomusicology Forum* 15:17–37.

Shryock, Andrew, ed. 2004. *Off Stage/On Display: Intimacy and Ethnography in the Age of Public Culture*. Stanford, CA: Stanford University Press.

Silverstein, Michael, and Greg Urban. 1996. "The Natural History of Discourse." In *Natural Histories of Discourse,* edited by Michael Silverstein and Greg Urban, 1–17. Chicago: University of Chicago Press.

Sinha, Mrinalini. 1996. "Gender in the Critique of Colonialism and Nationalism: Locating the 'Indian Woman.'" In *Feminism and History*, edited by Joan Wallach Scott, 477–504. New York: Oxford University Press.

Sohonie, Vik. 2017. "Sweet as Broken Dates: The Untold Story of the Somali Sound." Liner notes in *Sweet as Broken Dates: Lost Somali Tapes from the Horn of Africa*. New York: Ostinato Records. OSTLP003: USA.

Stasik, Michael. 2016. "Real Love versus Real Life: Youth, Music and Utopia in Freetown, Sierra Leone." *Africa* 86 (2): 215–36.

Sterne, Jonathon. 2003. *The Audible Past: Cultural Origins of Sound Reproduction*. Durham, NC: Duke University Press.

———. 2006. "The Mp3 as Cultural Artifact." *New Media & Society* 8 (5): 825–42.

Stokes, Martin. 1994. Introduction to *Ethnicity, Identity and Music: The Musical Construction of Place*, edited by Martin Stokes, 1–27. Providence, RI: Berg.

———. 2010. *The Republic of Love: Cultural Intimacy in Turkish Popular Music*. Chicago: University of Chicago Press.

Storey, John. 1997. *An Introduction to Cultural Theory and Popular Culture*. 2nd ed. London: Prentice Hall/Harvester Wheatsheaf.

Taylor, Ian. 2014. *Africa Rising? BRICS—Diversifying Dependency*. Oxford: James Currey.

Thomas, Lynn M., and Jennifer Cole. 2009. "Introduction: Thinking through Love in Africa." In *Love in Africa*, edited by Jennifer Cole and Lynn M. Thomas, 1–30. Chicago: University of Chicago Press.

Throop, C. Jason. 2012a. "Moral Sentiments." In *A Companion to Moral Anthropology*, edited by Didier Fassin, 150–68. Chichester: Wiley-Blackwell.

———. 2012b. "On the Varieties of Empathic Experience: Tactility, Mental Opacity, and Pain in Yap." *Medical Anthropology Quarterly* 26 (3): 408–30.

Turino, Thomas. 1999. "Signs of Imagination, Identity and Experience: A Peircian Semiotics Theory for Music." *Ethnomusicology* 43 (2): 221–55.

———. 2014. "Peircean Thought as Core Theory for a Phenomenological Ethnomusicology." *Ethnomusicology* 58 (2): 185–221.

Wacquant, Loic. 2004. *Body and Soul: Notebooks of an Apprentice Boxer*. New York: Oxford University Press.

Warner, Michael. 2002. "Publics and Counter Publics (Abbreviated Version)." *Quarterly Journal of Speech* 88 (4): 413–25.

Warsame, Amina Mahmoud. 2002. *Queens Without Crowns: Somaliland Women's Changing Roles and Peacebuilding*. Uppsala: Life and Peace Institute.

Weidman, Amanda. 2003. "Gender and the Politics of Voice: Colonial Modernity and Classical Music in South India." *Cultural Anthropology* 18 (2): 194–232.

———. 2012. "The Ethnographer as Apprentice: Embodying Sociomusical Knowledge in South India." *Anthropology and Humanism* 37 (2): 214–35.

———. 2014a. "Anthropology and Voice." *Annual Review of Anthropology* 43:37–41.

———. 2014b. "Neoliberal Logics of Voice: Playback Singing and Public Femaleness in South India." *Culture, Theory & Critique* 55 (2): 175–93.

———. 2021. *Brought to Life by the Voice: Playback Singing and Cultural Politics in South India*. Oakland: University of California Press.

Weiss, Brad. 2009. *Sweet Dreams and Hip Hop Barbershops: Global Fantasy in Urban Tanzania*. Bloomington: Indiana University Press.

Wenger, Etienne, and Beverly Wenger-Trayner. 2015. "Introduction to Communities of Practice: A Brief Overview of the Concept and Its Uses." https://www.wenger-trayner.com/introduction-to-communities-of-practice/.

Weston, Kath. 2017. *Animate Planet: Making Visceral Sense of Living in a High-Tech Ecologically-Damaged World*. Durham, NC: Duke University Press.

Wikan, Unni. 1992. "The Power of Resonance." *American Ethnologist* 19 (3): 460–82.

Williams, Raymond. 2015 [1977]. "Structures of Feeling." In *Structures of Feeling: Affectivity and Public Culture*, edited by Devika Sharma and Frederik Tygstrup, 20–25. Berlin: De Gruyter.

Wilson, Ara. 2012. "Intimacy: A Useful Category of Transition." In *The Global and the Intimate: Feminism in Our Time*, edited by Geraldine Pratt and Victoria Rosner, 31–56. New York: Columbia University Press.

Woodward, Kath. 2008. "Hanging Out and Hanging About: Insider/Outsider Research in the Sport of Boxing." *Ethnography* 9 (4): 536–60.

Woolner, Christina J. 2016. "*Hiddo Dhawr*: Singing Love in(to) Somaliland." *Camthropod: The Cambridge Anthropology Podcast*, Episode 5. https://www.socanth.cam.ac.uk/media/listen-and-view/camthropod#episode-5--hiddo-dhawr--singing-love-in-to--somaliland---by-christina-woolner.

———. 2018. "Singing Love in(to) Somaliland: Love Songs, 'Heritage Preservation,' and the Shaping of Post-war Publics." In *Music and Dance Research in Eastern Africa: Current Research in Humanities and Social Sciences*, edited by Kahithe Kiiru and Maina wa Mũtonya, 76–90. Nairobi: French Institute for Research in Africa (IFRA) and Twaweza Communications.

———. 2021a. "'Out of Time' and 'Out of Tune': Reflections of an Oud Apprentice in Somaliland." *Ethnomusicology* 65 (2): 259–85.

———. 2021b. "Preserving Somaliland's Auditory Heritage: An Introduction to HCC's Cassette Archives-in-Progress." *Dhaxalreeb* 17 (1): 16–22.

———. 2022. "Listening to Love: Aural Attention, Vocal Iconicity and Intimacy in Somaliland." *American Ethnologist* 49 (2): 178–90.

Zeleza, Paul Tiyambe. 2003. "Introduction: The Creation and Consumption of Leisure: Theoretical and Methodological Considerations." In *Leisure in Urban Africa*, edited by Paul Tiyambe Zeleza and Cassandra Rachel Veney, xii–xli. Trenton, NJ: Africa World Press.

Index

Somali artists and political figures are alphabetized by their most commonly used name (first name or nickname). Somali scholars are alphabetized as they are listed in the bibliography (usually by a second/third name). Songs are listed under the individual artists who contributed to them. Page numbers in italics refer to figures.

dress, sociality of: *cabaaya/jilbaab*, 6,
185, 190, 195; *dirac*, 2, 96, 169, 190–91;
macawis, 163; pastoral, 184; *shiid*, 95–
96, 163; women's head coverings, 23,
26, 94, 157, 169, 179, 184, 190–91
drums, 2, 41, 47, 173, 187, 191, *192*, 221n19,
225n9

emotion: as difficult to express, 2, 24,
35, 54, 57, 69, 72–73, 76–77, 89, 104,
108, 110, 123, 127, 140; as driving the
making/performance of love songs,
41, 53, 73–75, 77–80, 83–84, 86–87,
104, 107–8, 117, 157, 168, 195; as a
quality of sound, 47–48, 77–80, *81*,
82, 84–85, 89, 105–8, *108*, 110–11,
113, 136, 147, 165, 167–71, *167*, 197; as
residing in the liver and heart, 37, 41,
43, 135, 220n15; and singers' bodily
comportment, 84–85, 89, 195–97.
See also gender: and expression of
emotion; love-suffering, causes of:
difficulty expressing emotions; voice
empathy, 66, 74–75, 78–79, 82–84, 86–87
Englund, Harri, 223n4 (chap. 3)
entextualization, 12–16, 86, 206, 223n2
(chap. 3)
envocalization, 5, 15–19, 20, 203–6; listening as, 120, 144–45; music-making/
performance as, 148, 171–72, 174, 199–
200; song-making as, 65–66, 86–88;
talk about songs/singers as, 90–93,
99–100, 116–17, 223n2 (chap. 3)
Ethiopia, *xxii*, 5–6, 21, 34, 41, 127, 151,
217nn1–2
ethnographic praxis, xvii–xviii, 25–29,
147–48, 159–60, 201–2, 207–8

FanSan, 26, 68, 78, 156–59, 165, 169, 171,
188, 219n27
Faraax Murtiile (singer), "Han iyo
dookh," 58
Farxiya Fiska (singer), "Han iyo dookh," 58
Farxiya Kaboyare (singer), "Dhakac-
dhakac," 138–39
feeling-sharing. *See* dareen-wadaag
(feeling-sharing)
Feld, Steven, 201, 225n2

flutes, 47, 221n19
foorjo, 32, 79, 85, 215; "Leexo," 48–49

Gaarriye (Maxamed Xaashi Dhamac)
(poet), 63; "Uurkubbaale," 125, 207,
223n3 (chap. 4)
gabay, 32, 33, 35–36, 37, 41, 43–44, 50,
64, 69, 140, 187, 215, 221n23; poems
composed in, *45*
Gabobe, Jamal, 35, 36–39, 220nn7–8,
220n13, 220n16
geeraar, 32
gender: and development of Somali
music, 32, 43–44, 48–49, 50–52, 54,
56–58, 60, 95; and distribution of
song-making tasks, 50, 67, 69–70, 73,
75, 222n2; and ethnographic positionality, 27, 155–56, 163; and expression
of emotion, 24, 57, 69, 72–73, 75–77,
89, 110, 140–42, 207; love songs as
transcending or challenging norms of,
1, 4, 43–44, 48, 54, 71, 173, 175, 190–91,
195–98; and musical listening tastes/
strategies, 89–90, 110, 113, 117, 121, 129,
137, 140–41; and public space/speech,
21, 26, 32–33, 43, 51, 69–70, 95, 100,
183–85, 190, 192, 206
genre: affective dimensions of, xxvi, 5,
13–14, 218n3; as orienting framework,
13–14; in Somali orature, 11, 32–33, 63–
64, 78, 215–16. *See also* meter (in Somali
poetry); *and various named genres*
Gioia, Ted, 225n3 (chap. 6)
Gray, Lila Ellen, 14, 168, 217n5
Guddida Wanaag Farista iyo Xumaan
Reebista (Committee for Morality
and the Eradication of Bad Behavior),
22–23, 181, 185
guitars (acoustic, electric, bass), 50, 150,
155, 158, 163, 225n9

Hadraawi (Maxamed Ibraahin Warsame) (poet), xiii, 12, 29, 39, 92–93,
182, 218n9; "At the Grave of Cilmi
Boodhari," 34; "Beledweyn," 11–12,
135–39, 223n6 (chap. 4); "Haatuf," 39;
"Hud-hud," 39; "Jacayl dhiig ma lagu
qoray?," 92

.

www.ingramcontent.com/pod-product-compliance
Ingram Content Group UK Ltd.
Pitfield, Milton Keynes, MK11 3LW, UK
UKHW042115180325
456433UK00003B/213

9 780226 827391